Chalk Farm Railway Lands
A GUIDED TOUR 1830 TO 2030

Peter Darley

Grosvenor House
Publishing Limited

1. Stables Yard in 1943 (title page image)

All rights reserved
Copyright © Peter Darley, 2024

The right of Peter Darley to be identified as the author of this
work has been asserted in accordance with Section 78
of the Copyright, Designs and Patents Act 1988

The book cover is copyright to Peter Darley

This book is published by
Grosvenor House Publishing Ltd
Link House
140 The Broadway, Tolworth, Surrey, KT6 7HT.
www.grosvenorhousepublishing.co.uk

This book is sold subject to the conditions that it shall not, by way of
trade or otherwise, be lent, resold, hired out or otherwise circulated
without the author's or publisher's prior consent in any form of
binding or cover other than that in which it is published and
without a similar condition including this condition being
imposed on the subsequent purchaser.

A CIP record for this book
is available from the British Library

ISBN 978-1-80381-901-3

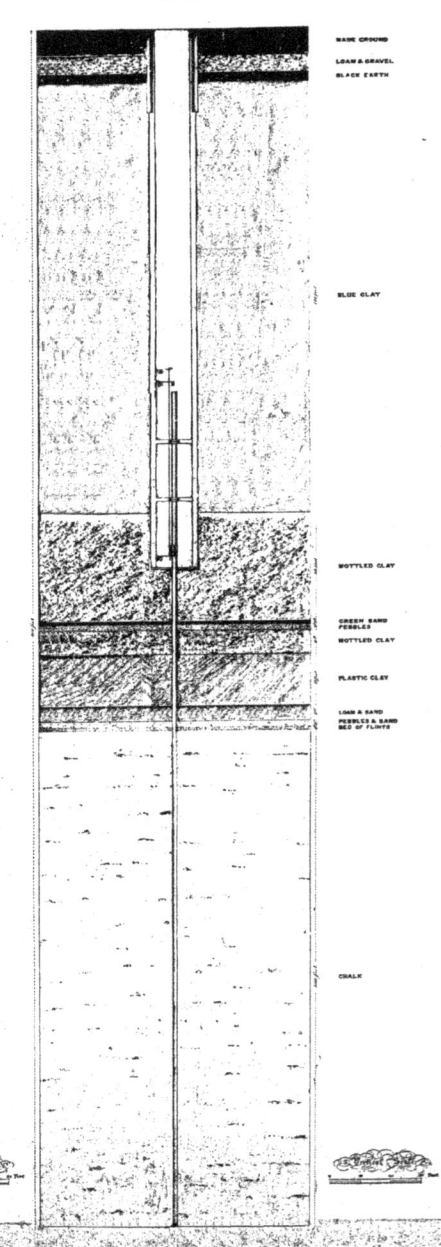

2. Section of artesian well drilled at Passenger Locomotive House, c1845

Camden Railway Heritage Trust (www.crht1837.org)

Camden Railway Heritage Trust (CRHT) is a charity ptomoting, for public benefit, the preservation and restoration of the railway and associated heritage, access to the heritage and the education of the public in the broad appreciation of the social and industrial history of the area.

The author's revenue from the sale of this book goes to Camden Railway Heritage Trust.

Contents

Foreword by Chair, Network Rail ... iv
Foreword by CEO, The Roundhouse ... v
Introduction ... vi
Acknowledgements ... ix
Abbreviations ... xi
Present and historical names ... xii
Time Line ... xiii
Purchasing power of the pound 1820 to 2023 ... xv

1. The Stephensons' Sunday stroll in 1830 ... 1
2. First inter-city to London ... 13
3. Building and opening Camden Station ... 25
4. Rope haulage on Camden Incline ... 45
5. Growth of traffic in 1840s ... 55
6. NLR and 1850s reconstruction ... 73
7. Stables complex ... 85
8. Camden Station from 1860s to 1900 ... 105
9. W & A Gilbey: the Camden story ... 119
10. Railway from 1870s to end of steam ... 141
11. Camden Depot from 1900 to end of steam ... 151
12. Transformation in later 20th century ... 167
13. Regeneration in the 21st century ... 177
14. The Railway Lands: a guided tour in 2030 ... 189

Bibliography, References and Sources ... 205
Image credits ... 210

Foreword by Chair, Network Rail

The history of the railway in Camden mirrors that of the railway in Britain – it changed the world as it was built, the results created enormous growth, jobs and housing, and the same is still happening, both in Camden, and more widely in the UK. From the beginning, earthworks were made, structures were built, torn down, rebuilt again, and both structures and land put to new uses as the railway and the economy changed. The story that Peter Darley tells is one of both continuous change, but also permanence, as the West Coast Main Line (WCML) has now had a constant presence in Camden for nearly 200 years.

As the custodians of today's railway infrastructure, Network Rail ought to respect its history, but adapt what we have to the times we live in. In any event, even when uses have moved on, the structures sometimes remain. No better case than the Winding Vaults, which as Peter describes, still sit under the WCML and await a new use – which we will find for them – befitting a monument of the railway age, albeit unseen, a bit neglected, but absolutely magnificent; an underground cathedral of steam. And plans for former railway land involve large scale residential development – a good thing, with a housing shortage; some actively being built, and more to come, as we rationalise the railway estate.

Personally, I am very glad the Roundhouse was saved, both as a building, and in support of the many cultural uses it has been put to. I am sorry my predecessors were so brutal with Primrose Hill station (which we would not have been today, guided by the Railway Heritage Trust, who if nothing else could have redeployed the decorative ironwork). That's not so true of the old Euston, which Peter mentions, as the Arch was in the way right in the middle of the station (and if you want to know where it was, we've marked its site on the ramp down to the suburban platforms); but if it had been threatened today, it would almost certainly have got moved, rather than destroyed.

As penance for the sins of my predecessors, I am Chair of the Euston Partnership, and I am expending much time with partners on what we all hope will be a new High Speed Two station at Euston, alongside a new concourse for the existing station, because as this railway moves towards its 200th anniversary, connectivity demands more capacity and faster travel on inter-city routes, and an appropriate terminal in the centre of the city is vital for the railway, and as an enabler of further economic growth next to and around the station.

This is a fascinating story, with great detail from contemporaneous accounts, and of uses long gone (like the enormous number of railway horses); and carried forward to the present day. I have enjoyed reading it, and whether or not you are familiar with the area, you will too. Peter Darley has done a great job.

Peter, Lord Hendy of Richmond Hill
Chair, Network Rail

Foreword by CEO, The Roundhouse

Camden Town has been and remains a place of invention and reinvention where buildings go up and in time they change or come down and something else is developed in their place. However, at the heart of this fascinating area are buildings, tunnels, roads and rail-lines constructed during the Victorian era that have shaped everything that has followed. This wonderful new illuminating book by Peter Darley releases details and secrets of its past that the millions of people who visit each year can barely imagine. Peter has brilliantly written a book which is not only for those interested in social history but a guide for everyone to enjoy and to understand the area where so many British firsts took place, that led, in time, to the creation of Camden Market, The Roundhouse and so many other spaces becoming famous internationally.

In this mysterious urban forest of caves and hidden treasures, the Winding Vaults and Wine and Beers Vaults are sleeping dragons waiting to be woken ready to draw breath and release the fire of life once again. From my office window I am witnessing the reimagining of Camden Goods Yard on a huge scale that would leave the original Victorian contractors of the area in stunned wonder.

Camden is a place steeped in history, a history of creativity, innovation, invention and reinvention. In every sense Camden is now reaching for the sky through the imagination of its people and through the Camden Goods Yard skyscrapers. Darley's book turns our attention to less visible infrastructure, among which a secret underground world awaits reawakening.

Marcus Davey CBE
Chief Executive and Artistic Director
The Roundhouse

Introduction

Before the arrival of the railway the area had barely started to be transformed from fields and market gardens. The Regent's Canal, which had arrived two decades earlier, prompted some industrial development, but Camden was still largely defined as a crossroads on the way to the higher and more salubrious environments of Hampstead, Highgate and Kentish Town.

With the opening of the London and Birmingham Railway (L&BR) in 1837, the first inter-city railroad to London, the capital was connected to the industrial heartlands of England, with the railway supporting the needs of the fast growing metropolis for the rapid movement of goods. A passenger terminus was established close to the New Road at Euston Grove, served by steam-powered rope traction from Camden, providing rapid long-distance transport. The expansion of the capital in turn stimulated the growth of a local railway network to serve passengers from the outer-lying suburbs.

The goods terminus was located on the Regent's Canal at Camden Town, an essential connection with the London Docks and hence to trade with the rest of the world. Camden Station was a pioneer in promoting goods interchange between rail, road and canal networks.

Geographically, Chalk Farm Railway Lands (CFRL) comprise a central body with a head and a tail. The tail is the incline from Camden to Euston; the head the cutting from the Regent's Park Road Bridge to the Primrose Hill Tunnel. The body is an area bounded by Chalk Farm Road, Regent's Park Road, Gloucester Avenue and the Regent's Canal. This area housed the goods yard, locomotive sheds, warehouses, stables and other infrastructure, as well as associated rolling stock, attracting industry and commerce to the area. It is shown in the annotated satellite image (§3).

Historically, the book charts the growth during the 19th century, the competition for trade, the later consolidation, the weakness between the wars, the high age of steam, and the subsequent decline under pressure from road transport. It examines the operations of a goods depot, the essential support role played by the horse, and how activities in the Railway Lands affected the neighbourhood. From being transported along the main line railway between Primrose Hill Tunnel and Euston, the story deviates into the many sidings at Camden Goods Station and branches onto the North London Railway (NLR) to connect with the Docks. The journey is one through both time and space and explores a number of side tracks.

W & A Gilbey, the wine and spirits merchant, occupied a vital part of this railway infrastructure for almost 100 years and was a major employer in Camden. Its Camden operations were intimately connected with the CFRL, yet all Gilbey chroniclers have focused on its more prestigious activities and locations. Gilbey's Camden story has never been told and this book attempts to fill this void.

Euston station is excluded from this historical and geographical panorama, being well covered in other publications. Nor is any attempt made to tell the wider story of the London and Birmingham Railway and the powerful executives that led the railway company, a story that has also been ably told elsewhere. The emphasis in this account is on the infrastructure created, rather than on tractive power or rolling stock. Simon Bradley expresses it admirably (*The Railways*, 2016):

> For those that have been initiated, a unique allure resides in the fabric and architecture of the railways, rather than in the trains themselves.

Robert Stephenson's role was central to the building of the Chalk Farm Railway Lands and to their surviving infrastructure and he must be embraced and celebrated in this account.

After the demise of steam, the CFRL area endured years of uncertainty. In the new millennium the area has become an immense construction site. A world of glass, steel and concrete is rising above the rich historical features that represent arguably the most important railway heritage complex in the country. The last chapters of the book seek to unite this new development with an appreciation and celebration of our industrial heritage. They address the recent past and look to the future for further repurposing and improved public access. The aim is to protect the heritage not only through better understanding but also by opening to the public what currently lies largely hidden and hence unappreciated.

While the area remains extraordinarily rich in historical features it is not always easy to tease out the threads that link past and present. For those who live, work or pass through this unfolding panorama or those interested in transport, railways or local history the book tries to provide these threads, showing how features have evolved.

To aid the reader a key plan below provides a local context and a snapshot in 1894 of many of the features that the book describes.

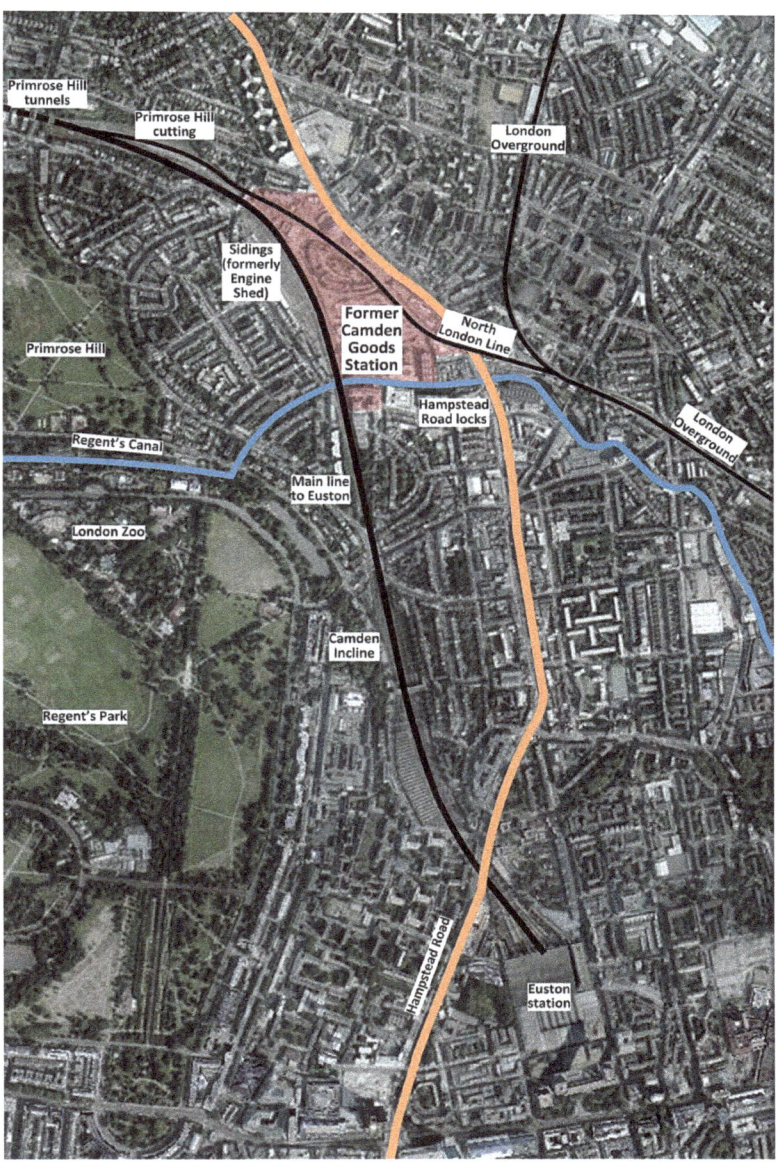

3. Location plan showing the main rail, road and canal infrastructure in the present day on *Google, Bluesky* image

INTRODUCTION

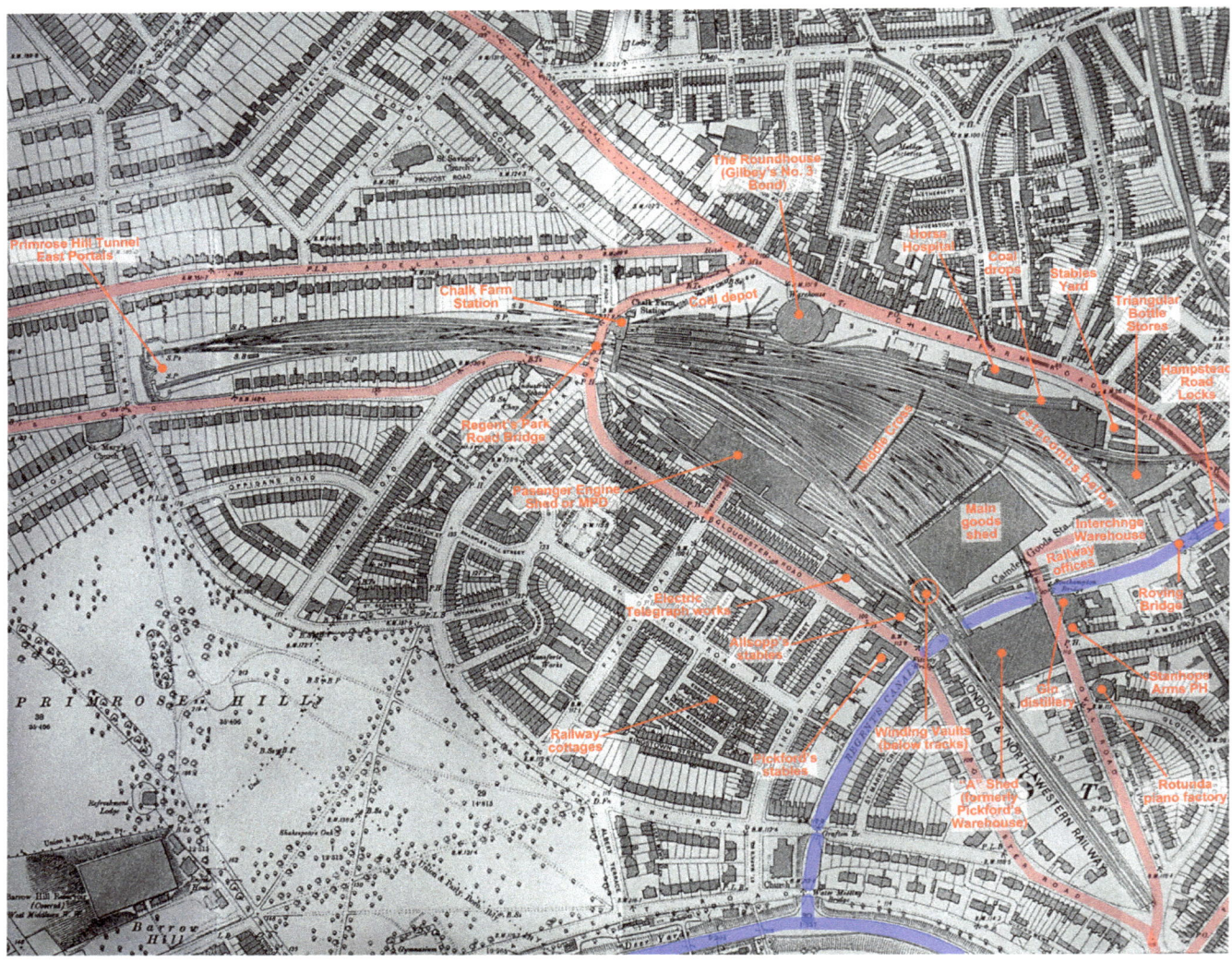

4. Chalk Farm Railway Lands, 1893, showing key features including roads and canal, based on *OS map edition 1894-96*.

The story of the Railway Lands is told through an extensive collection of images. It omits endnotes and footnotes and limits use of references that would break the flow of the narrative.

Acknowledgements

This book has had many years of gestation. Over that time, so many individuals have been generous with both their time, their advice and with their images. None more so than Malcolm Tucker who, over almost twenty years, has offered his in-depth knowledge and expertise as an industrial archaeologist, acting as a mentor and guide since the early days to tutor my limited understanding.

There are too many others who have enhanced the book by their contributions to mention each individually. I have had particularly valuable help with images from Eric Braun, David Thomas, Nick Catford, Brian Morrison and Dick Riley.

Special thanks are due to Network Rail, who generously sent me 600 historical images from their Archives in 2007, a resource on which I have drawn heavily in this account. While all the original images have been retained, I confess to an extensive use of software in order to select parts of images and enhance images to allow them to be read more easily.

My warm thanks also to Joanne McKerchar of the Diageo Archive who has facilitated the company's agreement to the use of its images. I hope that the Camden story of W & A Gilbey will merit this confidence.

Alison Kemp responded brilliantly to my request to animate the Pickford's Stables and the Railway Lands with four watercolours, one of which forms the front cover of the book. Special thanks are also due to the estate of the late Peter Green in granting permission for three paintings so evocative of a bygone era of steam locomotives.

The Tring Local History website and its 'The Train Now Departing, Notes and Extracts on the history of the London and Birmingham Railway' created by Ian Petticrew and others is a wonderful resource that I have tapped.

I have learned much about movements and servicing of passenger trains and locomotives from the Camden Shed topic on the railway modelling website RMWeb, whose members are always willing to share both their enthusiasm and knowledge.

John van Laun's comprehensive study of the techniques for construction of the London and Birmingham Railway through interpretation of the paintings, drawings and sketches of artists, notably John Cooke Bourne, deserves special mention.

Camden History Society (CHS) has been a springboard for many parts of this book, acting as a stimulus to developing ideas through talks arranged by Ruth Hayes and articles written for both the CHS Review and Newsletter, ably edited by David Hayes and Malcolm Holmes respectively.

The structure of the book owes much to two friends that have taken on an unpaid copyediting role. John Cottrell kept the book relevant when it was in danger of wandering into lengthy annexes and it was his suggestion that George and Robert Stephenson be the participants in an excursion to Primrose Hill at the start of the book. Keith Haydon not only questioned who the book was aimed at but placed himself firmly in the position of a discerning reader. He demanded more colour in the form of personal accounts and boldly advised which passages were not up to scratch. I am most grateful for both their interventions.

Finally, my wife Edith deserves special thanks not only for her diligent proof reading but also for her fortitude in bearing months of obsessive behaviour and even providing encouragement.

5. A scene of industrial dereliction in 1975. Former coal drops in foreground with Ale Stores (left), Horse Hospital (right) and Chappell's imposing piano factory in middle distance

Abbreviations

Where illustrations are referred to they are numbered by the chapter in which they appear prefixed by the symbol §. For example, those first appearing in Chapter 1 are §1.1, §1.2, etc. Where sections (sub-chapters) are referred to they are numbered similarly, prefixed by the symbol #.

BHO	British History Online
BR	British Railways
CFRL	Chalk Farm Railway Lands
CGY	Camden Goods Yard
Ch.	Chapter
CHS	Camden History Society
CLSAC	Camden Local Studies and Archives Centre
CRHT	Camden Railway Heritage Trust
DC	Direct Current
E&WIDL	East and West India Docks and Birmingham Junction Railway
EHV	Extra High Voltage
GJR	Grand Junction Railway
GNR	Great Northern Railway
GWR	Great Western Railway
HE	Historic England
HV	High Voltage
ICE	Institution of Civil Engineers
ILN	Illustrated London News
IWM	Imperial War Museum
L&BR	London and Birmingham Railway
LCM	London Canal Museum
LMA	London Metropolitan Archives
LMS	London Midland and Scottish Railway
LNWR	London and North Western Railway
MPD	Motive Power Depot
NA	National Archives
NLR	North London Railway
NR	Network Rail
NRA	Network Rail Archives
NRM	National Railway Museum
OS	Ordnance Survey
p.a.	per annum
PO	Post Office
RCC	Regent's Canal Company
SSPL	Science and Society Picture Library
TPO	Travelling Post Office
UECL	Up Empty Carriage Line
WCML	West Coast Main Line
WWI	First World War
WWII	Second World War
YCBA	Yale Centre for British Art

Present and historical names

Chalk Farm Railway Lands lie within Camden and Primrose Hill and the use of any of these geographical terms may be used for the same area.

Present name	Historical name(s) – more recent first
Camden Bank	Camden Incline; Euston Extension
Camden Lock Place	Commercial Place; Grange Road
Chalcot Road	St. George's Road
Chalk Farm Road	Hampstead Road; Pancras Vale
Dumpton Place	Fitzroy Place
Euston Road	New Road
Eversholt Street	Seymour Street
Gloucester Avenue	Gloucester Road; Southampton Road (north of Fitzroy Br.), Gloucester Road (south of Fitzroy Br.)
Historic England	English Heritage
Iron Bridge House	Stephenson House
Jamestown Road	Upper James Street
Parkway	Park Street
Prince Albert Road	Primrose Hill Road
Regent's Park Road	Chalk Farm Lane; Primrose Vale
Stables Market	Stanley Sidings; Stables Yard

Time Line

1816	Regent's Canal opens from Paddington to Hampstead Road
1820, August	Regent's Canal completed from Paddington to Limehouse
1825, September 27	Opening of Stockton and Darlington Railway
1829	Stephensons' 'Rocket' wins Rainhill trials
1830	Formation of London and Birmingham Railway Company
1830, September	George Stephenson and Son appointed by L&BR Company
1831, November	L&BR Company applies to Parliament for a private Act
1832, November	L&BR Company reapplies to Parliament for a private Act
1833, May 6	L&BR Act passed into law
1833, September	Robert Stephenson appointed Engineer-in-Chief for L&BR
1834, June 1	Start of construction of L&BR
1835, July 3	Extension to Euston authorised under Amending Act
1837, June 20	William IV dies and crown passed to his niece Princess Victoria
1837, July 20	Euston to Boxmoor section of L&BR opens
1837, July 24	First railway trial of Cooke and Wheatstone electric telegraph
1837, October 14	Start of rope haulage on Camden Incline
1837, October	Euston to Tring and Rugby to Birmingham opens
1838, 17 September	Euston to Birmingham line opens
1839, Spring	Camden Station opens for goods traffic
1840, August	First auction of Lord Southampton's property
1844, July 14	End of rope haulage on Camden Incline
1846, July	Amalgamation of L&BR, GJR and B&MR companies to form LNWR
1846-47	Phase 2 reconstruction of Camden Station
1851	Completion of E&WIDL (later name: North London Railway)
1856-57	Phase 3 reconstruction of Camden Station
1859	Death of Robert Stephenson
1864	Construction of main goods shed
1879, June 1	Opening of second Primrose Hill tunnel
1907, June 22	Opening of the Hampstead Tube
1921, August 19	Railways Act given royal assent

1923, January 1	Creation of London, Midland & Scottish Railway and three other consortia
1931	Enlargement of main goods shed and other major upgrades
1948, January 1	Four consortia nationalised under British Railways (later British Rail)
1962, September 9	Last day of steam at Camden Motive Power Depot
1963, March	Beeching Report *The Reshaping of British Railways*
1966, January 3	Camden Motive Power Depot closes
1972, May 20	Opening of Regent's Canal towpath in Camden
1994-1997	Privatisation of British Rail and creation of Railtrack
2002, October 3	Transfer of railway infrastructure to Network Rail completed

6. Time line of chapters

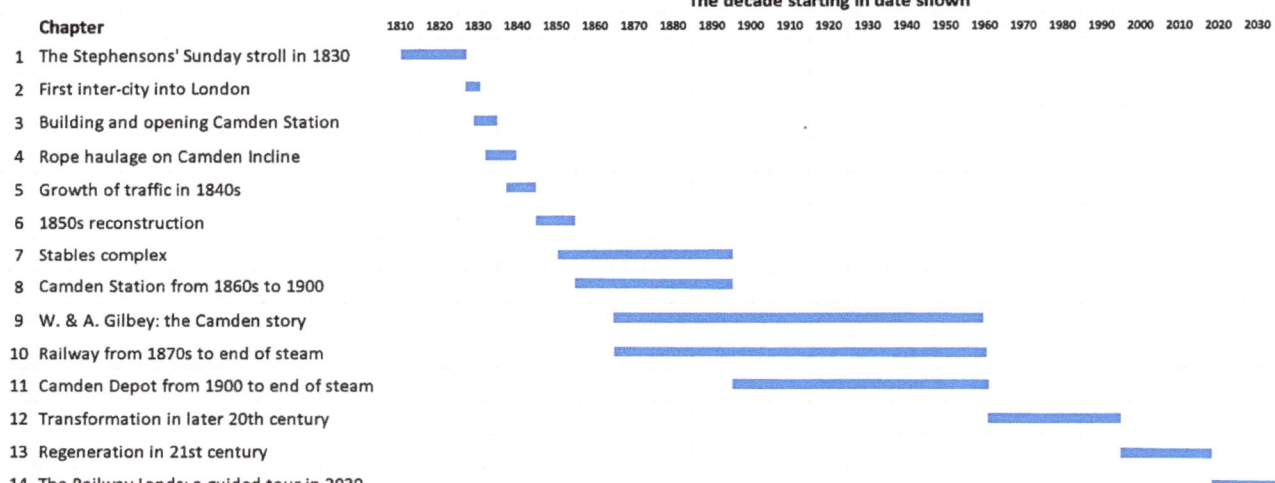

Purchasing power of the pound, 1820 to 2023

Comparing wages, salaries, contracts and other monetized values during the last 200 years can be difficult without some idea of how inflation (or deflation) in prices has affected the purchasing power of the pound. No such comparison can be anything more than very approximate. Expenditure patterns changed drastically over the period, as also did the quality of goods, and the method of determining the price index.

The chart uses standard sources for the retail price index and the relative purchasing power of the pound from 1820 to 2023. These are plotted to a logarithmic scale. It shows how the value of the pound was maintained relatively constant throughout the Victorian era and up to the start of WWI. There was an inflationary spike during and immediately after WWI, and a steady fall in prices from then almost up to WWII, since when inflationary pressures have caused a dramatic fall in the value of the pound.

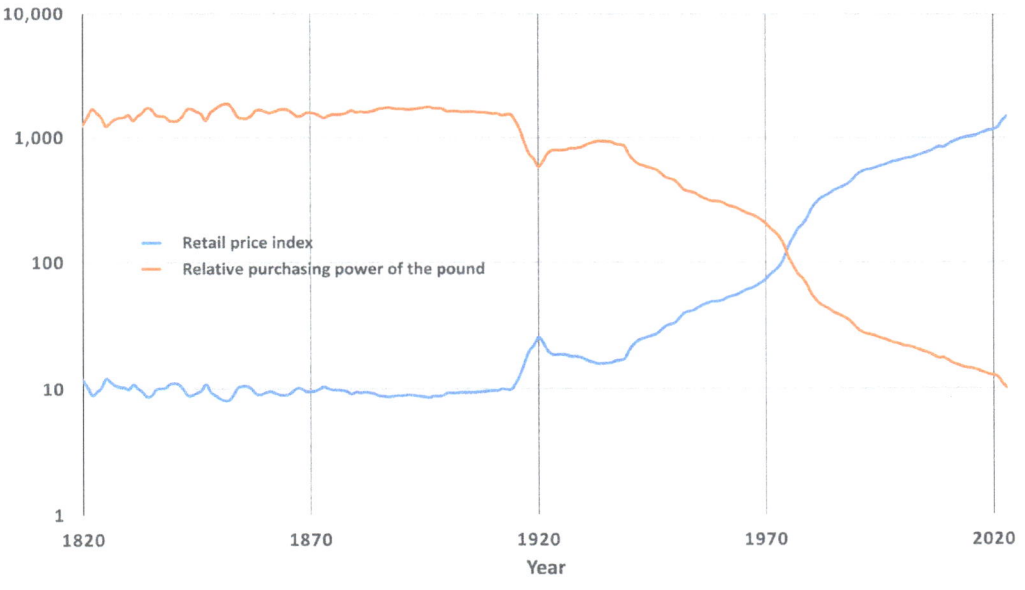

7. Retail Prices Index and relative purchasing power of pound, 1820 to 2023 (1974 = 100)

8. Industrial archaeologists could finally explore Camden Depot in the mid 1970s. Here they capture the barrel run used for trundling wine barrels, taken from bond in the Wine and Beer Vaults (foreground), across the Eastern Horse Tunnel and into the original 1839 vaulted sidings. The route is clearly defined by the railway sleepers. The sidings led in turn into Stables Yard, from where the wine could be bottled for export

1 The Stephensons' Sunday stroll in 1830

1.1 Appointment of George Stephenson & Son by L&BR Company
1.2 Stop for refreshment
1.3 The Colosseum
1.4 The Regent's Park
1.5 Regent's Canal
1.6 Primrose Hill
1.7 Chalk Farm Tavern
1.8 Sporting attractions
1.9 To Hampstead Road Locks
1.10 London terminus options

This chapter follows George and Robert Stephenson in 1830 as they pursue their remit from the L&BR Company to define the railway alignment and terminus. The choices they faced, described here, are recorded in Company minutes. To set the stage for the striking changes that would unfold over subsequent decades, the Stephensons are imagined on a Sunday excursion with its various diversions.

1.1 Appointment of George Stephenson & Son by L&BR Company

Surveys for a London and Birmingham railway had been carried out by John Rennie (later Sir John Rennie) in the 1820s, and two subsequent surveys had proposed different route alignments. Interest then languished in a hostile economic climate until revived by the opening, on 15 September 1830, of the Liverpool & Manchester Railway, the first inter-city railway, which had firmly established the reputation of George Stephenson and his son Robert.

The London and Birmingham Railway Company was formed in 1830 and In September of that year the civil engineering firm of George Stephenson & Son was appointed to make additional surveys as necessary, evaluate proposed routes and arbitrate between them, select the best route and carry the railway through obtaining a private Act of Parliament. The intention was to deposit the plans for the London and Birmingham Railway (L&BR) in the Private Bill Office by the 30 November 1830 deadline for the 1831 parliamentary sessions.

At the time, George was much concerned with other schemes, notably the Grand Junction Railway from Manchester to Birmingham. Robert was the

managing partner of Robert Stephenson & Co., the world's first locomotive factory, and designer of the Rocket which had decisively won the Rainhill locomotive trials for the Liverpool & Manchester Railway the previous year. Once George Stephenson & Son had submitted their route recommendations to the Board in that autumn of 1830, Robert would take sole charge of the project. As part of this handover, George took early steps to introduce Robert to his contacts in London and to the institutions with which he would be dealing.

Robert immediately set about seeking ways to refine the proposed route. One of the issues that the Stephensons had to consider was the location of the London terminus. A key determining factor was the Regent's Canal. This provided access to the London Docks at Limehouse, from where the railway would be connected with the growing markets of a large and expanding empire. A goods terminus could be sited anywhere along the canal, but particularly where it intersected one of the major roads leading from the north into the capital. The closer the terminus was to the Docks the more favourable to the Company for trade, but this advantage came at the cost of extending the railway through land that was becoming increasingly valuable as the metropolis expanded.

For the Stephensons, there were two initial contenders: a route from a terminus near the Paddington Basin (§1.1) leading up the Edgware Road to Watford and Hemel Hempstead; and a route from a terminus at Battle Bridge on the New Road at Islington to Hemel Hempstead. Battle Bridge was later to be renamed King's Cross after Stephen Geary's 1835 monument to George IV.

These two locations eventually became the London termini of the Great Western and Great Northern Railways respectively.

The route to Paddington was less costly in terms of earthworks. Together with some realignments of the L&BR further north, this was proposed by George Stephenson & Son to the Board in October 1830.

But Richard Creed, the Company Secretary, was adamant that a terminus at Paddington would not only involve double handling of goods destined for the Docks, creating dependence on the Regent's Canal Company, but would also be less convenient for passengers than a terminus closer to the City. Despite being a banker by profession, he evidently weighed the costs of building the line through London less conservatively than the Stephensons.

Richard Creed proposed a general route review to the Board, including options for a goods terminus nearer the Docks. He was subsequently charged with this undertaking.

Meanwhile, in that autumn, the Stephensons decided to look again at two options for a goods terminus east of Paddington Basin: Chalk Farm

1.1 Junction of the Regent's Canal and the Grand Junction Canal (middle right) with the canal to Paddington Basin (right foreground). The Grand Junction Toll Office is on the left, *T. H. Shepherd*, 1828

CHALK FARM RAILWAY LANDS: A GUIDED TOUR 1830 TO 2030

on the Hampstead Road and Battle Bridge on Maiden Lane leading to Holloway and close to the Horsfall Basin (now Battlebridge Basin) of the Regent's Canal. Having already familiarised themselves with Battle Bridge, they would combine a site inspection of Chalk Farm with leisurely enjoyment of the rural northern fringes of the capital on a fine day in late October 1830.

The route they took is shown on the extract from the Greenwood map of 1827 (§1.2).

1.2 Stop for refreshment

They walked along Regent Street and over Oxford Circus to Upper Regent Street, admiring the fine Georgian terraces that continued into Portland Place. This led to Park Crescent where they stopped at William Leftwich's ice cream parlour for refreshment.

Ice had traditionally been collected from frozen lakes or canals and stored over the course of the year. The source was not always clean. Ice for preserving perishables was initially only affordable by the wealthy.

Setting up his own business around 1810, William Leftwich appears to have traded as a high-class caterer, one that could meet the demand for iced drinks and ice cream. Following a hot summer in 1821, he imported ice from Norway as "the best and cleanest in England". The ice was transferred onto barges at Regent's Canal Dock and taken along the canal where it was lifted into one of his ice wells. From 1826, imported ice was stored in his new ice well at Cumberland Market, close to the Regent's Canal's Cumberland Basin, a market that had been established to serve the new residents of Regent's Park. He lived at 34 Cumberland Market from where he would deliver ice to residences, confectioners and fishmongers.

With an excavated depth of 82 feet (25m) and holding 1500 tons of ice, his Cumberland Market ice well continued to an overall depth of 300 feet (91m) as a water well into the Chalk, which would have made it self-draining for the disposal of melt water as well as providing a potable water supply (*The Pictorial Times*, 1845).

From about 1839 he also extracted ice from the Regent's Canal to store in an ice well at his wharf on Upper James Street that served less wealthy customers.

The earliest known large-scale commercial ice well was constructed in 1780, long before John Nash's Park Crescent was erected nearby. It has been designated a scheduled monument by Historic England. The ice well survives today (§1.3) at what was then Park Crescent Mews. William Leftwich had

1.2 Westminster to Primrose Hill, drawn on Greenwood map, 1827

1.3 Park Crescent Mews ice well, 2018

1.4 Park Crescent with the New Road, looking south, *Hughes*, 1831

been using this ice well to serve the high-class local clientele, including medical practices.

Another confectioner in the West End had marketed a product similar to modern ice cream in 1818. It can be readily imagined that Leftwich had opened premises to cater for those that would be seeking both fresh air and refreshment as they strolled up Portland Place towards Regent's Park.

Moving on, the Stephensons crossed the New Road (§1.4), stepping over the ordures that accumulated from the traffic on this busy highway. The road had retained the generous dimensions of its origins as a drovers' road to Smithfield. The first horse omnibus ('for all' in Latin) service had been established here by George Shillibeer the previous year, operating between Paddington and the Bank. It was an immediate success and had swiftly been followed by others.

1.3 The Colosseum

At Park Square East they walked past the Diorama, London's first, still attracting visitors to experience the large painted and illuminated tableaux it portrayed, many of overseas scenes. Entering the Regent's Park, they made for the Colosseum (§1.5).

Begun in 1824 from the designs of Decimus Burton to provide a space to exhibit Thomas Hornor's *Panoramic view of London*, this most popular of all panoramas was one of the first sights to which visitors to the capital were taken. It had been painted from sketches made in a temporary wooden cabin or 'crow's nest' erected in 1821 on the summit of the cross of St. Paul's. Painting the canvas took Thomas Hornor and many other artists more than four years.

1.5 The Colosseum, Regent's Park, *Hughes*, 1831

The panorama (§1.6) was viewed from two galleries, one above the other, intended to correspond with the two galleries in the dome of the cathedral, to create the illusion that the spectator was actually standing at that altitude. Above this was another staircase, leading to an upper gallery, the view from which was intended to represent the view from the cross at the top of St. Paul's.

The painting covered upwards of 46,000 square feet (4275 m^2), or more than an acre of canvas. The dome on

1.6 The geometric ascent to the galleries of the Colosseum (left) and birds eye view from the staircase and the upper part of the Pavilion (right), 1829, *R Ackermann & Co.*

which the sky was painted was thirty feet (9m) greater in diameter than that of St. Paul's and depicted an horizon that ran for nearly 130 miles (209km).

The Stephensons had a particular interest in tracing the Regent's Canal from Paddington to Limehouse to obtain an appreciation of the balance between the increase in trade that a terminus nearer the Docks would bring against the additional cost and complexity of routing the railway through densely built-up areas.

They then left the Colosseum to continue along the outer ring road of Regent's Park.

1.4 The Regent's Park

The Regent's Park is over 400 acres in extent and nearly circular in form. At that time, in 1830, the park was the private domain of the wealthy leaseholders of its large mansions. It first opened to the general public in 1835, initially for just two days a week.

The Zoological Society of London, which occupied part of the northern boundary of the park, was instituted in 1826. In 1831 William IV presented the Royal Menagerie to the Zoological Society, most of which was transferred from the Tower of London. Not until 1847 were the general public admitted to what had become the most extensive collection of animals in the world and which they soon christened the "Zoo".

The Broad Walk, which was to provide the main public entrance to the Zoo, had not yet been created and the public were confined to what is now known as the 'Outer Circle' of the park while work continued with its landscaping.

The Stephensons walked along this Outer Circle, impressed by the terraces of newly completed mansions: Cambridge Terrace, Chester Terrace and Cumberland Terrace (§1.7). Cumberland Terrace had become the second of the great terraces to come into occupation in 1828.

THE STEPHENSONS' SUNDAY STROLL IN 1830

1.7 Cumberland Terrace, Regent's Park, *Hughes*, 1831

It was not just British visitors that were impressed. In the words of the Vicomte d'Arlincourt, in his account of a visit to England in 1844 (*BHO*):

> The Regent's Park, above all, is a scene of enchantment, where we might fancy ourselves surrounded by the quiet charms of a smiling landscape, or in the delightful garden of a magnificent country house, if we did not see on every side a countless number of mansions, adorned with colonnades, porticoes, pediments, and statues, which transport us back to London; but London is not here, as it is on the banks of the Thames, the gloomy commercial city. Its appearance has entirely changed. Purified from its smoke and dirt, and decked with costly splendour, it has become the perfumed abode of the aristocracy. No artisans' dwellings are to be seen here: nothing less than the habitations of princes.

1.8 Gloucester Gate, Gloucester Terrace and St. Katherine's church, Regent's Park, *Hughes*, 1831

The Stephensons continued past Cumberland Terrace, past St. Katherine's church and Gloucester Terrace, and past the many street entertainers working the passers-by to reach the entrance to the park at Gloucester Gate (§1.8).

1.5 Regent's Canal

Leaving the park at Gloucester Gate, the Stephensons crossed the Cumberland Market branch of the Regent's Canal. This passed between Park Village East and West and continued past the Albany Street cavalry barracks to end in Cumberland Basin, lined with wharves and warehouses.

The original Hay Market near Piccadilly Circus moved to Cumberland Market at the south end of the Cumberland Basin in 1830, becoming the New Cumberland Hay Market. Hay and straw were brought in for sale to meet the needs of London's large population of horses (§1.9), not least those at the nearby Albany Barracks. Manure went in the other direction, back to fertilise the fields.

The Stephensons had reached Stanhope Terrace at the south end of Park Street, where the York and Albany Tavern overlooked the road junction, as it still does. They turned left into Primrose Hill Road (now Prince Albert Road) and continued along the Cumberland Arm of the canal until they reached Water Meeting Bridge. Here the Regent's Canal, approaching from the west along the northern boundary of Regent's Park, made a sharp 90 degree turn to the north, leaving the Cumberland Market branch of the canal to run alongside the eastern boundary of the park (§1.10).

1.6 Primrose Hill

1.9 Barge carrying hay from Cumberland Market passing Park Village East, view south, *T H Shepherd*, 1829

After crossing the bridge the Stephensons took the path to the summit of Primrose Hill. The approach to Primrose Hill was over fields – a network of footpaths leading up to Hampstead. The map extract marking their perambulations (§1.10) shows the road and 'intended road' across Lord Southampton's estate from bridges over the Regent's Canal, Southampton Bridge and Fitzroy Bridge, both of which remain, albeit with new structures.

In direct contrast to the aristocratic associations of Regent's Park, Primrose Hill has the character of a 'park for the people'. Its name bears testimony to when its sides were covered with hedges and brushwood that promoted an undergrowth of early spring flowers. It had long been a favourite resort of London's citizens who came for a day out to view the London skyline from there or from Parliament Hill.

In 1827, the Provost and Fellows of Eton College began to see that their property, located immediately north of Lord Southampton's lands, would soon become valuable, and they obtained an Act of Parliament enabling them to grant leases in the parishes of Hampstead and

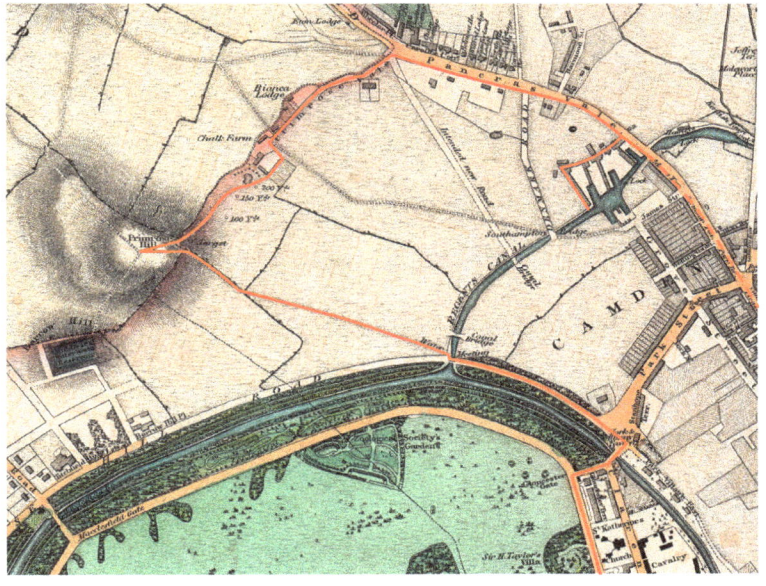

1.10 Approaches to Primrose Hill, from Greenwood map, 1827

Marylebone. Soon after the accession of Queen Victoria, endeavours were made to obtain Primrose Hill for the Crown, and a public act was passed by which Eton College received certain property at Eton and gave up all their rights in Primrose Hill. They retained the large area let to tenant farmers known as the Chalcots Estate.

The Stephensons approached Primrose Hill from the south. They observed Barrow Hill (or Little Primrose Hill) to the west with the Middlesex Water Works reservoir and pumping station that had caused the summit to be flattened (§1.11). On their right, Chalk Farm Tavern nestled in its gardens at the foot of Primrose Hill. A game of cricket was being played in the nearby field.

THE STEPHENSONS' SUNDAY STROLL IN 1830

1.11 A view of Primrose Hill from the southeast, *Hughes*, 1831

From the summit of Primrose Hill, the Stephensons were able to enjoy a panorama of the metropolis to the south, the houses forming a vast sea punctuated by the countless spires of churches. Curiously this extraordinary vista did not attract artists of the day, not even those of foreign origin that were culturally more engaged with urban realism than with the picturesque.

'The Prospect from Primrose Hill' was lyrically described in *The Gentleman's Magazine*, June 1749:

> 'Stella, my Muse! whose beauty prompts the song,
> To whom the poet and the lays belong...
> To Primrose Hill lead on the flow'ry way,
> And thence the matchless scenes around survey.
> Mean while the Muse shall sing, with fond surprise,
> The various prospects, as by turns they rise...

However, the Stephensons' interest lay to the north of Primrose Hill where the railway would have to be threaded between the higher ground of Primrose Hill and that of the Belsize Estate on the southern flank of Hampstead Heath, traversing Eton's Chalcots Estate. This would require substantial excavation in London clay to keep gradients within the limits George had specified, creating large quantities of spoil that would then have to be used to raise the ground locally.

They descended the hill to Primrose Vale and walked the short stretch of rough track to Chalk Farm Tavern.

1.7 Chalk Farm Tavern

The Lower Chalcots farmhouse, known earlier as the White House, began selling ale in the 17th century although farming continued until at least 1732. It had become the Chalk Farm Tavern by 1790.

The various types of hostelry can be confusing. Taverns sold food and wine to the well-off. Alehouses sold ale, and later beer, and simple food to the lower classes. Inns provided accommodation for travellers. The public house, as we think of it today, emerged in the middle of the 19th century and incorporated elements of each of these earlier types of building.

Chalk Farm Tavern stood almost alone on Primrose Vale and, with Primrose Hill nearby, was a popular destination for excursions by Londoners from the 17th century until 1865. From its proximity to Hampstead, it was the usual resort of holiday-folk on their return from the Heath.

It had been acquired by William Bowden in 1828 and extensively renovated (§1.12). The Tavern included pleasure gardens on the site now bounded by Berkley Road, Chalcot Square and Sharpleshall Street. These were a focal point from the 18th century. At the height of its fame the Tavern boasted a dance floor capable of taking one thousand people as well as a bandstand known as the Chinese Orchestra, which was 36 feet (11m) high. The large ballroom was decked with chandeliers and convex mirrors.

1.12 Chalk Farm Tavern c1830 showing new east wing

The peaceful meadows near Chalk Farm had been a favourite meeting place for duels in the 18th and early 19th centuries. With no houses between England's Lane and the Chalk Farm Tavern, and trees screening the fields, they provided perfect privacy. Those wounded in the duel would be carried to Chalk Farm Tavern.

Strong public opposition to duelling caused it to fade away, as did the gradual loss of the trees and hay meadows of Chalk Farm to new residential buildings.

By 1862, with development of Lord Southampton's estate well underway, the Tavern with its extensive grounds had been replaced by the current building (now the restaurant Lemonia), but the new tavern initially had grounds on either side that continued to provide space for outside entertainments.

1.8 Sporting attractions

To promote the attractions of Chalk Farm Tavern, William Bowden encouraged a number of sporting entertainments. What these had in common was the opportunity to place bets on the competitors. Such sports included Cumberland and Westmorland wrestling, pigeon shooting, target shooting and prize-fighting.

London and the City were magnets for people from all over the country. Those from Cumbria and Northumberland brought their wrestling with them and 'Mr Bowden's Grounds' were a centre for the sport during the 1830s (*Walford, 1978).*

Cumberland and Westmorland wrestling has its own particular rules and remains popular at country shows. The dress code then, as now, was white tights with hand embroidered pants over them and white tops (§1.13).

Live pigeon shooting was a very competitive sport, often with big money betting. The pigeons were released from a trap some way distant from the gun. To score, the bird had to be killed or brought down within a perimeter. Great accuracy as well as speed was needed for an elusive and unpredictable target. The modern clay pigeon shooting discipline mimics the live version.

1.13 Cumberland and Westmorland wrestling, heavyweight division, Grasmere sports, 1900

It is not clear how the birds were procured, but it is unlikely they were feral pigeons trapped in cities by enterprising urchins; more likely they were fast-flying homing pigeons bred for the purpose. How many of the shot birds would have been fit to eat is another question, touched on in David Stevenson's memoir when the Tavern became a staff canteen for those employed in Camden Station. There was a complaint that the pigeon shooting gave them "pigeon pies to satiety" (*Turner, 1891*). The birds were almost certainly too tough for the pigeon breasts to be served as fine fare.

Target shooting at Chalk Farm Tavern attracted the finest shots of the day. The range can be seen in §1.10 where markers have been laid on the ground at 100, 150 and 200 yards. As with all four of the sports mentioned here, there was direct competition between two or more competitors and a great deal of money was wagered.

Target shooting was also used for training soldiers from the Albany Street Barracks, detachments of 40 men of the 2nd Life Guards being marched each morning to the range.

Prize-fighting was heavily frowned on by most of the educated classes but hugely popular with the masses. Fights would often be arranged informally in the fields around the Tavern, which became a base for both participants and onlookers. Press reports of fights tended to focus on the violent or unusual. In 1825, following an inquest on a fatality, the coroner made a clear distinction between a quarrel and a prize fight, any fatality in the former having no malicious motive and therefore, while not legal, could be treated leniently: whereas in the latter it was wilful murder.

A second report, in 1834, concerned crowds flocking to a fight on the north side of Primrose Hill to place bets on two women of notoriety. The police got wind but were outnumbered by ruffians armed with cudgels, who may well have been navvies working on the Primrose Hill contract (#3.8); they had to enlist the help of reinforcements from the Albany Street station.

1.9 To Hampstead Road Locks

After lunch at Chalk Farm Tavern the Stephensons relaxed briefly in the gardens where they were entertained by a small group of musicians.

They now walked along Chalk Farm Lane (or Primrose Vale) to Pancras Vale, part of the Hampstead Road, and continued south and east along the road. They reached Commercial Place which led behind the basins and wharves concentrated here alongside Hampstead Road Locks. It formed part of the Regent's Canal towpath, skirting the first locks on the Regent's Canal downstream of Paddington Basin. Turning right to enter this section of towpath, as shown on §1.10, they noted the extent of open ground on their right side, land which all belonged to Lord Southampton. This area could comfortably accommodate a goods terminus. The drawback was that Lord Southampton was a known opponent of the railway and would oppose selling his land to the Company.

The two engineers paused on the north bank of the canal, just west of the wharves that surrounded the Hampstead Road Locks. From here they had a clear view back across the fields to Chalk Farm Tavern. Compared with Battle Bridge the site was too far from the City, although it might be possible, were Lord Southampton to become amenable, to extend the line towards the West End by taking it across the canal to the New Road or beyond. This would mean raising the level of the area they were inspecting so as to create sufficient clearance for barges to pass under a rail bridge over the canal – which they agreed could be a practical use of excess spoil from excavation through the Eton Estate.

Returning to the Hampstead Road, they took a coach back to their lodgings.

1.10 London terminus options

Although much effort had been put into identifying the optimum route, there was insufficient time to assemble a convincing case to place before Parliament in time for the 1831 session. It was therefore decided to defer application for an Act until the 1832 session.

Richard Creed was engaged from March 1831 in reviewing the route of the L&BR proposed by Robert Stephenson. Creed initially wanted the London terminus to be near the Limehouse Basin, bringing the railway through the Lea Valley. While this would have avoided the double handling of the Regent's Canal Company, it would have displaced several large factories, an added expense to an already longer route. He then considered a route from Kentish Town to the Docks at Limehouse with a branch for passengers to Battle Bridge. The route was to continue westward to the Paddington Basin before turning north to Harrow. When this also appeared costly and complex, he looked to the west end of the Docks, to City Road, for a goods terminus, retaining the passenger terminus at Battle Bridge.

1.14 Battle Bridge Gas Works, Maiden Lane, 1830 *unknown artist*

The Company first applied to Parliament for a private Act in November 1831 for the 1832 sessions. The route selected was that approaching London through Harrow, Willesden and Paddington, then turning east to pass between Camden and Kentish Town, before turning south to meet the Regent's Canal and the New Road at Battle Bridge where both passenger and goods termini were to be located. As seen in §1.14, Battle Bridge, with the major gasworks of the Imperial Gas Light and Coke Company, was rapidly industrialising.

When the Bill was laid before Parliament, much evidence from the growing experience of railway operations was produced in its support. Its promoters believed that they had established the railway was in the national interest. A large majority of the House of Commons committee voted in favour of the Bill and the chairman of the Lords committee found the application well prepared and convincing. But it was nevertheless vetoed in the Lords after an influential landowner declared, on behalf of a larger group of objectors, that a sufficient case had not been made to warrant 'forcing' the railway through the property of so many dissenting landowners.

At the London end, objectors included Lord Southampton and the Marquis of Camden, while William Agar, who fifteen years earlier had cost the Regent's Canal Company a great deal with his spirited dissent to allowing the Regent's Canal through his land, ominously deferred his opinion until he had seen the Bill. The Regent's Canal Company also opposed a London terminus at Battle Bridge, regarding this as a threat to its trade.

To placate such landowners, the Company was obliged to organise costly deviations and pay well above the market rates for land, in some cases three or four times its value. Landowners could be extremely devious, insisting on a series of bridges across the railway for access to their land, but then retracting on condition they were offered half the cost of the bridge in lieu of its construction.

This financial setback drove the Board to ask Robert Stephenson to find a less costly solution for the London terminus. Paddington was now becoming the focus of the Great Western Railway and he considered the most favourable site for the L&BR goods terminus was at Chalk Farm, the location that he had visited with his father in October 1830. Robert Stephenson therefore proposed a goods terminus at Camden Town alongside the Regent's Canal and adjacent to the Hampstead Road.

The passage of the first London and Birmingham Railway Act had caused attitudes towards railways to change. The sentiment expressed by the authors of Osborne's London & Birmingham Railway Guide (*Osborne, 1839*) summed up the feelings in the country that the rejection by the Lords Committee had engendered:

> When we consider that evidence had been laid before the committee sufficient to demonstrate to any reasonable persons, the overwhelming national importance of the realization of the proposed project, it will be palpable that the opposition arose from mere selfishness, and in ignorance or contempt and wilful violation, of the principle on which the tenure of land is based. The stoppage of this great national undertaking was extremely aggravating and vexatious to the public, and the placidity and sangfroid of the mode in which it was done, was not at all calculated to decrease the aggravation; on the contrary the rejection was so much more galling on that account.

2 First inter-city to London

    2.1   Act of Parliament
    2.2   London and Birmingham Railway
    2.3   Robert Stephenson, Engineer-in-Chief
    2.4   Terminus site
    2.5   Approach to Railway Lands
    2.6   Boundary road
    2.7   Extension Line
    2.8   L&BR and GWR
    2.9   Stephenson and Brunel
    2.10 Organisation of drawing office

2.1 Act of Parliament

If the capital to construct a railway was to be raised by public subscription — which in the railway-building era was the case — and/or its course was to lie across public land and that of individuals not associated with the scheme, a private Act had first to be obtained.

A provision generally found in a private railway Act gave the proprietors the legal power to acquire specified private land by compulsory purchase; in effect, to acquire it without the owner's consent but with fair monetary compensation. Other provisions and stipulations might include the right to cross public highways and divert rivers and streams, and the arbitration procedures to be applied in cases where land values were in dispute.

In addition to the documents deposited with the Private Bills Office, copies were also required to be deposited with the clerks of the peace in the counties through which the line was planned to pass, and with the relevant parochial authorities, while landholders had to be provided with a section showing the depth of cutting or embankment across their estates. Facsimiles had therefore to be made, a formidable task in the days before more sophisticated reproduction techniques were available. Conder (*1868*), whose pupil-master was Charles Fox, paints a vivid picture of the process of assembling the documents:

> Accordingly for some ten days the labour of plotting sections, copying plans, numbering and copying references, and the like, went on almost without intermission. At nine in the evening would appear mighty bowls of oysters, gallons of ale, and other materials of a rude but hearty repast. A respite of some three quarters of an hour would be filled up by uproarious hilarity and then a fierce objurgation from the chief — the moment before the chief reveller — for so scandalous a manner of wasting the company's time would set all briskly to work again . . . .

The actions of the Company to mitigate opposition to the Bill (#1.10) eased its passage through Parliament and it passed into law on 6th May 1833. Robert Stephenson, having guided the Bill through Parliament and obtained its Act for the Company, was appointed Engineer-in-Chief in September 1833.

Once the route had been approved by the Board, Robert took over the detailed surveying and planning of the line.

It was goods traffic that was the initial stimulus for construction of the London and Birmingham Railway (L&BR). In reaction to this threat to its trade, the Regent's Canal Company (RCC) had insisted that railways take goods traffic no further into London than the edge of the canal. The RCC considered the Camden Station location now proposed for the goods terminus would prove more advantageous for their business than that at Battle Bridge which it had opposed. Rail freight destined for waterside locations, including the Docks, could be transferred to the canal, while other freight and rail passengers would be discharged onto the road system at Hampstead Road.

The New Road (now the Euston Road) had already been deemed the obvious point at which to build a passenger rail terminus, but the Company had not wished to jeopardise their Bill by including this extension and upsetting the major landowner, Lord Southampton. However, after the first Act was passed, Lord Southampton became a railway supporter and, in late 1834, the L&BR Company applied for an extension over his land from Camden Town to Euston Grove. This extension for passenger traffic was authorised on 3 July 1835 under the Amending Act, which contained the following clause:

> That it shall not be lawful for the said Company to receive at their intended Station in Euston Grove, for the Purpose of Transport, or to deliver out therefrom, any Merchandise, Cattle, or Goods of any Description, save and except Passengers, Luggage and small Parcels.

The L&BR was the first railway authorised to extend into London as far as the New Road for passenger services; the opening of services from Euston in 1837 signalled the decline of longer distance commuting by road.

2.2 London and Birmingham Railway

The L&BR was London's first main line and the largest civil engineering project yet attempted in the country. The first railway of any major length, it changed the travel and commercial habits of the British people. The experience gained was to form the basis for much of the development of civil engineering in Britain. It also precipitated the railway mania of the 1840s.

The route of the line at the London end was dictated by the desire to reach the Docks. Forced by high ground to approach London from the west rather than the northwest, it made its way around the edge of the built-up area of Portland Town, heading slightly north of east, and passed between the southern flank of Hampstead Heath and Primrose Hill (§2.1). Gradients were kept low by nearly three miles of cutting and the 1120-yard (1024m) Primrose Hill Tunnel.

From there until Chalk Farm Lane Bridge the railway entered a deep cutting before turning south towards the Euston passenger terminus. Goods trains, on the other hand, were diverted to Camden Goods Station, shown in red on the map.

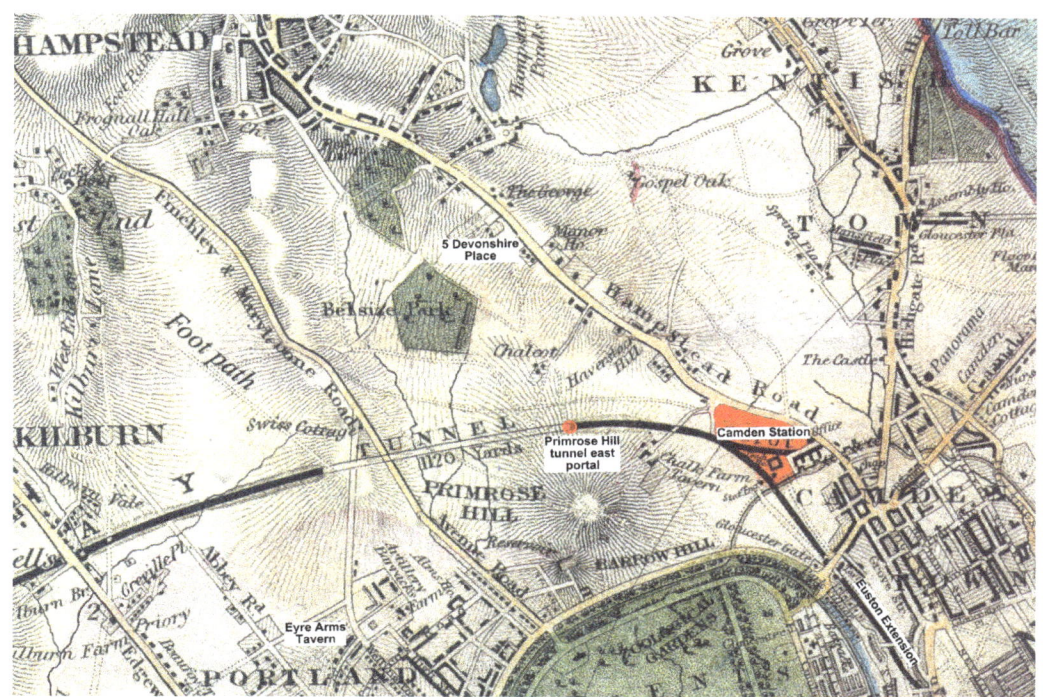

2.1 London approach of the L&BR, from Davies' Map, 1840

2.3 Robert Stephenson, Engineer-in-Chief

Robert Stephenson, as the son of George Stephenson, grew up in Newcastle-upon-Tyne in an environment dominated by the early development of the steam locomotive and his father's practical knowledge. As an infant he sat on Richard Trevithick's knee as his locomotive was being assembled in Gateshead for the 'steam circus' at Euston. His father determined that Robert should benefit from the education he never received, and this was combined with a natural diligence and aptitude, as well as the open nature of George and their joint passion for engineering. Intensive engineering training, working as his father's assistant, was combined with a short period at Edinburgh University.

When appointed engineer-in-chief for the L&BR in 1833 he was not yet thirty. He spent the next ten years working for the L&BR, living from 1834 to 1843 at 5 Devonshire Place (§2.2), one of a pair of semi-detached villas on the west side of Haverstock Hill, close to the corner with Belsize Grove; the location is shown on §2.1. The photo shows part of the turning circle in front of the house, which had a stable attached where a groom, a carriage, a phaeton for his wife and one or two horses were accommodated. The site is now part of a modern block of flats called Romney Court.

2.2 No. 5 Devonshire Place, 1903

Just like his father, Robert lost his wife when in her late 30s. Fanny, whom he married in 1829, died childless in 1842 and is buried in the cemetery of St John's, Hampstead, the church where they worshipped. This loss prompted Robert to move into the centre of London, where he could concentrate both his working and social life. He never remarried.

Robert Stephenson was appointed Chief Engineer for the L&BR on the basis that "his time and services should be devoted exclusively to the Company". This requirement departed from the usual arrangement whereby

2.3 Robert Stephenson

FIRST INTER-CITY TO LONDON

a Resident Engineer took charge of day-to-day operations, the Chief Engineer providing consultancy and occasional oversight, and charging his fee on a per diem basis. Instead, Stephenson was paid a salary, set initially at £1,500 p.a. plus £200 p.a. expenses, but later increased to £2,000 p.a. (about £320,000 today) to keep abreast of Brunel following his appointment as Chief Engineer of the Great Western Railway.

His gifts of leadership and organisation were needed in selecting and managing a large project team of assistant engineers, sub-assistants and draftsmen, collectively the 'Stephensonites'. Together they established the construction technology for the railway age.

He also took personal responsibility for the Primrose Hill contract, the first nine miles from Camden Town. This most difficult section of line, including Primrose Hill Tunnel and cutting, had driven the appointed contractor into bankruptcy after problems with ground conditions, particularly the swelling of blue London Clay exposed to the atmosphere. Stephenson must have walked this section of line innumerable times while supervising the direct labour the Company employed to replace the contractor's workforce.

The intense pressure of work, both at this time and later, led him to have frequent recourse to calomel, a toxic mercury-based chemical prescribed by doctors as a universal remedy. This took its toll on his health.

2.4 Terminus Site

The first businesses in the area followed the arrival of the Regent's Canal in 1816. They settled on the left bank along Commercial Place (shown as Grange Road in §2.4) and on the right bank along James Street, with wharves fronting onto the docks that had been created. The goods handled were not only for the construction activities that were gathering pace as London expanded rapidly, such as timber and stone, but also bulk goods for domestic and retail markets, such as coal and ice (§2.4).

The area the L&BR Company initially purchased from Lord Southampton was 25 acres (10 hectares) on the north side of the Regent's Canal (§3.11). Considered unwarranted by many directors when proposed by Stephenson, the area soon proved inadequate. Further land was subsequently purchased on the south side of the canal, on the southern boundary of the goods yard and on the north bank of the canal between Southampton Bridge and the present Roving Bridge. These additions created a goods yard of 33 acres (13 hectares), the area of which remained essentially unchanged for over 100 years to the end of the steam era in 1962.

2.4 Regent's Canal at Hampstead Road Locks from Goad Map of 1891

With the arrival of the railway, higher value goods could be moved more quickly and reliably. Camden Town enjoyed the transport advantages of ready access to canal and rail and became a centre from where goods carried by the L&BR and the Regent's Canal were dispersed by road to every part of London. The locational advantages of proximity to skilled furniture makers in the Tottenham Court Road area and proximity to West End retailers and a wealthy clientele helped Camden to become a centre of the piano industry. Collard and Collard were the oldest of the well-known piano manufacturing firms of the St Pancras area, having patented a form of upright 'square' piano in 1811.

The Camden Depot area, constrained between the Regent's Canal, the Hampstead Road, Chalk Farm Lane and Gloucester Road, had to be raised to the 'railway level'. This was dictated by the decision to carry the main line over the Regent's Canal, providing sufficient height for the passage of barges beneath the bridge.

Raising the ground at the depot was a practical way of using spoil, the waste material from construction. Stephenson will have calculated the balance of excavation and fill carefully. Material excavated from Primrose Hill Tunnel, from its deep approach cutting and from Camden Incline to Euston (the 'trench'), predominantly blue London Clay, was used to create a difference in level of up to 15 feet (4.5m) between the new railway level and the former ground level over not only much of the goods yard site but also some of its adjoining areas (#3.7).

The ground was also raised to this new level by vaults, the underground basements of buildings that were constructed at ground level to carry their loads down to foundations in the natural ground, providing spaces between the natural ground and the railway level that could be used for a variety of services, including workshops and stores.

This difference between the railway level and ground level is fundamental to understanding the topography and its impact on the features of the Goods Station. It is evident in all the following locations:

- the stairs at the Roundhouse from ground level up to the former locomotive turntable (now known as the 'Performance Space');
- the heights of the Great Wall of Camden, the retaining wall that ran along the Hampstead Road (§6.12), and the slightly lower retaining wall alongside the Regent's Canal towpath between Southampton Bridge and Fitzroy Bridge (§12.3);
- the rise from ground level in Stables Yard to the first floor level of the Horse Hospital, created by both the curved ramp (§7.21) and the horse road along the Great Wall (§7.24);
- the level of the Interchange Warehouse above Camden Lock Place;
- the stairs from the Camden Goods Yard redevelopment area down to Horse Tunnel Market.

2.5 Approach to Railway Lands

Until the 1820s the southern part of Hampstead was almost entirely rural. Apart from the Belsize Estate, the most notable feature of the area was the Chalcots Estate, 243 acres of land owned by Eton College with the manor house of Chalcott to the north, at the west end of the present England's Lane (§1.10).

In 1830 Eton College formed the first hundred yards or so of Adelaide Road at its own expense, named after William IV's newly crowned queen. Having a short section of Adelaide Road on the ground gave credibility to Eton's case that the railway proposed to cut through valuable building land. But it was not until 1839-40 that residential development really got under way.

The Company was involved in negotiations about running its line across Eton's Chalcots Estate from 1831. The College initially resisted the idea strenuously, primarily on the grounds of its adverse impact on landholders and the consequent reduction in the value of leases. That the College's solicitors were also the agents for the L&BR helped negotiations between the two parties. The Company maintained that:

> The railway will either pass under or over the great roads, never on the same level, will be carefully fenced everywhere, and ornamentally when in sight of gentlemen's residences; the carriages make little noise, the engines produce no smoke. Most convenient and elegant carriages will be provided for individual passengers and for families, whose carriages, horses, servants, &c. may be taken with them on the Railway, ready to drive off from any point at which they may wish to leave it.

The Company bought off college obstruction by agreeing to put the line in tunnel, thereby using little land and ensuring the least interference with building values. From an engineering viewpoint this was unnecessary as the rails were never more than 50 feet (15m) below the ground surface (similar to the tunnel approach cutting), and side slopes of 1 on 2 were specified initially, later flattened to 1 on 3 due to the nature of the ground. But for the College a tunnel had the merit of using no land, the surface being preserved for building. What is unclear is why Eton did not require the tunnel to be extended further to the east to provide even more building land.

Eton required a special provision in the Act:

> the Tunnel shall be constructed of sufficient strength to admit of buildings being erected thereon, except where the crown of the Tunnel is within 15 ft of the surface.

To make doubly sure, it was also provided that the tunnel had to be made by tunnelling and not by 'cut and cover' methods. Eton insisted moreover that:

> the mouth of the Tunnel at the eastern end shall be made good and finished with a substantial and ornamental facing of brickwork or masonry to the satisfaction of the Provost and College.

2.5 Primrose Hill Tunnel east portal, Lith. *C Rosenberg,* 1837

The proud classical elevation provided (§2.5) reflects the upmarket development intended for the neighbouring Chalcots Estate. It was the first tunnel nationally to treat a portal architecturally. The round-arched tunnel mouth is crowned by a dentillated cornice decorated with six carved lion masks linking to massive stone flanking piers with hipped capitals. The whole conveys the sense of a grand entrance.

2.6 Boundary road

Lord Southampton had powers to make two parallel roads from the Hampstead Road to the first and second bridges west over the Regent's Canal, through the ground sold to the Company, as shown in §1.10. He waived these rights on condition that the Company provided him with sufficient ground to realign his intended new road, so as to lead from Chalk Farm Lane Bridge (on right in §2.6) to Fitzroy Bridge over the canal (on left in §2.6). This road was essential to the auctions of Lord Southampton's estate in 1840-41.

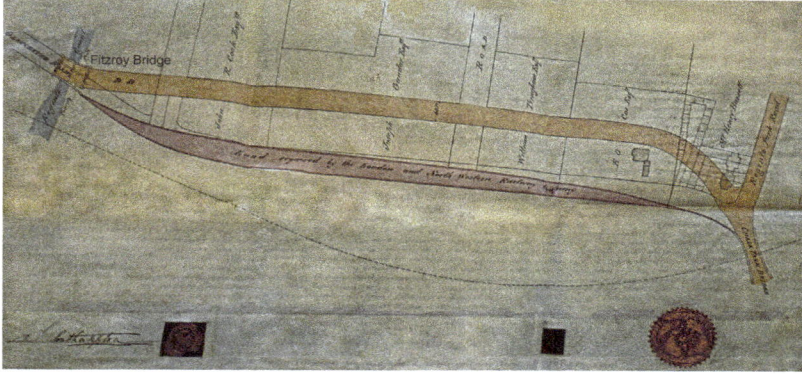

2.6 Southampton Road and its subsequent realignment

Stephenson considered that a road bounding the Company's station on the west and leading in a direct line across the Regent's Canal to the northeast entrance of the Regent's Park would be highly advantageous to the railway. This road became Southampton Road. With the purchase of an additional three acres of land to provide for the future Passenger Locomotive House, it was later to be moved further west again (§2.6) and be renamed Gloucester Road. This involved the loss of one of the earliest new villas on Regent's Park Road, built by Henry Bassett.

2.7 Extension Line

The Euston Extension, or Camden Incline, diverged to the south at Camden Goods Station to pass over the canal, pass under the street network and reach the Euston passenger terminus at ground level. The route is shown in the Introduction (§3). Later railways in the Camden area were to avoid such a steep gradient either by going under the canal, as at Kings Cross, or by raising the rail terminus on arches, as at St Pancras. This diversity of Victorian railway engineering can still be appreciated to this day.

The Regent's Canal had to be crossed at a height that allowed boats to pass below – a clear height of 10 feet (3.0m). The ground at Camden Depot therefore had to be raised, while that at Hampstead Road and six other road crossings had to be lowered for rail tracks to pass under the roadways, as required by the Committee of Metropolis Roads.

Initially Stephenson had proposed to run the Euston Extension on a viaduct, but influential landowners and wealthy residents in Park Village were concerned about the noise and smoke from locomotives toiling up the Incline and opposed any facilities at Euston to service and maintain locomotives. The Duke of Bedford and Lord Southampton required three special clauses in the new Bill, viz:

1st The Company not to erect Steam Engines, Forges and certain other buildings on the Estate of Lord Southampton south of the Regent's Canal.
2nd Similar Clause for the Duke of Bedford.
3rd Company not to carry heavy goods on the Extension Line.

There are many misunderstandings about the origins and justification for the solution that Stephenson adopted for the Extension Line. Although the gradients could be handled by the steam locomotives of the day, using banking engines if required to assist locomotives with heavier trains up the Incline, he deemed it wise to provide a rope-worked incline powered by stationary steam engines. This could be seen as a gesture towards the sensitivities of the major landowners, although the Company was always entitled to employ locomotives on the Euston Extension.

It is therefore worth hearing Stephenson's report to the London Committee on 26 October 1835:

> That he proposed working the Extension Line by a fixed Engine at the Camden Town Station.
>
> That whilst on the one hand the Euston Grove Depôt and the Railway would be relieved from the serious inconvenience of Locomotive Engines moving about in a space not more than is absolutely necessary for the disposal of passengers, the gradients of the Extension Line are on the other hand such that a Stationary Engine is better adapted for the Planes than an assistant Locomotive Engine which would otherwise be required.
>
> That he is of opinion that passengers are more conveniently landed on a Depôt by a Stationary than by a Locomotive Engine; that moreover the Company are prohibited constructing repairing Shops at Euston Grove Station whereas there is ample space for every accommodation of the sort at the Camden Town Station.

The Company therefore decided to work trains up the Incline, at an average of 1 in 85 the steepest section on the line, by an endless rope that ran around a driving wheel and four other large sheaves (rotating grooved wheels) that carried the rope (# 4.1).

Stephenson further minimised the impact of the railway by placing as much as possible in cutting, masked by the provision of extended overbridges at two of the major road crossings – Hampstead Road and Park Street. About 240 yards (216m) south of the bridge crossing the canal the railway sank into this cutting and a vignette accompanying the Parliamentary Deposited Plan shows it passing a villa in Park Village, sheltered from view by trees, boundary walls and the depth of the cutting (§2.7). The image was among those created by Thomas Allom, an English architect, who was known above all for his topographical illustrations. He was a founding member of what became the Royal Institute of British Architects.

2.7 Euston Extension at Park Village, from 1834 Deposited Plan, *Thomas Allom*

The cutting itself, made through the treacherous London Clay, necessitated massive and costly retaining walls but these and the accompanying overbridges were designed with a disarming elegance and grace (§3.20) and could be seen as an ornament to the landscape once they had weathered in.

2.8 L&BR and GWR

The Great Western Railway (GWR) Bill, before Parliament in 1834, reflected a ban imposed by the Metropolitan Road Commissioners on the line crossing certain highways to the west of London. Robert Stephenson's evidence before the Commons Committee on the GWR Bill prompted overtures by the GWR in September 1834 to ascertain whether a junction of the GWR and the L&BR would be to their mutual advantage.

There was little further contact before the GWR received its enabling Act of 31 August 1835, which specified a terminus near today's Willesden Junction (§10.1). The intention was that the line would continue over shared track to a terminus adjacent to that of the L&BR at Euston.

Soon after, in October 1835, the GWR's London Committee proposed:

- GWR to be tenants on the L&BR, initially for 7 years;
- GWR to pay for use of the railroad, with equal rights of way to L&BR;
- GWR to receive sufficient land at Euston and Camden for passenger station and goods depot;
- L&BR's Engineer to consider accepting carriages of greater axle width.

Stephenson had been instructed in April 1835 to consider both two and four lines of rail on the Euston Extension, reporting in October that he was recommending four lines of way. The extra pair of tracks, while not prompted by the GWR, helped the negotiations and, in November, Stephenson was instructed to report on arrangements at Camden and Euston whereby GWR traffic would interfere as little as possible with L&BR traffic. Later that month he tabled enlarged plans of the two depots.

In December, while negotiations with GWR were ongoing, the contract for the Extension Line was awarded to William and Lewis Cubitt. The quality of their work on the Euston Extension was much admired and ten months later, in September 1836, they were able to negotiate a contract for the Winding Engine House and its chimneys.

How Stephenson would have accommodated broad gauge in the two track Primrose Hill Tunnel, for which construction had started some 17 months earlier, is not clear. Operationally, the tunnel would have needed a pair of extra rails on both up and down lines but, given the greater width of broad gauge trains, this would not have been a viable solution. There would also have had to be at least a single extra rail extending west beyond the tunnel up to a GWR/L&BR junction at Willesden.

While the terminus at Euston Grove could accommodate the GWR, it is more difficult to see how GWR goods traffic could have been accommodated at Camden Depot. Although discussions continued, there is little sense of either company taking the proposals very seriously. A deadline of February 1836 for agreement on the size of carriages to be allowed on the line appears to have triggered one barrier: GWR's insistence on broad gauge. But it was disagreement about the length of lease at Euston that became the formal reason for the breakdown of negotiations on 2 March 1836. The two additional tracks that had been provided on the Euston Extension on Stephenson's recommendation were soon to be appreciated by the L&BR.

Yet the negotiations between Stephenson and Brunel in the mid 1830s were the start of a 20-year association between the two engineers, who had become both friends and commercial rivals.

2.9 Stephenson and Brunel

Robert Stephenson and Isambard Kingdom Brunel were appointed Chief Engineer to the two largest projects of their day before reaching their 30s. They had each achieved a high level of professional competence, helped by their close working relationship with their famous fathers.

Over the years that followed, the two engineers were rivals competing for commissions in the rapidly expanding railway network and for influence over its technical evolution. Yet they shared a strong professional respect for each other and, despite great differences in their character and upbringing, this warmed to support and friendship.

Among many examples of such support, here we see Isambard Brunel, John Locke and other eminent engineers in 1849 discussing Stephenson's bold plan to float the tubes into position for Britannia Bridge (§2.8). This hangs in the Institution of Civil Engineers (ICE). It was painted by John Lucas, Stephenson's favourite artist, who was given a number of other commissions, including a portrait of Robert and one of Robert and George, also hanging in the ICE.

2.8 Meeting of eminent engineers to discuss flotation of tubes for Britannia Bridge, 1849, *John Lucas*, 1849

The Great Exhibition of 1851 was another endeavour that brought the two engineers together. Both were involved in organising the exhibition, and their projects were prominently displayed in the British Pavilion, enshrining their places in the pantheon of Victorian engineering. A GWR broad gauge steam engine dominated the heavy machinery area, while the main avenue featured a large model of Stephenson's Britannia Bridge.

The launch of the *Great Eastern* in 1857 proved a most testing time not only for Brunel but also for his friend, whom he wanted at his side. Stephenson, although unwell, went to great lengths to provide support, writing to say:

> I shall always be at hand happen what may to aid and do everything in my power without shirking any responsibility if need be.

They met for the last time on Christmas Day 1858 for dinner in Cairo, Stephenson having sailed to Egypt on his yacht *Titania,* while Brunel was recovering from the stresses of the *Great Eastern,* on holiday with his family. Each was attempting to restore his health after a lifetime of overwork, but a year later, within a month of each other, both were dead.

Many engineers in that era failed to reach their sixtieth birthdays, perhaps a reflection on the rigours of civil engineering. The cost of the English railways included the lives of many eminent men (*Conder, 1868*).

2.10 Organisation of drawing office

The engineering team for the L&BR was initially based in Kilburn. In May 1834 the office staff moved to the vacant Eyre Arms Hotel at 1 Finchley Road at the junction with Grove End Road (§2.9), named after the major landowner in the area. This later became the Eyre Arms Tavern. Its location is shown on §2.1. The Eyre Arms Tavern was demolished in 1928. Now the site of a block of flats, a plaque on the wall recalls its past.

The grounds were later shared with ladies and gentlemen practising jousting for the 1839 Eglinton tournament, a re-enactment of a medieval joust and revel held in North Ayrshire, as well as early balloon attempts, the last in 1839.

The main lounge was adapted as the drawing office and became a classical example of the organisation of engineering work, with 20 to 30 draughtsmen producing an average of 30 drawings a week, all signed by Robert Stephenson. Under intense pressure from the Company, the draughtsmen worked in two shifts — the day shift sleeping in the rooms the night shift had vacated.

2.9 The Engineer's Office at the future Eyre Arms Tavern, *unknown artist*

Very little of this drawing output has survived, but a typical drawing is that of the Locomotive Engine House (§2.10).

The cover drawing of the 1834 Deposited Plan for the Euston Extension is an example of the exquisite nature of some engineering drawings. Only part of the original colour drawing has been found and the b/w version of the plan is shown here (§2.11). Note the Oval that was part of Lord Southampton's building plans before the arrival of the railway bisected the western half.

When Brunel was preparing for construction of the GWR he borrowed Robert Stephenson's plans as the best system of draughting. From that time they became recognised models for railway practice (*Jeaffreson. 1869*).

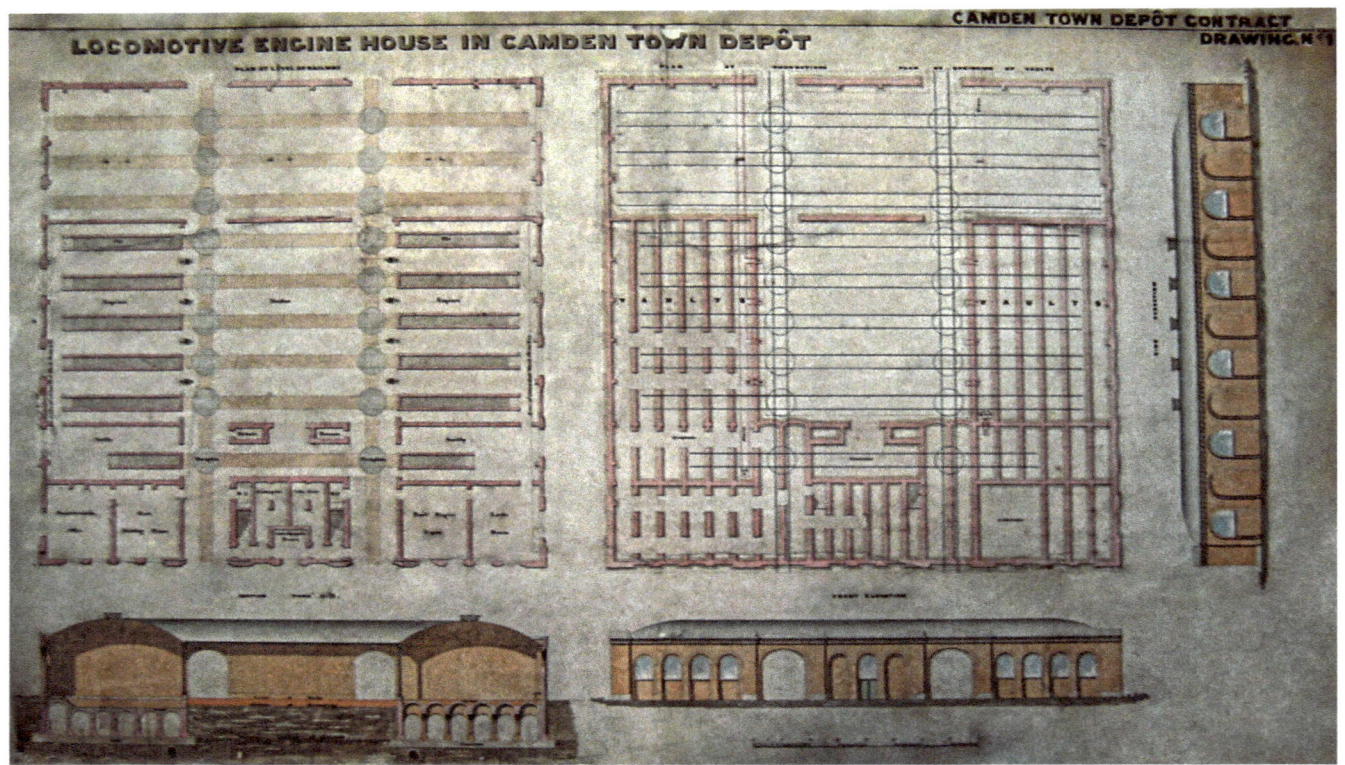

2.10 Locomotive Engine House, Drawing No. 1 of the Camden Town Depot contract

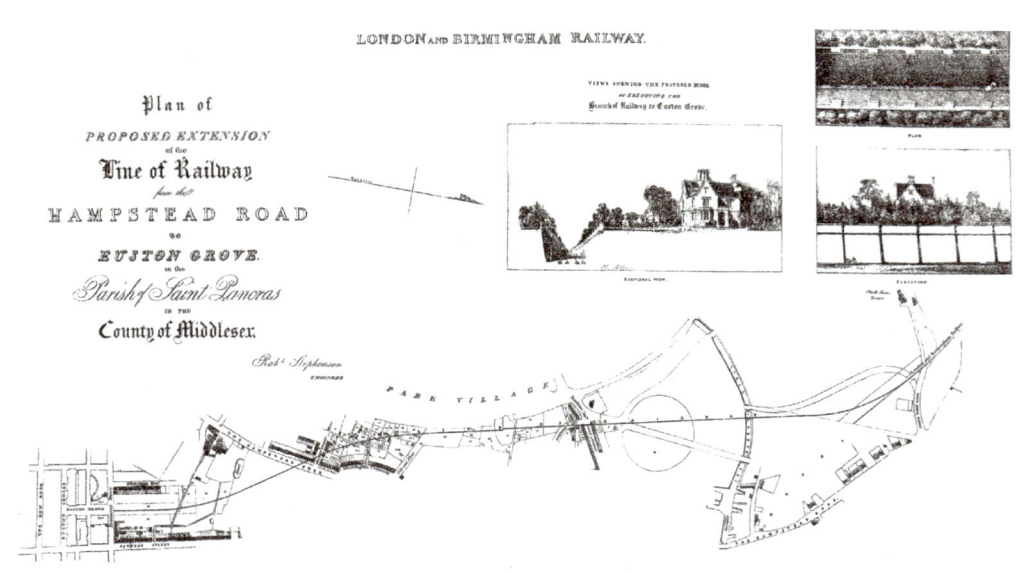

2.11 Cover drawing of 1834 Deposited Plan

3 Building and opening Camden Station

3.1 Organising the work
3.2 Primrose Hill Tunnel
3.3 Bridge on Chalk Farm Lane
3.4 Euston Extension
3.5 Stationary Winding Engine Vaults
3.6 Camden Station
3.7 Balancing cut and fill
3.8 The navigators
3.9 Opening the line
3.10 Early operations – railway
3.11 Early operations – Camden Station
3.12 Electric telegraph
3.13 The drawing record

3.1 Organising the work

From an early stage the L&BR Board realised they would need to raise more capital than first estimated to complete the largest civil engineering project yet undertaken. Such was indeed the case, with the final bill coming in at £5,500,000 (£745M today), well above the parliamentary estimate of £2,500,000.

Several factors had conspired to drive up the cost and introduce delay. To a general rise in the retail price index of about 20% in the mid 1830s must be added the impact of other railway projects that started at that time, increasing the competition for scarce resources and raising wages and material costs well beyond estimates.

However, Lt. Peter Lecount R.N. took a more cynical view (*Lecount, 1839*):

> The way in which these things are usually got up for Parliament is so vague and undetermined, as to merit no other name than a guess, and not a good one either; hence has arisen the common saying with all great undertakings of this kind, 'halve the receipts and double the expenditure if you wish to know anything about it'

John Britton, a strong supporter of railways, took a similar view (*Britton, 1839*):

> engineers were aware, if they apprised the shareholders of the whole cost attending such undertakings, the latter would never embark on any of them.

To stimulate the necessary interest and raise the project's profile in the eyes of its investors and of the general public the Board directed that:

the portion of the line at the London end ... be executed with all the expedition which may be found consistent with the stability of the work, and other considerations, from a conviction that the novelty and convenience of a railway contiguous to the Metropolis cannot fail to excite a general interest, and consequently to prove an early and productive source of revenue to the Company.

Charles Fox was appointed as the Assistant Engineer to supervise work on the Extension Line, in which Stephenson took a particular interest. During the progress of this portion of the line, the contractor, William and Lewis Cubitt, had no less than 1,000 men employed upon the mile and a quarter of ground.

The management structure that Stephenson put in place was much the same as would apply to a similar project today. The railway was divided into a number of Districts, each being placed under the direction of an assistant engineer. Each District was then further divided into sections under the supervision of sub-assistant engineers.

Two sections concern this account: the first the Euston Extension and the second the first section of District No. 1 which extended from Camden Station to Primrose Hill Tunnel. Overall District No. 1 extended from Camden Town for about nine miles and was reserved for the Engineer-in-Chief's personal supervision. The assistant engineer under Stephenson was John Birkinshaw.

Towards the end of the project, the number employed in Stephenson's team in various capacities had grown to fifty-five. Stephenson developed a strong personal attachment to his pupils when they were young men of capacity and character. He never forgot or lost sight of them. Four of these – Peter Lecount, Francis Conder, Robert Dockray and Herbert Spencer – appear in the Bibliography and References at the end of the book.

3.2 Primrose Hill Tunnel

3.1 The Birmingham Railroad constructing near Chalk Farm, June 1836, *George Scharf*

The first sod for the L&BR was cut at Chalk Farm Lane on 1 June 1834 at the east end of the Primrose Hill Tunnel approach cutting.

The Primrose Hill Tunnel passes through 1100 yards (1000 metres) of stiff London Clay "the most unmanageable and treacherous of all materials" (*BHO*). Up to that time the short Highgate Tunnel had been regarded as almost a miracle.

Apart from about 21 yards (19m) at each end built in 'cut and cover', the Tunnel was excavated from four eight-foot (2.4m) diameter shafts, the working face not being allowed to advance more than 6½ feet (2m) ahead of the brickwork lining. George Scharf's sketch of the eastern end of the Tunnel (§3.1) shows much construction detail, including the rotary horse engines or 'gins' over two of the four shafts. These were used to lift spoil from the tunnel shaft to the surface and to lower materials to those working in the Tunnel. From the surface, spoil was deposited into wagons running on temporary rail tracks and hauled by horses to the Depot to be used as fill.

The cut and cover section was dug by hand, with the spoil being removed by barrow over duckboards that led to a wagon tipping area, from where spoil was again removed by horse drawn wagons on rails. All of this can be seen in the sketch. No spoil was allowed to be deposited on Eton Estate land.

Lecount (*1839*) maintained that hatchets and cross-cut saws were the most effective tools to cut the hard London Clay, while spades, pickaxes and blasting proved to be of little use. But when exposed to the atmosphere, the clay moistened and swelled, the pressure of the moist clay on brickwork causing mortar to be squeezed from joints and crushing bricks brought into contact. Attempts to save money by omitting the structural support provided by the arched invert of the tunnel were quickly abandoned when the clay was observed to rise menacingly to fill the excavation area.

The Primrose Hill contract, a 5¾-mile section that included the Primrose Hill Cutting and Tunnel, a tunnel at Kensall Green, and a long embankment across the Brent Valley, had been let to Jackson and Sheddon in May 1834. The ground conditions and rising costs rapidly bankrupted the contractor and in November 1834 the contract was taken over by the Company using direct labour and its own plant and materials.

To resist soil pressure the tunnel arch thickness was increased from 18 inches (457mm) to 27 inches (686mm), and stronger paving bricks were used in place of London stocks, substituting quick-set Roman cement for lime mortar. The slope of the eastern approach embankment was increased from 1 on 2 to 1 on 3.

Public apprehension about tunnels was not set at rest until a trial trip was made into Primrose Hill Tunnel carrying engineers and doctors to blow off steam for 20 minutes, an expedition with which all expressed themselves delighted.

The original Primrose Hill Tunnel, completed in January 1837, was London's first railway tunnel and considered a great feat of engineering in its time. Crowds gathered both to watch the construction of the railway and to stroll along the railway cutting to admire the trains in operation (§3.2). A Sunday stroll could be completed at Chalk Farm Tavern.

3.2 Watching trains emerge from Primrose Hill Tunnel, 1837, *J H Nixon after J Cleghorn*

The L&BR, as a long-distance line, did not create a demand for housing in its vicinity. Nevertheless, Eton College took advantage of the public's attraction to the entrance to the Primrose Hill Tunnel to alert people to the healthy situation of the future Chalcots Estate.

BUILDING AND OPENING CAMDEN STATION

Boundary walls were provided at the foot of the cutting and the Eton Estate retained ownership of the land up to these walls, at least until the railway was widened ten years later. This unusual feature encouraged the public to the site without trespassing on the railway.

3.3 Bridge on Chalk Farm Lane

The first bridge over the railway on Chalk Farm Lane was a brick-built arch as seen in the engraving (§3.3).

The image shows some of the first wagon workshops beyond the bridge as well as the twin chimneys of the stationary winding engines and that of the coke ovens on the right. The open carriages suggest the engraving dates from 1837. People were evidently encouraged to stroll along the cutting to admire trains in operation.

3.3 Primrose Hill approach cutting and Chalk Farm Lane Bridge over L&BR, 1837, *Engr. J Fussell*

Initially passengers were unable to alight at Camden Station as Pancras Vale (part of the Hampstead Road) was considered unsuitable. A passenger station was created at Chalk Farm Lane Bridge for passengers both to board and alight.

3.4 Euston Extension

Robert Schnebbelie's watercolour of 1837 (§3.4) is looking from Regent's Park towards the Camden Station of the L&BR. In the foreground is the Cumberland Market Branch of the Regent's Canal, constructed in 1816, that led to the Cumberland Basin, where the hay market that took over from that in the West End was established in 1830.

The northern end of the Euston Extension is on embankment for the first 200 yards (180m) south of the main arm of the Regent's Canal. The chimneys of the Winding Vaults and the Locomotive Engine House are prominent. The tall building is the Stanhope Arms, which had just been built on the corner of Oval Road and Upper James Street in the expectation that Camden Station, as the railway terminus, would require a railway hotel to accommodate passengers (#5.11). The basement remains to be backfilled to bring the ground level up to railway level (#3.7).

3.4 Camden Station viewed from Regent's Park, 1837, *R B Schnebbelie*

Moving south, the scene near Park Street (now Parkway), immortalised in

Dickens' *Dombey & Sons*, shows the bridge and the curved retaining walls under construction in September 1836 (§3.5). Bourne has captured the labour intensity of construction. The spoil in the rail wagons is destined for a spoil tip to the south of Camden Station (#3.7) as the wagons cannot escape from the cutting until about 180 yards (165m) north of Park Street.

3.5 Construction of Euston Extension, looking north to Park Street Bridge, 1836, *J C Bourne*

Between Park Street and the Hampstead Road the cutting was driven through London Clay. Characteristically, as described earlier, this would stand for a short time after being cut, but then bulged outwards with force as it absorbed moisture.

Stephenson laid down exactly how the excavation was to proceed — on no account was the face to be carried on more than 40 feet (12m) in advance of the completed retaining wall without the Engineer's written permission. The construction sequence of excavating the cutting just ahead of lining with stone and brickwork can be appreciated from the detail in Bourne's drawing, down to the curved forms for the brick lining.

3.6 Construction of Euston Extension, May 1836, *George Scharf*

Construction work at Hampstead Road was captured by George Scharf (§3.6). His drawing can tell us much about the evolving landscape and the rapidly advancing construction of the Euston Extension, which was approaching Euston Grove at the time. On the left is the church of St Mary the Virgin in Seymour (now Eversholt) Street, still extant. His drawing shows how the ground had to be lowered for rail tracks to pass under the roadways. The arched viaduct at the Euston end of the line is the approach to the short-lived Wriothesley Bridge.

3.7 Rhodes Farm showing Euston Extension approaching Euston Grove, June 1836, *unknown artist*

Whereas George Scharf was an artist who drew the expanding city with strong urban realism, the watercolour of Rhodes Farm (§3.7) has a truly rural feel, very much in the realm of the 'picturesque' despite its setting in the expanding fringes of the

BUILDING AND OPENING CAMDEN STATION

3.8 Extract from Deposited Plan (§2.11) showing Rhodes Farm on the Hampstead Road and the approach of the L&BR to Euston Grove

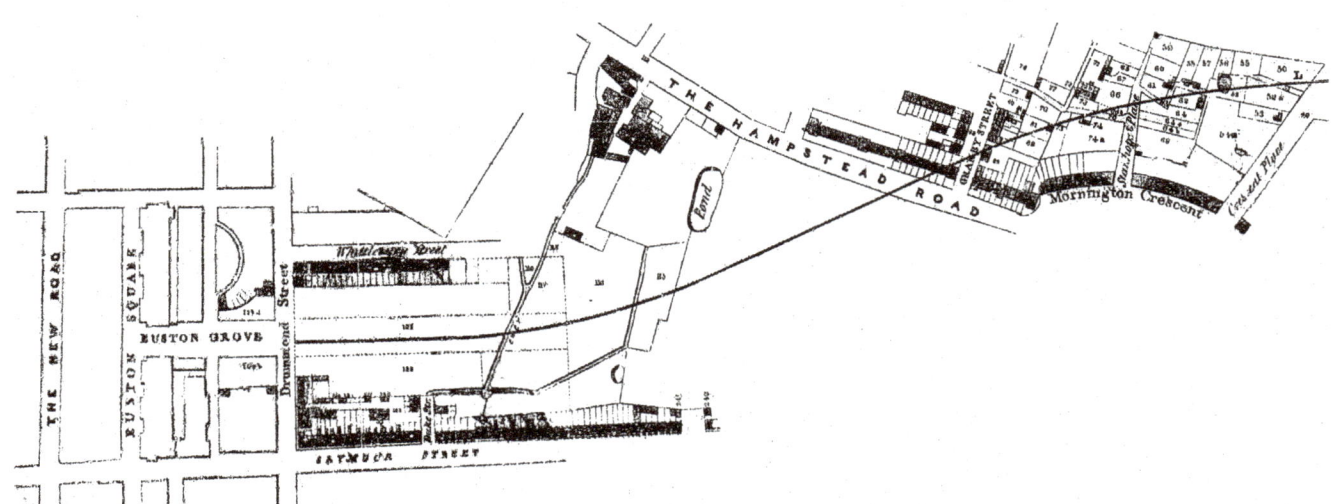

metropolis. The painting dates from very soon after the George Scharf sketch, perhaps June 1836, as the approach to Wriothesley Bridge is now filled and embanked with earth. St Mary the Virgin church is again prominent.

Rhodes was a major landowner in North London and leased a number of farms to tenant farmers. This farm was evidently used for fattening livestock before it was driven to Smithfield along the New Road. It occupied the land opposite Varndell Street, now part of Euston Station. The plan (§3.8) shows the pond and the fencing enclosing the farm that are seen in the watercolour.

3.5 Stationary Winding Engine Vaults

At the top of the Euston Extension is the Regent's Canal rail bridge, seen in Bourne's drawing of 1837 (§3.9). To meet the requirement of the Regent's Canal Company (RCC) for a ten-foot (3.0m) clearance, the depth of the bridge deck was minimised by employing a bold design, a bowstring arch bridge, whereby the railway was entirely suspended by rods from the arch ribs, the first railway example of this principle. This bridge is generally attributed to Robert Stephenson but has also been attributed to Charles Fox (*Conder, 1868*).

3.9 Regent's Canal railway bridge, 1837, J C Bourne

The Winding Engine House formed a large vaulted underground structure, located below the main line just north of the Regent's Canal rail bridge. It was built by William and Lewis Cubitt under their contract for the Extension Line. They requested RCC permission to land materials on the sides of the canal as neighbouring wharves near the Hampstead Road were too distant to be effectively used. Bourne's drawing indicates that much of the building material was delivered by canal, to the benefit of the RCC, the alternative being to cart it from the Thames. It shows the diverse traffic – ordinary barges, lighters, sailing barges and narrowboats – the contractors used to land materials for construction of the Winding Engine House.

3.10 Construction of Stationary Winding Vaults 1837, *J C Bourne*

Another Bourne watercolour of 1837 shows the construction of the Stationary Winding Engine Vaults (§3.10). It is drawn from the site of Fitzroy Bridge over the Regent's Canal. The centring for the two transverse vaults, one that houses the engines and the 20-foot driving wheel and the other the return wheel, is in place and both transverse vaults are being clad with bricks. The chimneys are starting to rise in the two far corners. On the right the centring is for the eastern coal stores. Counterforts for the outer wall of the coal stores are evident on the left. Bourne has used artistic licence to emphasise the scale of construction, the workers appearing like ants in the landscape.

The Locomotive Engine House, a drawing of which is shown in §2.10, is seen on the built-up railway lands beyond.

3.6 Camden Station

The L&BR and its Camden goods sidings were carried on an embankment above the local street level. Railway buildings in Camden Depot were generally founded on mass concrete rafts or footings from which vaults raised the buildings to railway level. The vaults played an important role in goods warehousing and later in wine and beer storage, stabling and goods interchange.

The Camden Goods Depot in 1839 included:

- the stationary engine house with boilers, condensing engines, winding gear and chimneys;
- a locomotive engine house accommodating 15 engines, with fitting shops and offices;
- eighteen coke ovens with a tall chimney to make smokeless fuel for locomotives;
- two goods sheds, stores and a wagon building and repair shop;
- cattle pens;
- stabling for 50 horses;
- offices.

The plan (§3.11) shows the original goods station plus some early additions. The curious kink in Southampton Road at Fitzroy Bridge over the Regent's Canal was caused by diversion of Southampton Road from its intended line (seen in §1.10) to avoid crossing the railway. This was described in #2.6.

3.11 The original Camden Goods Station, with some later additions

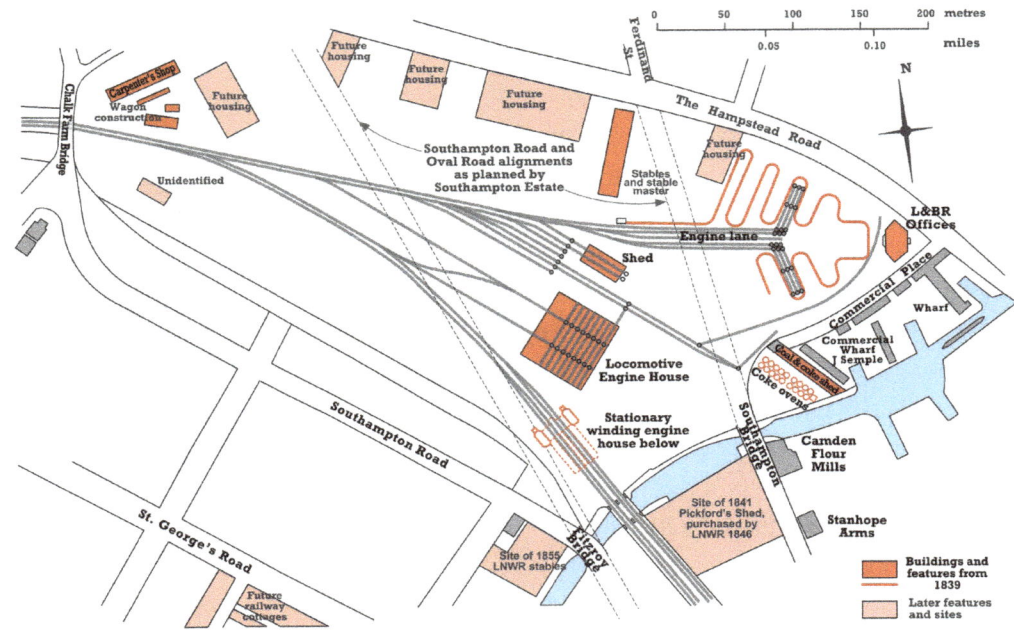

The goods sidings were constructed in a curious pinnate form, with spur sidings branching out on either side of a 'stem' at angles of about 60 degrees. Both sidings and the No. 1 Goods Shed, on the southern side of the stem, were supported by vaults that were arranged to fit within these lobes. This arrangement is shown in one of only two sketches of Camden Station under construction (§3.12), this one drawn by George Scharf on 10 June 1837, shortly before the main line from Euston to Boxmoor opened. The goods depot would not be fully operational for another 22 months, until April 1839.

3.12 Construction of Camden Station, 10 June 1837, *George Scharf*

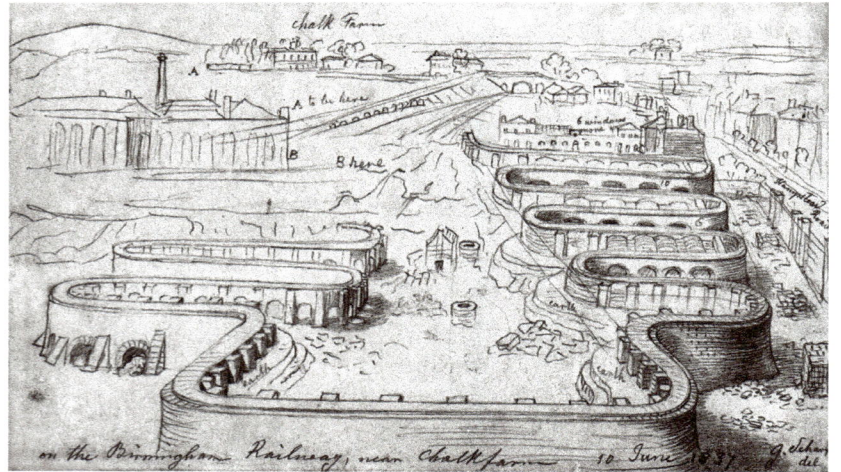

George Scharf's sketch was drawn from the tower that rose above the two-storey trapezoidal office building located in the angle formed by the Hampstead Road and Commercial Place. This building, shown in §3.16, was originally intended for the passenger booking office before the extension of the railway to Euston. It did not survive the arrival in 1851 of what became the North London Railway.

The retaining wall along the Hampstead Road appears to end at an entrance to the goods depot just beyond the most distant lobe. Here there may have been a road entrance alongside a building where Scharf has added "6 windows more", a note believed to relate to a complex of stables with the horse-keeper's house at the end furthest from the Hampstead Road.

The vaults on which the goods sidings were raised were constructed of red brick on concrete footings. The main span of the vaults was 12 feet (3.7m), the distance between pairs of rail tracks. In the direction of the rails, the modular

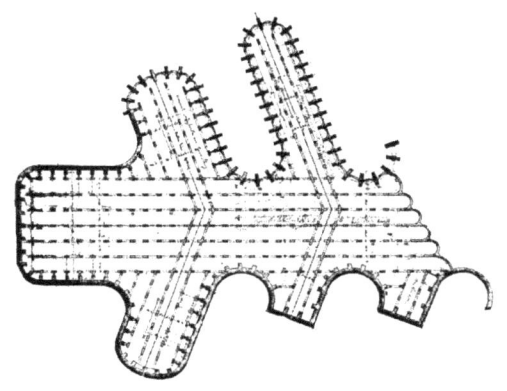
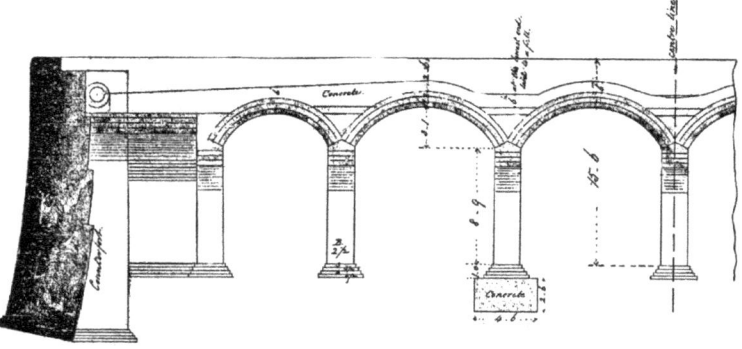

3.13 Vaults supporting the goods sidings, extracts from original plan and details of the vaulting

distance of the arched openings was 10 feet (3.0m), made up of arches 6ft 3in (1.9m) wide and arch piers 3ft 9in (1.1m) wide. A plan and elevation of the vaults and retaining wall are given in §3.13. They show a height of 15ft 6in (4.7m) from ground level to the level of the rails for the main vaults under the goods sidings. The height of the major arches is 11ft 10in (3.6m), and that of the side openings is 7ft 3in (2.2m).

The second artist that drew the Camden Station under construction was Robert Schnebbelie. By 26 July 1837, the date of his sketch (§3.14), seven weeks after that of George Scharf (§3.12), the mainline railway had opened – not the impression given by the sketch. He shows two features quite clearly: the L&BR Offices and the Stanhope Arms. Their alignment suggests that the view was drawn from Camden Station close to the locomotive shed. This is the only sketch that features the L&BR Offices, and these are shown enlarged in the extract in §3.16. The spur sidings shown by Scharf appear to have been filled. A further seven weeks later, the layout of the Depot looked much more established in a Bourne drawing (§3.21).

3.14 Camden Station under construction, 26 July 1837, R B Schnebbelie

The layout of the new station was largely in the hands of Joseph Baxendale, a director of Pickford who later served as the L&BR's Goods Superintendent for a few months in 1839. From the start of 1839 freight was hauled between London and Birmingham for Pickford & Co. and Chaplin & Horne, who had become carriers for the L&BR. From 15 April that year similar services were offered to other firms.

The Act had specified that all locomotives and stationary engines should consume their smoke. Therefore coke, which burns cleanly, was used initially, produced by the coke ovens located alongside the canal with the chimney at the canal end. Coal could be delivered by barge. There was a store on the east side of the ovens with coal at the canal end and coke at the western end. Stairs led down from railway level and all the coke produced had to be raised

BUILDING AND OPENING CAMDEN STATION

manually to the level of the goods depot. Only later, when firebox efficiency had improved, could coal be used as a fuel.

The complex of temporary buildings erected near Chalk Farm Lane Bridge in early 1837 included a stores/office and wagon shed/workshops, seen on George Scharf's sketch (§3.12). These workshops produced third class carriages, goods wagons and trucks. First and second class carriages were built at Euston (#3.9).

One of the first to work at the Chalk Farm Lane complex was David Stevenson, a young man who entered the service of the L&BR at age 16 in June 1837. He became the first clerk to the first manager of the line, taking on any tasks he was given: collecting cash bags, working in the office, and engaging policemen or porters.

Stevenson was then assigned to the workshops/stores. He describes the experience graphically *(Turner, 1891)*:

> I was drafted from the Manager's office at Euston to Camden Station, in connection with the Stores and Construction Departments. This was a change for the worse as regards my personal comfort. The office was a rough wooden erection, with an earthen floor, and contained, by day, myself in my great coat, the stores of all kinds, a table, a small cabin stove, and the mice. Chalk Farm was in the country then, and I had to prepare my meals at the small stove, and to consume them assisted by the mice, who evidently had a great contempt for my presence. The place was always muddy. The station had been raised from the road by the earth from the Primrose Hill Tunnel, and this new clay produced a Slough of Despond, which I have only seen at the Royal Agricultural Show at Kilburn a few years ago.
>
> Still the building of waggons for the intended goods traffic went on. Chalk Farm Tavern was then at the end of a lane near my office and it still retained some of its faded grandeur, as a place of resort for dancing and fêtes. The large ball-room was decked with chandeliers and convex mirrors. An elevated gallery led to the tea-garden, at the entrance to which two soldiers were painted. The Chalk Farm Fair had not yet begun, but the navvies, during the making of the tunnel, had lowered the character of the place.
>
> As a number of rats joined the mice and me in our shed, and the rain began to damage the books and goods, it was found necessary to find accommodation for me in the office of the engineer and timekeepers, beneath an arch of Chalk Farm Bridge; and then we organised a daily ordinary at the Chalk Farm Tavern, which suited me better than the cabin-stove feasts.

William Bowden, the owner of Chalk Farm Tavern, must have done very well from the L&BR, serving the many visitors to the railway, the railway staff and construction workers, and the rail passengers that embarked or alighted at Chalk Farm Lane, as well as from the various entertainments the Tavern offered. The east wing appears to have been enlarged from its 1830 form (§1.12), the balcony strengthened and the approach road fenced (§3.15).

Improved office accommodation became available in August 1839 when Joseph Baxendale was appointed manager of the line. He moved the manager's office into the

3.15 Chalk Farm Tavern in 1840s

CHALK FARM RAILWAY LANDS: A GUIDED TOUR 1830 TO 2030

trapezoidal building, once the intended passenger booking office (§3.16), that is shown as 'L&BR Offices' in §3.11. Robert Stephenson's office was also transferred into this building from the design office in St John's Wood, which took on a new purpose as the Eyre Arms Tavern. The stores and engineer's departments were likewise brought into the manager's building.

3.7 Balancing cut and fill

Given the difference between the original ground level at Camden Station and the railway level to which the ground had to be raised, balancing cut and fill would have been an important exercise, albeit one involving fairly simple mathematics.

From the 1837 plan of the goods station, it is estimated that about 60% of the area was raised to railway level in this first phase, mostly on fill but about 15% on vaults, creating an area to be filled of about 12.5 acres (5ha). The height of fill varied from about 11 feet (3.4m) to 16 feet (4.9m), averaging perhaps 14 feet (4.2m), and leading to a fill volume estimated at 210,000 cubic metres (m^3) – it is simpler to work in metric units here. Clay in its natural state is some 10% denser than clay fill. Some 190,000m^3 of excavation would therefore have been needed.

The sources of excavated material and the approximate volumes they yielded were:

Primrose Hill Tunnel	62,500m^3 (some of which was deposited at the Kilburn end)
Tunnel approach cutting	150,000m^3
Euston Incline	125,000m^3

The Euston Incline, with its four lines of rails, was enclosed by curved and battered retaining walls, shaped so as not to take more land than necessary. Primrose Hill approach cutting had only two lines of rail but was banked at 1 on 3 and therefore took more land.

Contemporary accounts suggest that all of the fill at Camden Station was provided from the excavation of the tunnel and approach cutting. This is confirmed by the volumes of excavation determined above. Little or none of the Euston Incline excavated material would have been needed for fill at Camden Station. A part, perhaps 10%, could have been used for brick making. There were a number of brickworks south of the upper end of Park Street (now Parkway), an area through which Albert Street and Delancey Street now pass.

This would still leave over 100,000m^3 of cut, or over 110,000m^3 of spoil, to be used for fill and raises the question of where this material was deposited. The wagons hauling spoil up the Euston Incline, either under locomotive or horse power, could only exit from the cutting some 180 metres beyond Park Street bridge. If spoil heaps were to be created the obvious location was an area then known as Britannia Field.

An 1834 sewer plan (§3.17) shows that, shortly before the L&BR drove its railroad through the landscape, plans were being laid for this part of the Southampton Estate. The most important feature was the Oval, where the centre, which had been part of Britannia Field, was to be retained as green space.

3.16 L&BR Offices, extract from §3.14

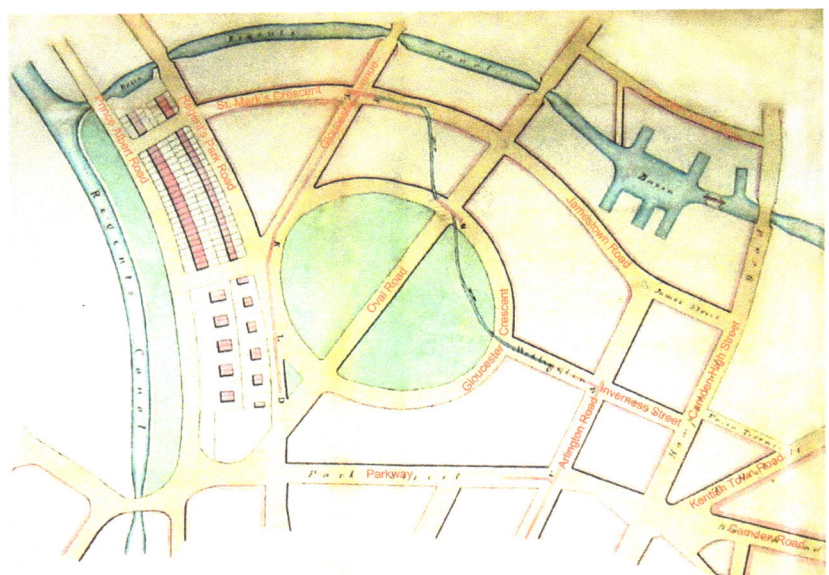

3.17 Proposed sewer on Lord Southampton's Estate, 1834

These plans were not to be realised as the L&BR carved through the western part of the Oval. But the landscape structure, while altered by the railway, remains essentially recognisable. The present road names have been superimposed on the plan. It is worth noting that all five bridges over the Regent's Canal had already been built and remain to this day. The plan shows the towpath diversion around the basins and wharves on the north bank of the canal.

The railway ran through the northern part of what had been Britannia Field on embankment before entering a cutting to pass under Park Street. This transition provided a short length of track that was close to natural ground level, and this dictated where much of the spoil was subsequently placed. However, there is little mention in contemporary documents of large spoil heaps disfiguring the landscape, nor of extending rail sidings into the area. The only account that refers to spoil heaps in this area is that of Herbert Spencer, a polymath who become a notable philosopher, biologist, and sociologist. As a 17-year old, Spencer joined Charles Fox's team at Camden Town in November 1837 and both the timing and his description of his duties suggest he was closely involved with the spoil heap (*Spencer, 1904*):

> It was, indeed, disagreeable in muddy weather to make measurements of 'spoil-banks,' as are technically called the vast heaps of earth which have, here and there, been in excess of the needs for making embankments, and have been run out into adjacent fields

3.18 'With a distant view of Primrose Hill, Chalk Farm & its environs, taken from Park Street', 1837, *A F Edington*

A F Edington's stylised engraving of 1837 (§3.18). shows the Stanhope Arms, the prospective terminus hotel, waiting for Oval Road to be raised to turn its lowest floor into a basement. This must have been the plan from as early as December 1835, when the contract for the Extension Line was let.

The spoil that was to raise levels locally can be seen in the enormous heap that had been deposited on what was then Britannia Field. It only intrudes marginally into the view that Edington wanted, not spoiling the picturesque scene, and has been unremarked on hitherto.

Oval Road had to be raised to railway level to create a level approach to the goods station. The changes in level can be appreciated by walking up Jamestown Road from natural ground level at Camden High Street to railway level at Oval Road. The natural ground must have been raised by a wedge of made-up ground from the railway embankment (seen in §3.4) to some way east of Oval Road. Were the 110,000m^3 of spoil to be spread to an average depth of two metres (6.6 feet) it would cover an area of more than five hectares (12.4 acres).

3.8 The navigators

Up to 12,000 men were engaged in construction of the L&BR at its peak. Many of these were skilled or semi-skilled men from the building trades but large numbers were labourers or muck-shifters, excavating the cuttings and tunnels by hand. Of these, some were locally based, living in nearby lodgings but many were itinerant, either living in lodgings or more often in rudimentary shacks thrown up by the contractors. They detested the name 'navvies'.

The greater proportion were English, but typically some 30% were Irish. There was always a strong tribal element to gangs of navvies and tensions arose spontaneously with little pretext, for example if the Irish were suspected of driving down wage rates. Conventionally, the navvie was as free with his fists as he was thirsty for beer and this convention was amply confirmed in the account of navvies working on the L&BR in District No. 1, described below.

The distinctive dress of navvies, their many strange dialects and colourful nicknames, and their general irreverence heightened the alarm of the local population when the railway approached a settled community and its relief when the work passed on.

Yet the navvies could be highly disciplined and relished the challenge of hard and difficult work. Drunk or sober, the work was dangerous and injuries and fatalities were accepted as inevitable. Every mile of the L&BR cost an average of three lives, with a far higher toll in tunnels and cuttings. The Primrose Hill Tunnel and its eastern approach cutting were among the first to start construction, before the treacherous nature of the ground had been fully appreciated. Although there are no figures available, there were many fatalities. The Chalk Farm Tavern was usually the first resting place of navvies killed in this section of the works.

Off duty, navvies would spend their wages freely on beer, much of it sold in 'tommy shops' run by the contractor. Chalk Farm Tavern was much frequented by the navvies on the Primrose Hill contract, which must have changed the tone of the establishment. Over their beer, their singing at night could be heard far away.

There is a full description of navvies on the L&BR in *Household Words* (*1856*), one of the journals that Charles Dickens edited. As a young man, H J Brown, after finishing schooling at 16, where he was fascinated by the railway construction works nearby in Harrow, left home in March 1835, over his guardian's objections, resolved to become an engineer.

He found accommodation in lodgings locally and worked initially as a driver on the Boxmoor embankment until he drove the loaded horse van over the tip-head. He then worked at a gin on the Watford Tunnel, steering buckets down into the shaft, before joining a typical gang of about 40 navvies working in the Tunnel. He describes his experiences vividly, from teaching an illiterate gang member to read and write (who later became a sub-contractor); receiving his protection in return; the shanty accommodation and the old crone that ran the 'tommy shop' that fleeced the navvies; the vicious battle with a new gang of Irish and the torching of their shanty; the collapse of the Tunnel, burying 30 men and the unremitting day and night efforts over 21 days to recover the last body; and the extraordinary irreverence of the navvies at a funeral.

There is space here to mention just one incident described by Brown that captures some of the navvies' behaviour that so alarmed the general public.

> Shortly after Christmas, when another man was killed, his ganger proposed to raffle the body. The idea took immensely, and was actually carried out. Nearly three hundred men joined in the scheme. The raffle money, sixpence a member, was to go towards a drinking bout at the funeral, the whole expense of which was to be borne jointly by those throwing the highest and lowest numbers. The raffle took place, and so did the revel; but the funeral, after a fortnight's delay, was performed by the parish.

His account ends by describing the gradual improvements introduced by enlightened contractors such as Thomas Brassey and the rather less successful efforts of missionaries.

3.9 Opening the line

Princess Victoria ascended to the throne on 20 June 1837, following the death of William IV. The new era that this ushered in was swiftly boosted by the opening of the London and Birmingham Railway on 29 July, two events that must have been a source of great pride and expectation to the nation.

3.19 Opening of the L&BR, view from Stanhope Bridge towards Euston, July 1837, *R B Schnebbelie*

Crowds gathered at Hampstead Road Bridge to witness the opening of the Euston to Boxmoor section of line (§3.19). Robert Schnebbelie's painting anticipated the endless rope on all four tracks, which raises doubts that he was actually there. The spire of St Pancras New Church is seen just off the line of the cutting and the Euston train sheds and Coach House (see §3.21 below) are also seen. The train on the right set of tracks is horse-drawn.

From July until October 1837, when rope haulage started, a pair of locomotives drew trains to Camden Town, where the banking engine at the rear would disengage. Thomas Talbot Bury captured this in September 1837, looking south towards Euston from under Hampstead Road Bridge (§3.20). He also shows the actual configuration of the endless rope running on sheaves, but only on the eastern pair of tracks.

The elegance of the massive curved retaining walls in the 'trench', formed from 16 million bricks, and the handsome stone and iron bridges are seen in both paintings (§3.19 and §3.20).

In 1837 there were three trains a day in each direction pulled by small and slow locomotives. First class passengers travelled in comfortable covered coaches with six passengers and numbered seats. Second class coaches were covered, but without cushions or divisions, and carried eight passengers on un-numbered seats. Third class wagons were open, without windows, curtains or seat cushions and carried four passengers on each bench seat.

Third class wagons can be observed in Bury's painting of the arrival (right) and departure (left) platforms at Euston Station in October 1837 (§3.21), as can the absence of locomotives, indicating that rope haulage had just started. Third class was stopped that month, the wagons being converted into second class carriages. It was resumed three years later with third class trains and closed carriages.

The Coach House, where first and second class carriages were built, can be seen beyond the arrival platform.

The 32-mile (52km) line from Euston to Tring (Denbigh Hall) and another section from Rugby to Birmingham were opened in October 1837. Due to the delayed completion of Kilsby Tunnel, London passengers and mail had to travel the 36 miles (58km) between Denbigh Hall and Rugby by horse-drawn coach or omnibus, a service entrusted to Chaplin & Horne, before completing the journey by rail to Birmingham. The through line from London to Birmingham opened for public service on 17 September 1838, the first passenger train taking 5½ hours to complete the 112½ mile (181km) journey.

The L&BR was originally planned to open at the same time as the Grand Junction Railway (GJR), Britain's first trunk railway, linking Birmingham to Liverpool and Manchester. Sharing a terminus at Curzon Street, Birmingham, the two railways between them provided the first high speed, high capacity transport link between London and the industrial regions of the Midlands and the North-West of England. But the difficulty in overcoming the large bed of quicksand found at the southern end of Kilsby Tunnel in Northamptonshire delayed completion of the L&BR, and it was over 12 months after the GJR opened on 4th July 1837 before a through service between London and the North-West was established.

3.20 Camden Incline looking towards Euston from under Hampstead Road bridge, September 1837, *T T Bury*

3.21 Euston Station, October 1837, *T T Bury*

3.10 Early operations – railway

The main line to Euston curved to the south between the chimneys of the Winding Engine Vaults with a large and stylish Locomotive Engine House in the angle

3.22 Locomotive Engine House, September 1837, *J C Bourne*

3.23 Entrance to Locomotive House, 1837, *J C Bourne*

between the main line and the sidings to the goods station (§3.22). Designed by Philip Hardwick, architect for the Euston terminus, it was built by W & L Cubitt under a six month contract dated December 1836 for £14,123 (£2.1M today). This was the principal feature in contemporary views of the site since the stationary engines and rope mechanism were accommodated in vaults below the railway.

The engine house was built on the up side. Rail tracks led to entrances to the three engine house units and onto turntables by which locomotives were turned into their parking bays. Points in the foreground directed locomotives to the top of the Incline, where one can be observed in §3.22.

Emerging from the engine house in §3.23 is a Bury-type 2-2-0 locomotive, being directed to either the main line or the goods depot by the points operator.

At the start of operations the site where passengers could alight at Camden Station was close to Chalk Farm Lane Bridge, but this was soon moved to a ticket office near the Locomotive Engine House. There must have been a path providing access from there to the Hampstead Road, but this remains to be identified.

W S Penson was employed as a ticket collector at the ticket office and appears to have had the spare time for some painting. His unusual and rather stylised view of Primrose Hill, dates from around 1842 (§3.24). What appears to be a kiosk on the distant summit of Barrow Hill is the pumping station for the reservoir that had been constructed some fifteen years earlier and is seen more clearly in §1.11. Chalk Farm Tavern is seen on the right with its fenced gardens.

The wall in the centre ground is the original boundary wall of Camden Station, set back from Southampton Road (later Gloucester Road) and separating the goods depot and railway from future residential land. The wall with its piers is shown in §5.4 although the piers have been obscured by the thickness of the new line drawn. The boundary wall was rebuilt ten years later about 25 metres further west, closer to the present Gloucester Avenue. Much of this later wall remains.

The gate in the wall seen in Penson's painting (which can be detected in §5.4) appears to have connected Camden Station with Chalk Farm Tavern. Staff from the depot would eat and drink at the Tavern, which became their canteen, as we learned from David Stevenson's account in #3.6.

The parallel lines running across the tracks in the foreground are surface drains created by digging finger trenches for gravel in the heavy clay fill and leading these trenches to a main drain. By contrast, at King's Cross the contractor fired some of the excavated clay to create a substantial granular permeable layer about 15 inches (380mm) in depth to provide a working surface.

3.24 View west to Primrose Hill from L&BR ticket collection platform, with mail train in foreground, c1842, *W S Penson*

The train depicted is a 'mail' train, timetabled to carry Royal Mail letters. In 1837, prior to the adoption of wagons that sorted mail, mail trains were passenger-carrying trains that included a mail coach, run by agreement between the railway and the Post Office (PO). The railway company built the carriages and operated the train, which could only leave when the PO allowed.

Post Office railway carriages included in these trains were modelled on the horse-drawn Royal Mail coaches, a two abreast, four inside narrow-bodied form that had been running on the Liverpool & Manchester Railway since 1831. They were luxuriously fitted and charged premium fares for providing an exclusive form of transport. A traveller's personal carriage was carried on a separate wagon as seen in the painting.

The introduction of sorting carriages became recognisable as the Travelling Post Office (TPO) when they acquired the mail bag apparatus to collect and drop bags along the line. Mail coaches could be attached to all trains that had first class carriages while the TPO only passed up and down the line initially once a day.

David Stevenson *(Turner, 1891)* is candid regarding the early problems faced by the line. The rails were found to be too light for the traffic. The clatter caused by the stone sleepers, used before wooden sleepers replaced them, added to the unpleasantness of the journey. Fires to luggage on the tops of the carriages were frequent. Guards, adhering to road coach usage, rode outside on the top of the carriage where, amidst other discomfort, their clothes sometimes caught fire. Signals by flag and hand lamps proved insufficient and signal posts were contemplated. Stones were frequently thrown from bridges along the Extension Line despite the notices offering rewards for the apprehension of offenders, and some of the company's police in plain clothes had to be stationed locally in readiness.

3.11 Early operations – Camden Station

Paintings of Camden Station are very scarce. Penson's painting is therefore notable, a view with the centre ground occupied by houses on the Hampstead Road that were imminently to be demolished to make way for the expanding Goods Depot

3.25 View east to Hampstead Road with Highgate Church in distance from L&BR ticket collection platform, c1842, *W S Penson*

(§3.25). It dates from about 1842 and was probably drawn from the same location as that in the previous section, namely the ticket office where he worked.

Highgate Church dominates the landscape, with Highgate Road/Highgate West Hill forming the ridge on the right. The finger drains described above are again seen here and must have been continuous over the site. The locomotive has been stopped over an ash pit and its fire is being dropped. A hose has been attached to a hydrant to the right and there is a further hydrant to the left.

The Goods Depot became fully operational in April 1839. As traffic grew, more sidings were needed, in turn creating a need for more turntables and for adapting those existing to the growing layout. The discarded turntables in Penson's painting suggest just such progressive reconfiguration ahead of the major restructuring in 1846-7 described in Chapter 5.

The livestock wagons seen in Penson's painting are drawn up at the Cattle Landing, which was located on the south side of the villas in the Hampstead Road (§5.4) until it was relocated to Maiden Lane Station, near to the Metropolitan Cattle Market in 1856. David Stevenson (*op. cit.*) describes the escape of cattle and other animals:

> The cattle traffic necessitated the erection of a large cattle station at Camden. The animals, who always, in their excitement, ran the wrong way, often escaped onto the main line and charged the trains, getting, of course, the worst of such encounters. The cattle landing was ultimately removed to Maiden Lane Station, which reduced, but never entirely stopped, such casualties. These were not confined to bullocks from the cattle pens. A sharp watchman, in a dimly lighted goods shed at Camden, once found a bear, which had escaped from Euston, crouching against a wagon, and, taking it for a thief, he pounced upon it, but retreated in dismay, unhurt.

A fuller account of operations in the 1840s is given in Chapter 5.

3.12 Electric telegraph

The first use of Cooke and Wheatstone's electric telegraph was on 25th June 1837, when Robert Stephenson introduced it on a trial basis for the Camden

Incline (*The Post Office, 1867*). It had only been patented the previous month. Professor Wheatstone, seated in a small ill-lit room at Euston Station with Robert Stephenson and other notable people, held one end of the wire, whilst Mr. Fothergill Cooke, was at the other extremity in Camden Town. David Stevenson (*op. cit.)* describes how

> two copper wires were laid between Euston and Camden and the two quiet inventors placed themselves one at either end and conversed.

However, the Directors were only prepared to lay down telegraph lines between London and Birmingham provided their counterparts at the Grand Junction Railway Company continued the circuits northwards to Liverpool, which they refused to do. They therefore informed Cooke that the trial was limited to Camden Incline. Even then, Stephenson decided to retain the pneumatic telegraph (#4.5) and it was July 1845 before Cooke was asked to establish the electric telegraph between Euston and Camden Stations.

3.13 The drawing record

The railway era began well before the age of photography. The enormous impact of railways on the popular imagination had therefore to be captured by artists and engravers during these early years. Their sketches, drawings and paintings have formed an essential resource for describing the dramatic changes that were underway. Over thirty drawings from more than a dozen artists and engravers are included in Chapters 2 to 5 of this account. The earliest reproducible photographs from negatives date from the 1850s.

But one should be conscious of artists' choice of subjects and the way that they chose to express these. There was a large market for the 'picturesque'. Most railway prints from this period produced neat and ordered views for publication. Figures, if they appeared at all, were usually groups of the admiring well-to-do (§3.4, §3.15, §3.18, §3.21). The choice of what to show was the artist's, often reflecting what the artist thought the market wanted rather than what he saw (§3.19).

Most artists steered well clear of Dickens' realities in portraying the railway – whether through commission or through choice:

> There were a hundred thousand shapes and substances of incompleteness, wildly mingled out of their places, upside down, burrowing in the earth, aspiring in the air, mouldering in the water, and unintelligible as any dream. (*Dombey & Son, 1846-8*)

Two notable exceptions are George Scharf (*Jackson, 1987*) and John Cooke Bourne (*van Laun, 2021*), both of whom were interested in the detailed processes of construction. Bourne's works remind us that it was human labour that built the railways, from the muck-shifters to the skilled workmen and the tools they employed. When construction of the Euston Extension began near his home, Bourne started drawing the excavations, subsequently moving further along the line. The drawings impressed the noted antiquarian and topographer John Britton (*1839*) who, as a railway supporter, believed their publication would help to win over people sceptical of the railways.

4 Rope haulage on Camden Incline

4.1 Winding mechanism
4.2 Motive power
4.3 The rope
4.4 Up trains
4.5 Down trains
4.6 Winding Engine House
4.7 System operations
4.8 Phasing out rope haulage
4.9 Water supply and drainage

4.1 Winding mechanism

The stationary winding engines started service on 14 October 1837. From then until 1844 trains of up to 12 coaches weighing about 60 tons were worked up the Camden Incline by an endless rope that ran around a 20-foot (6.1m) driving wheel and other large sheaves and pulleys. At a maximum ground speed of 20mph (32km/h) the driving wheel rotated at 30rpm. The mechanism is illustrated schematically (§4.1).

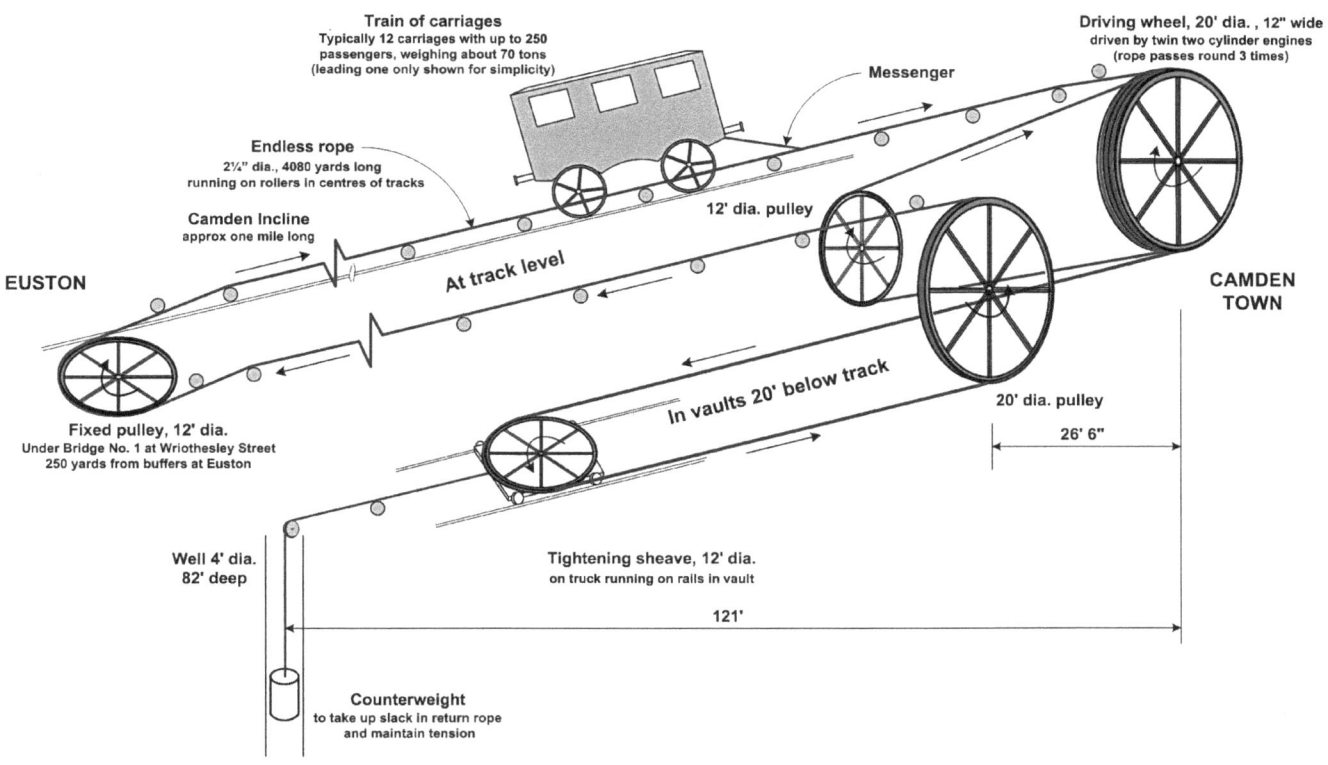

4.1 The winding mechanism for rope haulage on Camden Incline illustrated schematically

4.2 Inclined sheave, from Wishaw, 1842

The continuous rope of tarred hemp rested for most of its length on a line of iron sheaves (rollers) placed centrally between the rails at intervals of 24 feet (7.3m), as seen in §3.20. Inclined sheaves (§4.2) guided the rope around bends.

Only the eastern pair of lines was so equipped: the western pair was worked by locomotives when the rope system was not available.

The tarred hemp rope was kept taut by means of a counterweight sunk into a well at one end of the vaults. The tightening sheave was designed to cope with variations in rope length arising from loading and fluctuations in humidity. It was mounted on a four-wheel carriage running on a pair of rails and moved under the opposing actions of the haulage rope and the tensioning weight sliding up and down its 82 foot (25m) deep, four foot (1.2m) diameter brick well (§4.3). The weight may have been fully immersed in water to smooth its movement.

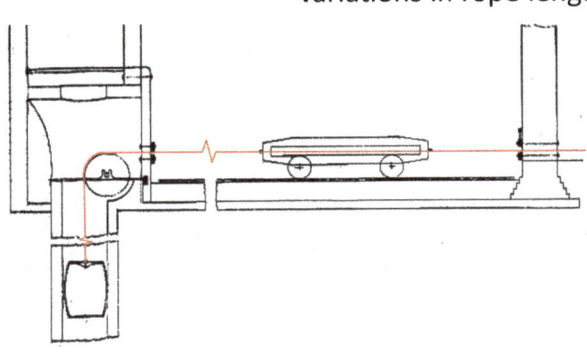

4.3 Rope tensioning mechanism, extract from original drawing

To accommodate the carriage movement, the tensioning chamber was made 80 feet (24m) long from its north wall to the centre of the well, giving the 15 foot (4.6m) long carriage approximately 50 feet (15m) of free travel. Given that the haulage rope was some 2.3 miles (3.7km) long, this may have proved barely sufficient.

4.2 Motive power

Two marine boilers 18 feet (5.5m) long, 7ft 6in (2.3m) wide and 8ft 9in (2.7m) high, were installed in the eastern boiler room. Two twin flue circular boilers 20ft 6in (6.2m) long and 7ft 8in (2.3m) diameter were installed in 1838 in the western boiler room with 100 feet (30m) of 9.5 inch (240mm) connecting steam pipe. The boiler rooms were built to be open to the atmosphere and were encircled with palisades for security.

Between the two boiler houses is the transverse vault, 72 feet (22m) long by 30 feet (9m) wide, which housed two condensing beam steam engines of 60hp working side by side on a common shaft driving a flywheel. The cylinders were 43-inch (1090mm) diameter, with a stroke of 48 inches (1220mm). Stephenson considered these capable of drawing 20 first class carriages with 360 passengers up the one mile long Incline in five or six minutes. In practice the distance from the canal bridge to the winding vaults restricted the length of train that could be rope hauled to 12 carriages.

The winding engines were supplied by Maudslay, Sons & Field of Lambeth. Delivery was delayed by repairs to the Regent's Canal and from July until October 1837, when the winding engines were commissioned, a variety of Stephenson and other locomotives worked trains up the Incline.

4.3 The rope

British shipping was almost completely dependent on Russian hemp (*cannabis sativa*). High quality hemp was more important to Russia's exports than fur, wood or iron.

Napoleon, through the Peace Treaty of Tilsit with Tsar Alexander in 1807, had tried to weaken Britain by embargoing Russia from trading with Britain. In 1811, after Russia resumed such trade, Napoleon put an army of 680,000 men into the field and began his march on Moscow, starting the so-called 'hemp war'.

Tenders for the endless rope required for the winding engine mechanism were invited from companies at the forefront of rope manufacture. The requirement was for a seven-inch (178mm) circumference rope of 4080 yards (3730m) for the Extension Line in one length without a splice. The rope was furnished from the works of Huddart and Company of Limehouse. It cost £477 (£71,000 today) and weighed 11.75 tons (*Whishaw, 1842*).

As seen in §4.4, a rope was made from hempen fibres twisted and wound together in stages. The number of yarns largely determines the ultimate size of rope or cable, with larger cables being made of several hundred yarns. At each stage the fibres are twisted in an opposite sense from the preceding stage.

Rope-making factories such as that at Chatham Dockyard had been making rope the old-fashioned way for centuries, using a 'rope walk' up to 1200 feet long to make a ship's cable, by hand and without a joint.

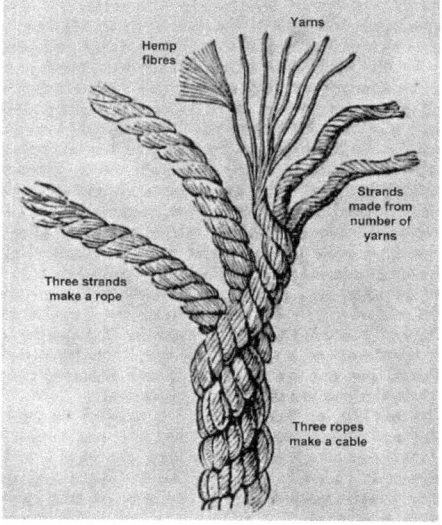

4.4 Constituents of a hemp rope

Huddart's machinery not only eliminated the rope walk and automated the production of rope but ensured that all the fibres were under the same strain when the rope was fabricated. The yarns were wound onto bobbins and placed in a large frame (§4.5).

For naval purposes ropes are generally tarred, the tarring being carried out while in the yarn stage, the fibres passing through a vessel containing molten tar with pressure driving the tar into the fibres. For most land-based purposes ropes are used in the 'white' or untarred state.

Trials of the extension engine found that the resistance had been much increased by what Stephenson considered excessive tar employed in the rope's manufacture. As a spare rope was to be kept, he recommended a trial be made of a white rope manufactured by Huddart & Co. with only as much tar as necessary to protect it from changes in the weather.

4.5 Huddart's manufactory at Limehouse

4.4 Up trains

Passengers on the up line, whether alighting at Camden Station or continuing to Euston, had to surrender their tickets. Trains from Birmingham would stop at

Camden Station for tickets to be collected. Here the locomotive was detached from the front of the train and turned into a siding while tickets were being collected and the train was prepared for its descent to Euston. The same locomotive or another was then shunted to the rear of the train to give it an impetus towards Camden Incline. The train, now controlled by a brakeman or 'bankrider', travelled under gravity down the slope to Euston Station at a maximum intended speed of 10 mph.

This can be seen in the annotated engraving (§4.6) where the locomotive, detached from the train, has just provided an impetus to its former train of carriages which is now descending to Euston. The locomotive is seen between the twin chimneys of the stationary engine house which, at 133 feet (41m) high, tapering from 12 feet (3.7m) diameter at the base to six feet (1.8m) at the top, were a major local feature. Commonplace in the industrial heartlands of Britain, they became an attraction to Londoners.

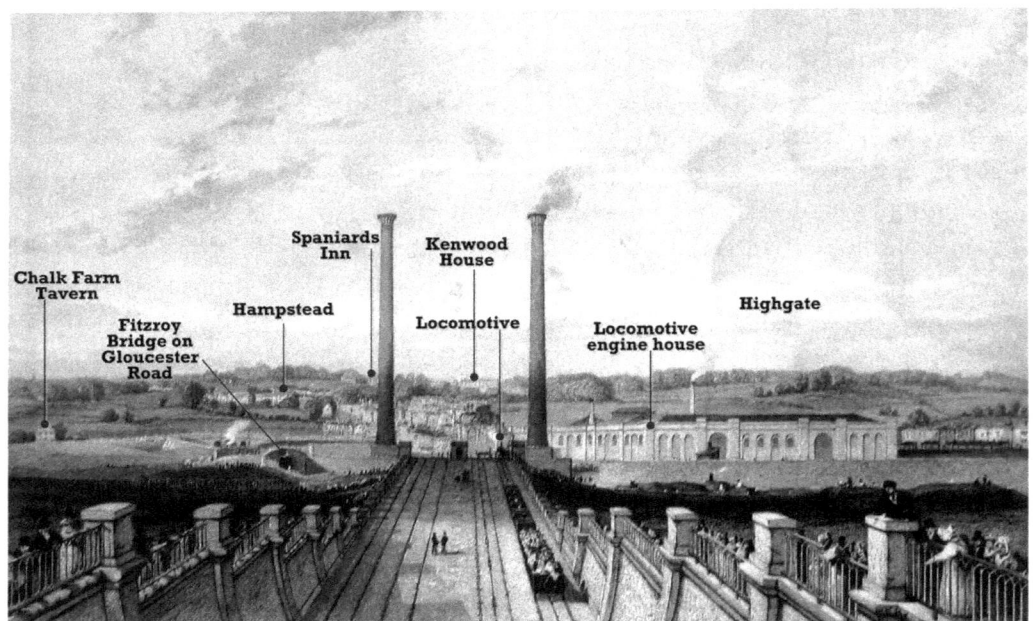

4.6 Up train descending to Euston controlled by 'bankrider', 1838, B Duncan

The image shows the line of railway initially on embankment but descending into the cutting that continued almost to Euston.

David Stevenson, whom we met in #3.6 and who later became a director of the London and North Western Railway (LNWR) Company, gives us a graphic description of how staff treated the descent to Euston (*op. cit.*):

> Railway managers of this day would be shocked at the free-and-easy use of the main line between Camden and Euston at this time. Thus, the manager rode to Euston on a waggon which he lowered himself; and any superior officer had the power to adopt this method of making the journey, quite regardless of what might be in the way. All hands were proficient at this braking, for we used to make small wagers as to stopping the waggons or carriages to an inch on the turntable at the bottom.

Stevenson was himself sometimes asked to act as brakeman from Camden to Euston, notably when the French Ambassador, Marshall Soult, Napoleon's celebrated general, paid a visit. The Duke of Wellington was keen to impress his old adversary, and the Euston-Birmingham journey arranged for the Marshall was the fastest of its era.

4.5 Down trains

The pulley system could not cope with the sharp curve at the Euston platform end. The train of coaches and passengers waiting at the departure platform was held in check by a clerk before a signal was given to indicate that it could be released.

It then moved the 250 yards (230 metres) to the first rope sheave under Wriothesley Bridge under gravity, aided by the slight fall that had been engineered for this purpose and no doubt by an initial human impulse. At Wriothesley Bridge the front carriage was attached to the endless rope using the 'messenger' (§4.7) and a communication sent to the winding engine house that rope haulage should commence.

Communication between Euston and Camden was by pneumatic telegraph, an organ pipe operated by compressed air. Guards at Euston would operate a plunger that activated an audible and visual signal at the winding engine house about four seconds later. The rope haulage system would be started and the train hauled up the Incline. It took 3-4 minutes to draw the train over the mile or so from Euston to Camden.

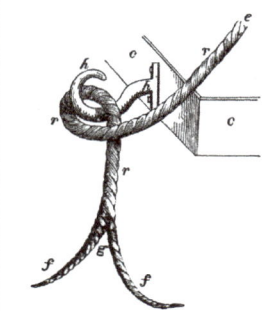

4.7 The 'messenger', from Osborne, 1839

At Camden the train from Euston arrived at the bridge that carried the railway over the Regent's Canal (§4.8). The bankrider jumped off the leading carriage just before the train reached the twin chimneys and the winding engines below. The messenger was cast off and carriages were allowed to run along the line until they met and were harnessed to the waiting locomotive engine by which they would continue their onward journey.

The rope system had been designed to haul a maximum of 12 carriages, representing the distance from the summit of the Incline to the stationary engines. A longer train had to be split, with all the attendant delay of separate ascents followed by shunting and recoupling at the summit. Assistance by banking engine on the eastern set of tracks was not possible because the sheaves prevented locomotives running on the roped track (*Jack, 2001*). This proved an increasing impediment as trains grew longer.

4.8 Down train arriving at Camden for rope to be cast off, *T T Bury*

From Camden Station passengers continued their journey by locomotive under Chalk Farm Lane Bridge and through Primrose Hill Tunnel East Portal, the western boundary of Chalk Farm Railway Lands. From the Stationary Engine House to Chalk Farm Lane Bridge the gradient was engineered to a slight fall, in order to give an impetus to a train leaving London (a down train) and to check the speed of a train coming into London (an up train).

4.6 Winding Engine House

The location of the Stationary Winding Engine House is revealed by the above ground features shown in §3.11 and §5.4.

The plan of the Winding Engine House, as originally built, is symmetrical (§4.9). It measures about 170 feet (52m) long by 135 feet (41m) wide. Only the eastern half of the engine house was fully equipped with machinery, the western half, once intended for the GWR, being largely redundant.

The boilers were supplied from coal stored in vaults 116 feet (35m) long, 15 feet (4.6m) wide and 20 feet (9m) high running south-east towards the Regent's Canal. The boiler rooms are 44 feet (13m) long by 24 feet (7.3m) wide, with workshops of 20 feet (9m) by 15 feet (4.6m) on their south sides.

Three openings on the south side of the engine vault lead to longitudinal vaults, two of which are similar in size to the coal stores. The eastern vault of these two housed the rope tightening mechanism. At the far end of these vaults are the wells into which the counterweight was sunk for the eastern vault.

The central vault is six feet (1.8m) wide with seven arched openings to the rope tightening vaults on either side. The floors are invert vaults, the inverted arches providing additional strength. The arrangement of the pulleys

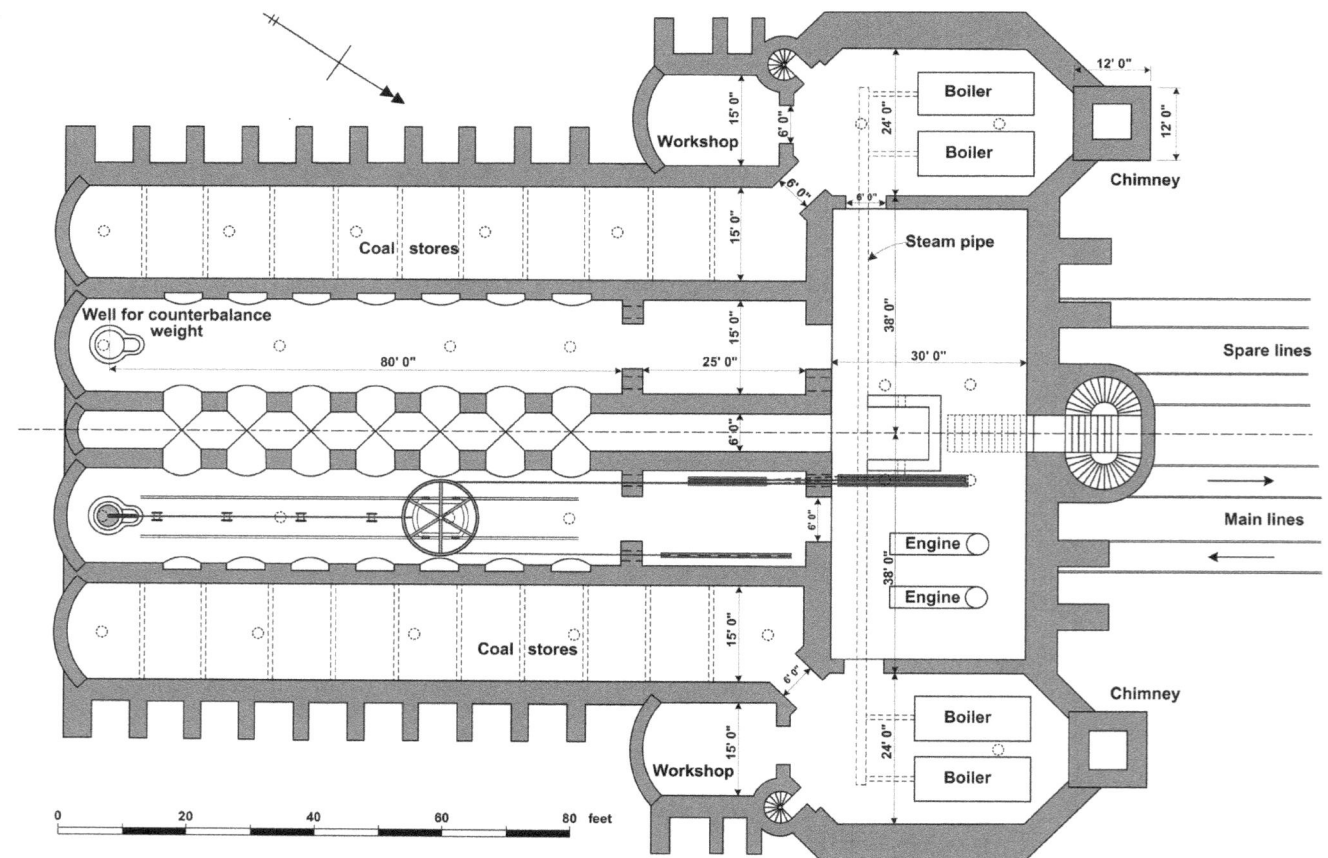

4.9 Plan of Stationary Winding Engine House, redrawn from original

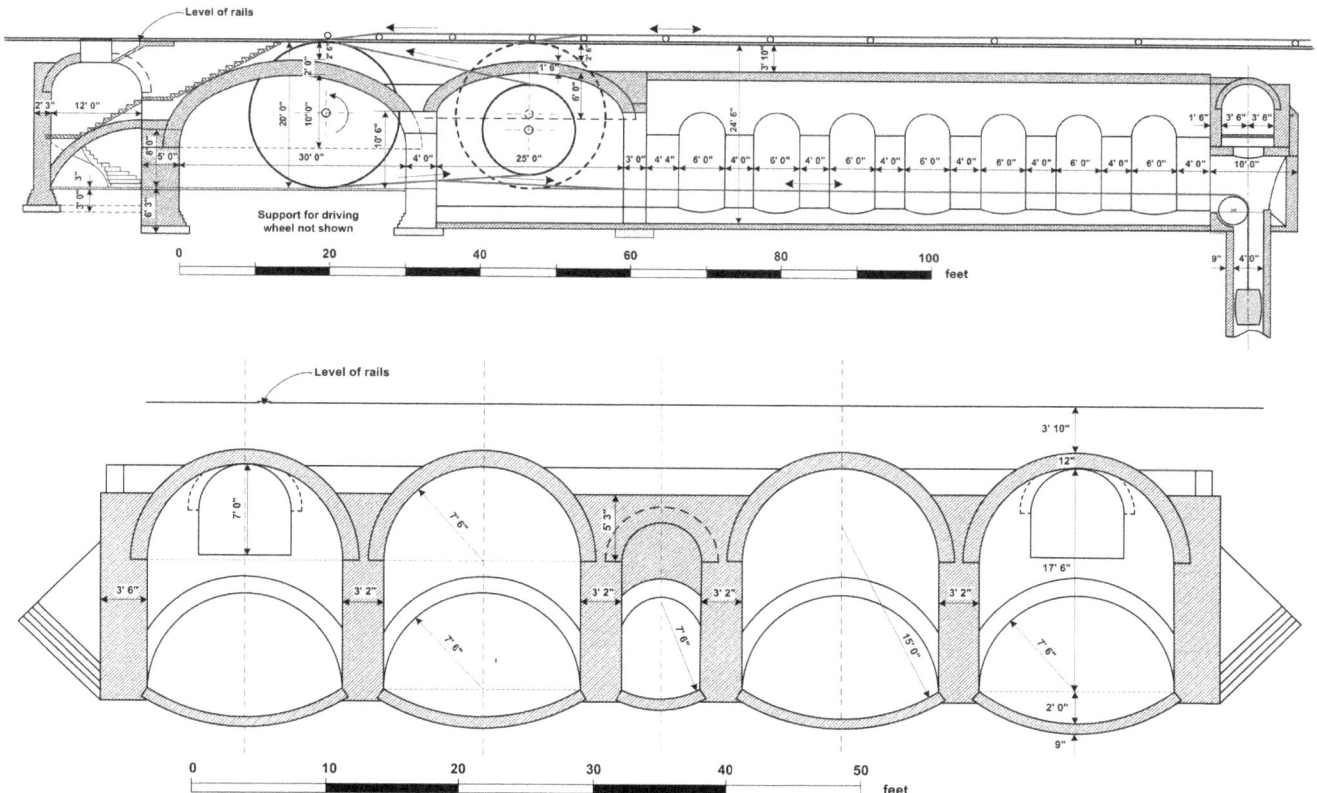

4.10 Longitudinal section A-B of Winding Engine House, redrawn from original (top image)

4.11 Cross-section C-D of Winding Engine House, redrawn from original (bottom image)

and tightening mechanism is shown in the plan (§4.9) and longitudinal section (§4.10). A cross-section is also shown (§4.11).

On the north side of the transverse vault is a staircase that was used for communicating with the signalman who supervised the movement of trains up the Incline.

Problems must have arisen with the tensioning system as, in July 1839, Robert Stephenson presented plans for a new well in the eastern tensioning vault, some 30 feet (9m) beyond the original. The new well was wider than the original and provided with a system of guide rails for the weight, suggesting a problem with friction or binding in the earlier well. A small tunnel was driven at the south end of the eastern rope tensioning vault (or winding vault) to the new well.

4.7 System operations

Access to the Stationary Winding Engine House is shown in the plan (§4.12). Coal (anthracite) was transported by canal and offloaded near the rail bridge over the canal. From here it is believed to have been moved by wagons running on narrow gauge rails through the coal supply tunnel connecting the towpath to the coal stores in the vaults, where the rails would have continued across the cast iron beams spanning the coal vaults at regular intervals.

The original entrance to the coal tunnel was set some way back from the present one, leaving more handling space on the towpath than is now apparent. The present retaining wall is an 1856 structure, replacing a sloped embankment.

The Camden Incline was economical in its use of manpower, with Whishaw (*1842*) recording in March 1840 an establishment of just one engineman and

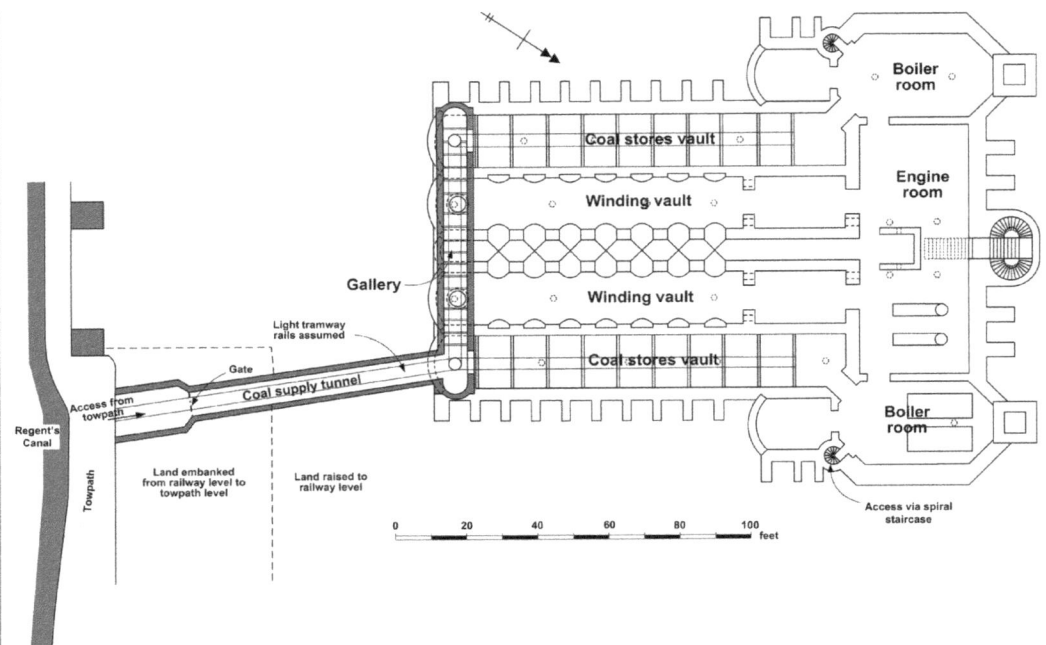

4.12 Locational plan showing access to Winding Engine House, redrawn from original

one stoker plus a rope splicer and assistant, a sheaves oiler and two cleaners, who may also have doubled as trimmers in the coal store. Trimmers used shovels and wheelbarrows to keep coal level in the bunkers and move the coal to the stoker who fuelled the furnaces. The repair of ropes must have been an important and routine task.

The main access for the engine room operator was via an archway in the north wall and stairs leading up to a tall oval room. The stairs then curve up either side to meet at a landing before doubling back as a straight flight, carried on the outside of the engine-room vault, to emerge in the 10-feet (3m) wide gap between the two pairs of running lines where the operator would have had his shed (§4.10). Secondary access was originally provided by spiral stairs down into each of the two boiler rooms.

Given Stephenson's experience of coal transport, some form of gantry or staging was presumably provided within each coal vault, borne on the surviving cast-iron beams (§13.17), to facilitate stacking and movement, while discharge chutes may have been employed to minimise coal breakage when tipping into the vaults. The boilers ran on Welsh coal (anthracite) which had low tar content. Coal consumption is recorded by Whishaw (*1842*) as three tons of Welsh coal daily when working 11 trains up the Incline.

4.8 Phasing out rope haulage

Some five years after the start of rope haulage, with trains becoming longer, faster and more frequent, rope working had become an operational constraint. In particular, the adoption of longer trains, which had to be divided to go on the Camden rope, made the Incline an operational bottleneck.

The Locomotive Committee reported in October 1843, after consulting Edward Bury, the Locomotive Superintendent, that they considered that the working of the Euston Incline with locomotive power was practicable,

CHALK FARM RAILWAY LANDS: A GUIDED TOUR 1830 TO 2030

employing supplementary banking engines when necessary. A trial on the spare line was to be started promptly. If permanently adopted, the construction of two locomotives with low driving wheels was foreseen, to be used behind the trains, in the front of which the engine intended for the journey would be attached at Euston Station so as not to slacken speed at Camden.

Trials started in November 1843, initially to accelerate only Mail Trains. These trials confirmed that newer and more powerful locomotives would be able to manage the Camden Incline, often with a second locomotive at the rear of the longer trains. A saving of ten minutes in time and a reduction in operating costs was expected. Rope haulage therefore ceased on 14 July 1844. The stationary engines and associated equipment were decommissioned the same year. New locomotives were only introduced after that date.

Within 18 months the equipment was removed from the vaults through the open boiler room and was sold at auction in 1847 (§4.13), the two engines going to a flax mill and a silver mine in Russia (*Jack, 2001*). Huddart's offer for the old rope had been accepted in July 1845. The chimneys were demolished in 1849. Cross walls were added to the boiler rooms to support new vaulting to seal the roof, which had previously been open to the atmosphere.

> LONDON AND NORTH-WESTERN RAILWAY COMPANY.
> STEAM-ENGINES FOR SALE BY AUCTION.
> On Tuesday, the 15th of June, at Camden Station, on the London and North-Western Railway, if not previously disposed of, TWO LOW-PRESSURE STATIONARY ENGINES, 60-horse power each, made by Maudslays. These Engines are in good working order, and have duplicate Pistons, also Five Fly and Rope-Wheels and a Travelling-Frame; Two Circular Boilers, 20 ft. 6 in. long, 7 ft. 8 in. diameter, with two tubes in each, 2 ft. 8 in. diameter; Two Marine Boilers, 18 ft. long, 7 ft. 6 in. wide, and 8 ft. 9 in. high; 100 feet of 9½ in. Steam-Pipe, Safety-Valves, Dampers, Frames, &c. complete.
> Office, Euston Station, April 17, 1847.

4.13 Sale of winding engine equipment, 1847

4.9 Water supply and drainage

The water supply to the winding engine boilers was taken from the header tank situated in the nearby Locomotive Engine House. This tank was supplied initially from a well sunk beneath the building, a well that did not penetrate the Chalk but terminated in the Greensand formation (now referred to as the Thanet Sands). The well water proved unfit for locomotive and boiler use because it was too hard and an arrangement was made to take the supply from the Regent's Canal, the Company returning an equal quantity from their well to the canal. This return flow ceased when the well supply diminished.

Given the increasing demand for water, it was decided to sink a new well 400 feet into the Chalk under the southwest corner of the Passenger Engine House (*The Builder 1846),* the water being raised in two stages to two tanks, one on each tower (#5.9). A drawing of the profile of this well is shown (§2); the description that follows relies on Dockray (*1849*).

Down to a depth of 180 feet (55m) there was a hand dug shaft, eight feet (2.4m) in diameter, lined with brickwork in cement. The upper 25 feet (7.6m) was lined with cast-iron to keep out the surface water, especially that which moved along the interface between the original and the made-up ground.

This portion of the well terminated in a cast-iron plate with a central circular opening through which boring continued down to the Chalk. This lower portion was lined with a 12 inch (305mm) diameter cast-iron pipe extending 20 feet (6.1m) into the Chalk. The boring continued for a further 125 feet (39m) without a lining. A pipe was then fitted above the plate rising to a level above that to which the artesian pressure in the Chalk caused water to rise, which was 144 feet (44m) below the ground surface.

However, the water was found to be charged with an unusual proportion of sulphate and carbonate of soda, an anomaly attributed to the influence of the great breweries in London. In those days, before water softening technology, the well water proved unsuitable for locomotives, but was excellent for supply of Euston hotels. Locomotives continued to receive water from the canal.

A degree of groundwater seepage into the vaults is visible today and raises the question of how they were drained originally. A key issue is whether the original drainage was a gravity system or always relied on some level of continuous pumping, which ceased when the vaults were abandoned.

Not having control over the sewer that ran through Camden Station, the Company had built its own wastewater system, including a sewer under the Regent's Canal. The original Locomotive Engine House had an extensive, and partially surviving, system of underground oval brick drains to handle rainwater which fed this sewer. Recent work has exposed an iron pipe by which the water was channelled from these into the eastern boiler pit of the winding vaults.

This raises the tantalising possibility that the vaults were central to the drainage of the goods depot. Given the care which Stephenson lavished on the design of drainage systems, we are at some disadvantage in not understanding his arrangement for draining the vaults and dealing with wastewater.

5 Growth of traffic in 1840s

5.1 Carriage of goods
5.2 The Regent's Canal
5.3 Warehouses
5.4 Handling the goods traffic
5.5 Passenger and goods traffic conflict
5.6 London & North Western Railway
5.7 Planning the second phase
5.8 Luggage Engine Shed
5.9 Passenger Engine Shed
5.10 Wagon construction and repair
5.11 Operations on Camden Incline
5.12 Movement of retaining walls
5.13 LNWR's first interchange operations
5.14 Roving Bridge
5.15 Hampstead Road Locks
5.16 Housing the company's servants

5.1 Carriage of goods

When Camden Station opened for goods traffic, the Company was short of management resources and expertise. It had intended to arrange goods traffic through its own salaried agents, but this was opposed by the public carriers of goods, to whom the Company had to turn for assistance in the first few years.

Pickford was the first carrier to obtain the rights of carriage and distribution of goods on the L&BR. Key Pickford officers were appointed to senior positions. Baxendale was appointed Superintendent of the Line, responsible for traffic. The first Goods Manager was also from Pickford. Baxendale instituted the forms and processes by which goods conveyed were tracked from the consignor to their destination, the basis of the carrying business for the next century.

Chaplin & Horne, as coach proprietors, were equally forward thinking, taking early steps to connect with the railway establishment. They joined Pickford as agents for the L&BR, taking on parcel carriage and omnibus services.

From the start of 1839 freight was hauled between London and Birmingham for both Pickford and Chaplin & Horne. From 15 April that year similar services were offered to other firms, although they were used mainly by the two large operators.

Pickford, the largest of these carriers, was particularly strong in the canal trade, operating in London from a base on the Regent's Canal at City Road. Joseph Baxendale, Pickford's director, realised that future growth would come from carrying for the railways. An opportunity arose, at the first of Lord Southampton's land auctions in August 1840, to acquire a large site on the south bank of the Regent's Canal, directly opposite Camden Station. The warehouse he built on Oval Road (§5.1), the road entrance to Camden Station, was 'twice the area of Westminster Hall'. It emphatically expressed his conviction that the future lay with railways.

The overall charges for carriage were initially set by the carriers. On the L&BR, carriers conveyed their customers' goods from source to destination, paying the Company a toll per ton for use of its railway, its railway wagons and its tractive power. They also paid L&BR a lease for terminus facilities unless, like Pickford, they owned them. As several railways might be traversed from source to destination, carriers would have accounts with each railway company, paying per ton for the extent of railway traversed.

This was essentially the same model that Pickford and other carriers operated on the Regent's Canal, a trade Pickford dominated, and a large share of which the railway was keen to capture. The model gave Pickford, and other businesses that had invested in canalside facilities, little incentive to transfer traffic from the canal. As Baxendale was also a director of the Regent's Canal Company, he faced a clear conflict of interest. Goods traffic increased little in the years up to 1845, even after inducements had been offered to canal carriers to transfer their business to the railway. Carriage rates were higher than they would have been with more aggressive competition.

The railway companies faced a greater challenge in capturing goods traffic from the canals than they did in capturing passenger traffic from the stagecoach operators, who could not compete with the superior speed and relative comfort of rail travel.

When tolls were reduced in 1845 for both passenger and goods traffic, in order to capture the bulk of the general trade hitherto sent by canal, goods traffic tonnage handled by the Company increased rapidly.

By contrast, the Grand Junction Railway (GJR), operating between Birmingham and Manchester, which had started operations at the same time as the L&BR, employed a different model. It did its own carrying, setting its own charges and using agents to collect and deliver the traffic it carried. This caused Pickford serious disadvantages in moving its goods traffic between London and Manchester, resulting in a lengthy legal battle between Pickford and the GJR. Chaplin & Horne, on the other hand, had less to lose and became the GJR's main agents in March 1843.

As cooperation between the L&BR and GJR grew towards their eventual merger, the different ways that the two rail companies operated was thrown into sharp relief. There were many complaints that the carriers on the L&BR were not passing on the benefits of reduced tolls to their clients. Following their amalgamation and incorporation into the London & North Western Railway (LNWR) in July 1846, the GJR model was adopted and former carriers for L&BR

lost the right to set rates, becoming agents for the new company. This was a major setback to Pickford's corporate ambitions and the company had to jettison its plan to become a major carrier, accepting a more limited role serving the LNWR. The LNWR purchased Pickford's shed at this time.

The benefits to LNWR's customers of its new role as carrier were:

- greater punctuality in delivery, as wagons could be loaded expressly for a town with goods that had previously been divided by carrier;
- less petty fraud that resulted from the carriers charging what they could get;
- equality of charges to all parties;
- interchange of traffic, merchants knowing the cost of transit to any part of the kingdom;
- more ready settlement of claims for loss or damage with none of the former division of responsibility between the Company and its carriers;
- more timely and reliable delivery of goods.

The growth of trade and the lower margins for carriage stimulated the already intense rivalry between Pickford and Chaplin & Horne, spurred on by the characters of their chief executives. Benjamin Worthy Horne of Chaplin & Horne threw all his excitable and inexhaustible energy into the combat, as did Baxendale and his three sons at Pickford.

Anticipating the impact of this competition on their business, Pickford withdrew from canal carriage after 1847 to concentrate on railways. (The name 'Pickfords', now that of the international removals firm, appears to have evolved from Pickford & Co. in the late 19th century. The present company of that name has retained little of the history of its forebears as its current website illustrates.)

5.2 The Regent's Canal

The Regent's Canal Company (RCC) had addressed its perennial water supply problems, aggravated during a series of dry years in the 1830s, by building a reservoir on the Brent River, which became the Welsh Harp reservoir. It also deepened the canal and lined it with stone walling. But water shortages continued until the reservoir had been enlarged in 1857.

By the mid 1830s the traffic from the Thames through Limehouse Dock for the RCC was three times greater than that arriving at its Paddington Basin entrance via the Grand Junction Canal. The infrastructure upgrades described proved timely as Thames barge movements increased and barges became wider, not least because of the increase in construction traffic (#3.5).

While the RCC traffic to and from the Docks had less competition, traffic arriving at the Paddington Basin entrance to the canal faced strong competition from the railways from the end of the 1830s. The Grand Junction Canal Company, under pressure from carriers, reduced its rate to Paddington by one penny per ton-mile. A further defensive move was for the canal companies to become carriers on their own account, competing with the railways on price. While this provided some flexibility, the low tariffs hurt the canals more than the railways, as the railways had the advantage in those early years of balancing the profit derived from passenger traffic against the losses incurred in the conveyance of goods.

Despite the rapid growth in goods traffic conveyed by the railways in the 1840s, the quantity carried by the Regent's Canal increased by about 40% in the first decade after the opening of the L&BR compared to the years prior to the opening. Aside from the general growth of the economy, much of this increase in traffic would have been between the Regent's Canal Dock at Limehouse and the railway goods yards operated by L&BR and GWR at Camden and Paddington respectively. A further high proportion was coal supplied to the several bankside gasworks.

5.3 Warehouses

Goods sheds had to be provided by the Company for each individual carrier except Pickford which had built its own shed. From 1842 the aim was that each carrier be provided the means of working his goods independently, paying rent for the accommodation. Seven new sheds were to be erected at that time, to be let to the regular carriers, but the only shed immediately built was that for Chaplin & Horne. Those carriers that only used the railway at intervals were accommodated in the shed built alongside the lobed sidings. The carriers had all become company agents in 1847.

Pickford's was the first interchange warehouse with goods interchange between rail, road and canal. Designed by Lewis Cubitt, it opened in December 1841, just fifteen months after the site had been purchased (§5.1). The shed

5.1 Pickford's interchange warehouse c1842. View east along Regent's Canal towpath, with chimney of coke ovens and Camden Flour Mills either side of Southampton Bridge, *unknown artist*

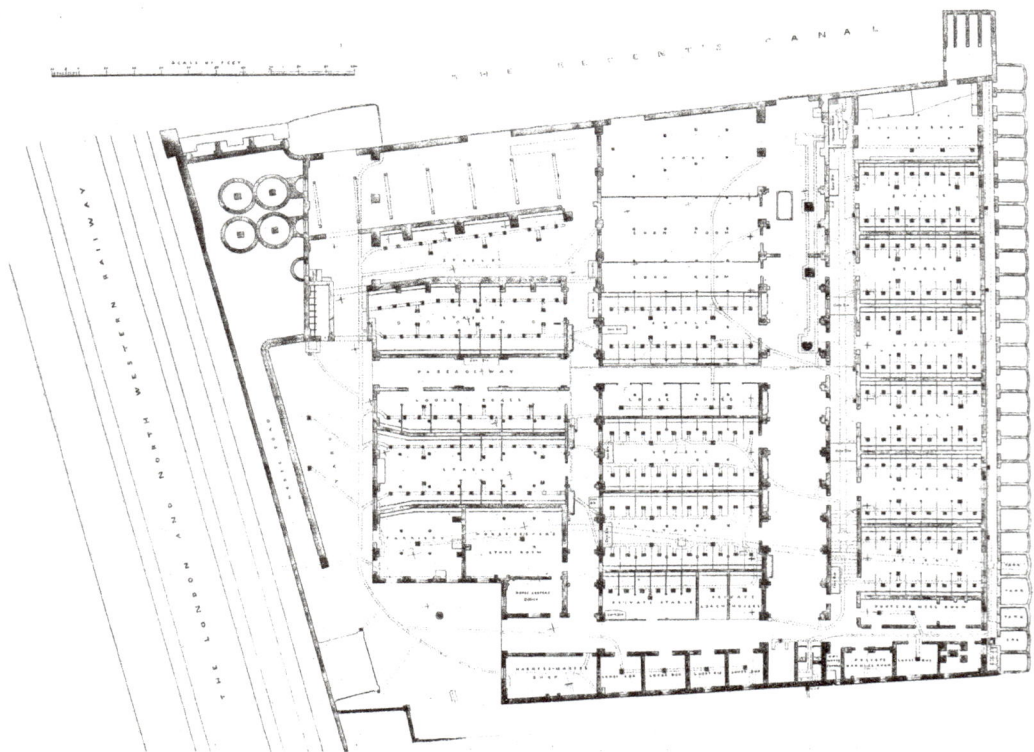

5.2 Plan of the Camden Station of Messrs. Pickford & Co., basement storey shewing drains, 1847

had extensive stabling in the basement and a rail connection with the goods yard on the north bank. The western side had a temporary enclosure, to be removed on future enlargement of the building.

With the rapid growth of traffic from 1845, Pickford's warehouse, owned by LNWR from 1846, needed to be enlarged. The basement footprint of the shed, as enlarged by LNWR in 1847, is shown in §5.2. At the same time, new and larger warehouses were built by the Company for Chaplin & Horne and other railway agents.

5.4 Handling the goods traffic

The Company's agents sent their carts to all corners of the metropolis in search of goods to carry. Cart loads of merchandise and boat loads of goods were transported to the agents' warehouses to be transferred into railway vans or brought to their general receiving sheds. To prevent mistakes, all invoice forms and wagon labels for Pickford were printed in black, those for Chaplin & Horne in red.

5.3 Pickford's warehouse showing goods handling c1842

The scale and organisation of Pickford's operations are seen in §5.3. Rail tracks, sidings and turntables criss-crossed the building while cranes and hoists assisted with loading and unloading. Goods were placed on a raised platform at a level that aided loading into rail wagons.

During the day, the contents of horse drawn vans that entered the warehouse were unloaded, to be left on the raised platform or ranged around the walls in large compartments, labelled according to their destination: 'Glasgow', 'Birmingham', 'Manchester', 'Leicester', 'Nottingham', 'Coventry', &c. On arrival and unloading, each bale or parcel was registered by a clerk, its weight recorded, and a printed charge sheet for conveyance attached. After reloading into the appropriate railway wagons the item was ticketed off. The operation needed to ensure that goods went out by rail wagon as fast as they came in by horse drawn van in order to avoid costly congestion.

Once the agents had loaded their wagons, labelled them and covered them with waterproof and fire-proof tarpaulins, they were moved into open sidings where they passed into the hands of the railway company's Goods Department. Under the Superintendent's direction, they were drawn by horses over a weigh-bridge to receive their weigh-bills, and then to a series of turntables to be turned into thirteen rail sidings, where they were marshalled into trains for their various destinations.

The up goods traffic was handled similarly. As soon as an up luggage train arrived at Camden Station, its loaded wagons of merchandise were placed under the care of the Goods Department Superintendent. They were drawn by horses along sidings to the point where they were transferred to Pickford and Chaplin & Horne, according to which the different wagons were addressed. The safe onward delivery of the goods was the agents' responsibility. Wagons thus deposited in the open were handled by drivers and horses belonging to the two agents, who brought the goods to their own warehouses, where porters unloaded, marshalled and dispatched the goods by horse drawn vans to their destination.

The Company increasingly turned to the use of its own wagons, constructed in Camden Station as described below, because of limitations of suspension, strength, security and weather protection in the former carriers' own wagons. The Company's wagons were placed in a siding, from where its agents turned them into their respective sheds. Occasionally the Company supplied tarpaulins for the wagons, for which a charge was also made. When trade was brisk and wagons were in high demand, there could be a pitched battle for the vehicles between the carriers' men.

5.5 Passenger and goods traffic conflict

The increase in speed and length of passenger trains meant that their longer, more powerful locomotives could no longer be accommodated in the original locomotive shed, which occupied a space that was now needed for goods traffic.

Goods trains were also increasing in length, prompted partly by the Company deciding to become carriers of coal (#6.6) but also by general increase in traffic. The Company, concerned at the risk of interruption to passenger trains from the increased number and length of goods trains, explored what additional sidings could be provided. With the rapid growth of passenger and goods traffic, the risk of disruption from conflicting movements of trains had been serious for some time.

The need to separate goods from passenger services was accentuated by a fatal accident in July 1845 when an early morning mail train approaching Chalk Farm Lane Bridge in heavy fog collided with a goods train whose departure had been delayed. The goods train being assembled extended beyond Camden Station and along the main railway tracks, as was normal practice. But the accident aroused a major outcry in the national press.

5.6 London & North Western Railway

In July 1846, the London and Birmingham Railway Company merged with the Grand Junction and the Manchester and Birmingham railway companies to form the London & North Western Railway (LNWR). Robert Stephenson had become the Consulting Engineer of the L&BR Company from September 1842, at a retainer of £100 (£15,000 today) per annum, in addition to charges allowed for his time and expenses when providing services. He retained this role in the new company.

The LNWR faced the immediate task of upgrading Camden Station, with the following aims:

- separation of goods and passenger traffic;
- engine sheds that would allow goods engines to be mobilised rapidly and passenger engines to be serviced to a regular timetable;
- improved facilities for construction and repair of goods wagons;
- provision of the Company's own road-canal-rail interchange facility, anticipating the proposed rail connection with London Docks that was to become the North London Railway.

5.7 Planning the second phase

The rapid development of railway systems since opening the line, the increase in volume of goods traffic and the Company's growing experience in railway operations rendered it necessary to sweep away much of the first phase and entirely remodel Camden Station.

Planning of the Camden Station reconstruction was led by Robert Dockray, resident engineer for the L&BR and then for the Southern Division of the LNWR. The general plan (§5.4), one of the contract drawings for which he was responsible, shows the original features and their progressive upgrade over 1839-1846 in a fainter form, while the major new works of 1846-7 – the Roundhouse, Construction Shop and Passenger Engine Shed – have been drawn in bolder lines. Annotations are by the author.

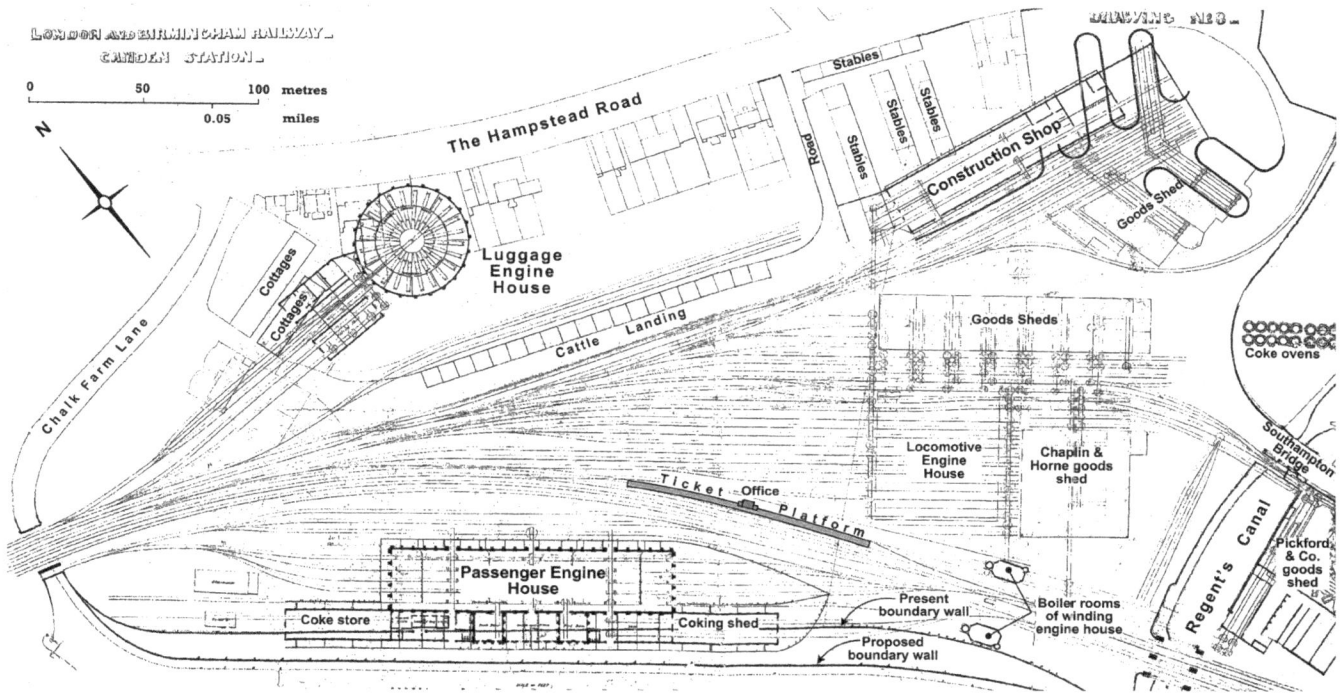

5.4 L&BR Camden Station, Drawing 8 of reconstruction, 1846-7, with annotations

The works included:

- The Passenger Engine House, complete with coking shed, coke store, offices, stores and fitters' shop.
- The Luggage Engine House or Roundhouse to service goods engines, complete with similar coking facilities to the Passenger Engine House.
- A Construction Shop for building and repairing goods wagons, consisting of carpenters', smiths' and fitters' shops as well as offices.
- Stabling in four freestanding stable ranges along Chalk Farm Road. with stalls for an estimated 168 horses. Other stables included the basement of Pickford's warehouse (§5.2) and stabling in the arches under the Construction Shop making total provision for over 427 horses.
- An additional three tracks between Chalk Farm Lane Bridge and Primrose Hill Tunnel.
- A new bridge on Chalk Farm Lane across five rail tracks instead of the original two.
- A cattle landing area with cattle pens and access road from the Hampstead Road.

The plan in §5.4 shows the complex created for the company's agents, with warehouses for Chaplin & Horne and the seven smaller warehouses (one

GROWTH OF TRAFFIC IN 1840s

double) for other agents. The original Locomotive Engine House was destined to be moved to make way for goods sidings that would improve the marshalling of traffic.

Stephenson planned for the original locomotive shed to provide each engine with an individual stable road, reached via a small turntable off one of two through roads. This soon proved inconvenient as the turntables were only large enough to handle an engine without its tender.

New engine houses were built on opposite sides of the main line near the western extremity of Camden Station, for passenger locomotives on the down side (south) and for goods engines (the distinctive 'Roundhouse') on the up side as shown in §5.4. Passenger trains were now passing at full speed through the station and this arrangement reduced the risk of collision.

To further separate passenger and goods traffic, the two tracks from Camden Station to Primrose Hill Tunnel were augmented by two additional tracks on the south side which became the down side lines, the tracks being merged to go through the tunnel. A fifth track was provided to allow longer goods trains to be assembled clear of the main line. The widening of the cutting gave a length of double line reserved for goods traffic of 2500 feet (762m).

The new bridge on Chalk Farm Lane was 60 feet (18.3m) across and spanned five rail tracks, allowing longer goods trains to be assembled with less risk of collision. Completed in March 1847, the bridge used early wrought-iron box girders to Robert Stephenson's general design. It was the first such bridge he erected and may have been the first such bridge anywhere of a significant span.

The engraving of the goods depot (§5.5) is one of the few images of Camden Station. Viewed from Chalk Farm Lane looking east, it shows the Roundhouse in the foreground with offices, coke store and entrance siding. These obstruct the view of the Construction Shop, the west entrance of which can just be seen in the far ground. Various goods sheds and the original Locomotive Engine House that was taken out of service are seen in the distance. On the far right is the Passenger Engine House, with its five lines of rail and coke store. In the middle distance, people appear to be waiting at the ticket collection platform; how they got there safely across the goods sidings is not clear.

5.5 Camden Station showing Roundhouse and other buildings, 1849, *unknown artist*

5.8 Luggage Engine Shed

Dockray's solution for the goods or 'luggage engine' shed, given the limited space on the north side of the yard, was in the form of a round house, with stalls radiating from a single large turntable.

The Roundhouse could hold 23 engines, one between each pair of columns, with the 24th track left clear for entrance and exit. In the centre was a turntable 41 feet (12.5m) in diameter on to which the engines were run to be turned into their berths over the ash pits. The elegance of the cast-iron columns, perforated spandrels, tension rods and other ironwork was widely admired by contemporary architects (§5.6). Sir George Gilbert Scott (*1857*) wrote that it and its rectangular companion (#5.9) "could hardly be bettered".

5.6 The 'New Great Circular Engine House', December 1947, *Illustrated London News*

The Roundhouse, 160 feet in diameter, is one of the oldest surviving former locomotive engine sheds in the country and one of the first examples of a truly circular engine shed. The first roundhouse, dating from 1837 was at the Birmingham Curzon Street terminus of the L&BR and was followed by the Derby Roundhouse of 1839, with each of which Robert Stephenson was closely involved. Both have polygonal sides that create the rounded form.

Below the Camden Roundhouse were brick vaults, founded at natural ground level, which raised the turntable and engine storage bays 15 feet (4.5m) to the railway level (§5.7). Below the turntable, and central to the basement vaults is the Hub, a circular space 36 feet (11m) in diameter. From the Hub eight

5.7 Basement of Roundhouse: Hub (left) showing radial passages; inner circular passage (centre); and one of 24 radial passages for removing ash (right)

GROWTH OF TRAFFIC IN 1840s

passages radiated to an inner circular passage from which 24 passages, corresponding to the locomotive bays and ash pits, radiated to an outer circular passage. These passages provided the means of removing spent fuel and other waste.

The Roundhouse served its intended function for only a few years. The next stage is described in #6.3.

5.9 Passenger Engine House

The Passenger Engine House was located on the down side of the mainline as it enters Camden Station from Euston before curving west around Primrose Hill. It was orientated northwest-southeast but, for simplicity, will be described as having west and east ends.

A further three acres of land were purchased to provide for an engine shed of internal dimensions 397 feet (121m) by 90 feet (27m). There were five doorways at each end and five lines of rails running through the building, locomotives diverting directly from the main line to pass into the straight shed and subsequently out through the west end (§5.8). It could hold 40 locomotives and their tenders of the largest class.

5.8 West end of Passenger Engine House, 1905

5.9 Passenger Engine Shed, extracts from Drawing Nos. 4 and 5 of reconstruction 1846-7

The various functions associated with the engine shed were carried out in extensions to the shed's south side, or rear of the building, which ran behind the wall along Gloucester Road (§5.9). These extensions to west and east

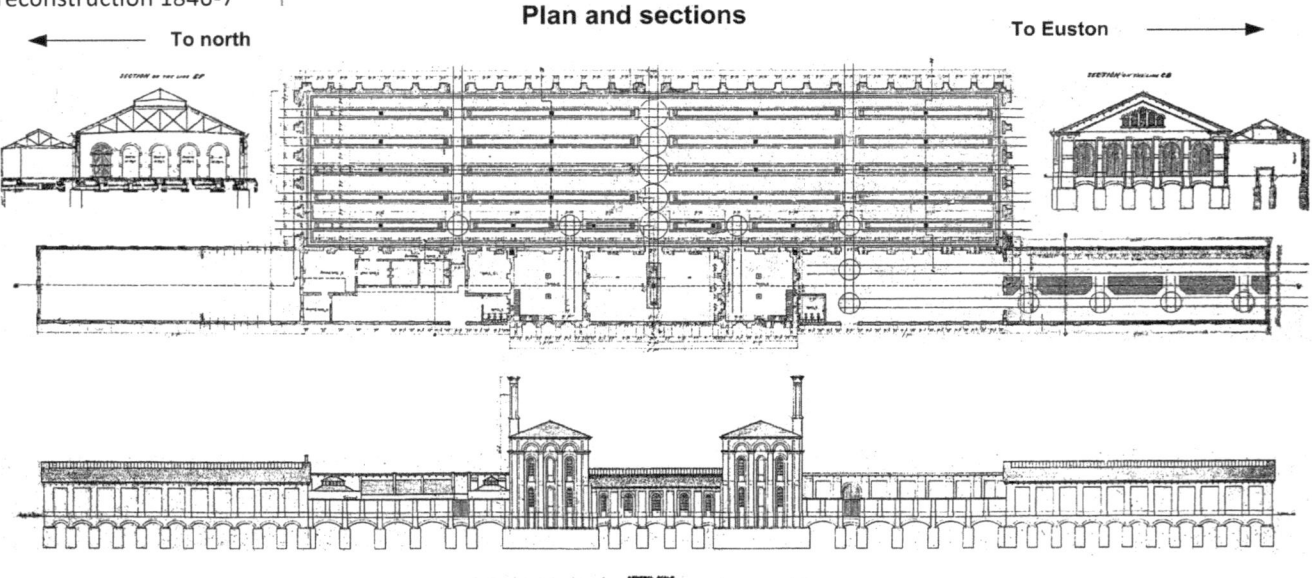

← To north

Plan and sections

To Euston →

Rear elevation to Gloucester Road

CHALK FARM RAILWAY LANDS: A GUIDED TOUR 1830 TO 2030

were each 152 feet (46.3m) long, resulting in an overall shed length of 700 feet (213m) The eastern extension housed the coke shed where tenders were loaded. Next to this was the two-storey tank house, intended for the carpenters' and coppersmiths' shops. Above was a tank holding 38,673 gallons (176,000 litres), one of two such tanks, filled by steam-driven pumps from an artesian well close by. The next building, and between the two tank houses, was the fitters' and smiths' shops. The western extension was a coke store for 2000 tons of coke (§5.9).

5.10 View along Fitzroy Road to Passenger Engine Shed, c1910

The rear elevation faced Fitzroy Place (now Dumpton Place). Residents looking along Fitzroy Road would have seen part of the classical rear elevation with its twin towers rising above the wall (§5.10). The tall building on the left is J & J Hopkinson's piano factory. The engine shed rose 45 feet (14m) above the level of the rails and could readily be mistaken for one of the ornate Victorian terraces springing up along Gloucester Road. Fifty years after its original construction, an additional storey is seen in §5.10 to have been added between the towers. The date of this is uncertain.

5.10 Wagon construction and repair

The Construction Shop, for building and repairing goods wagons under the supervision of Edward Bury as Locomotive Superintendent, complemented a wagon shop at Wolverton and carriage construction at Euston. There was room to build and repair 100 wagons at the same time.

Now that it was responsible for carriage on the railway, the Company wanted to build better wagons both to reduce theft and breakages and to reduce maintenance and replacement costs. The wagon-building department at Camden therefore built and patented a durable covered wagon with buffers, using galvanised iron, combining strength with lightness, which made pilferage much harder and reduced maintenance. British oak was the favourite wood for the frames of railway wagons.

The Construction Shop would have employed a large number of skilled men. They could access the site from the Hampstead Road where there was a side road into the goods depot that survived from 1839 to 1856, until the building of the massive retaining wall, or Great Wall.

To make way for the Construction Shop, some of the lobe-shaped structures that had been built for spur sidings to the north-east of the original No. 1 Goods Shed (§5.4) were cleared away.

The building measured 435 feet (133m) long by 70 feet (21m) wide and was covered by a roof in two spans. It stood on the northern edge of the 1839 vaults, which extended about 25 feet (7.5m) further south to back onto the embankment of the goods depot. It was brought up to the level of the rails on

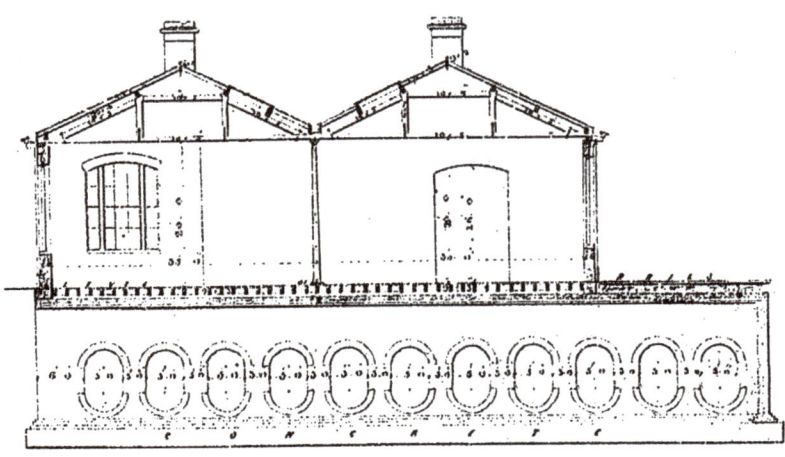

5.11 Cross-section of Construction Shop showing minor vaults, rail access and sidings alongside, extract from Drawing No. 1 of reconstruction 1846-7 (left image)

5.13 Transverse vaults of 1846–7 (right image)

vaults which were used for stables and general stores. A cross section through one of the 25 main vaults (§5.11) shows the original 11 minor vaults.

The main vaults are arches with a 14ft 3in (4.3m) clear span and are 12 feet (3.7m) from ground level to the crown with three feet (0.9m) piers (§5.12). The minor vaults in the form of transverse arched openings are five feet (1.5m) wide with three feet (0.9m) piers. They are only about six feet (1.8m) high from ground level with inverted arches on top of the footings providing structural support. The view at §5.13 is through the transverse arches two decades after they had been vacated by W & A Gilbey, which had used them for storage of wine in barrels (§9.12).

5.12 Longitudinal section through rail sidings showing main vaults with elevation of Construction Shop, extract from Drawing No. 1 of reconstruction 1846-7

5.11 Operations on Camden Incline

Locomotives continued to be taken off trains to Euston north of the canal after the winding engines were decommissioned in 1844; and until 1857 bankriders controlled the descent to Euston. Thereafter delays in clearing the arrival platform at Euston led to the introduction of pilot engines for the descent of main line trains, while their locomotives continued to be detached at the Camden ticket platform. Taking the locomotive off at Camden also meant it could be refreshed with coal and water at the nearby Passenger Engine Shed before heading down to Euston to pick up its next train.

The LNWR had expanded at Euston into the space originally reserved for the GWR, including building the Great Hall. The train shed extension adopted similar roofing to the original but was set somewhat higher. The original roof had been designed by Charles Fox, the Assistant Engineer on the Euston Extension, whose distinguished career included being knighted for his contribution to the construction of the Crystal Palace for the Great Exhibition of 1851. Despite raising the roof, locomotives would almost certainly still have had

5.14 The top of Camden Incline with ticket collection platform and bankriders' waiting room, 1848, *W H Prior*

to be taken off prior to the train entering Euston station. This was common practice in terminal stations with low train shed roofs, as at Euston, which did not allow adequately for the dispersal of smoke and steam. In a remarkable exercise carried out in 1870 Fox's original roof was jacked up by about six feet.

As part of the reconstruction of Camden Station in 1846 the ticket collector's platform and office and the bankriders' waiting room were moved immediately south of the railway bridge over the Regent's Canal. The platform can be seen beyond the four tracks in W H Prior's 1848 watercolour (§5.14) from a south-westerly viewpoint. This also functioned briefly as the short-lived Camden Town Station passenger platform. Access from Oval Road for those boarding or alighting here cannot have been ideal in what was a congested industrial landscape.

The painting shows Pickford's enlarged shed with its western façade stepped back twice. Chaplin & Horne's new warehouse, built in 1845 by William Cubitt, is seen on the other side of the canal, on which the mast of a Thames barge can also be seen. Collard & Collard's first piano factory on Oval Road is on the right. Beyond that, on Oval Road, was the Stanhope Arms, which the proprietor had built in the expectation that it would become the terminus hotel for Camden Station. It was put on the market in 1842, with typical estate agent hyperbole, advertising that:

> This valuable Property was erected by the present Proprietor and Occupier, at an Expense upwards of £8000 (£1.2M today), and contains every Appendage and Convenience for carrying on a large Trade. There is also in contemplation the erection of a Passengers' Railway Station, which will abut on these premises. The Outbuildings comprise Stabling for Six Horses, Coach Houses, Dry Skittle Ground, etc.

5.12 Movement of retaining walls

In May 1842, within five years of the Extension Line opening, Stephenson found himself once again addressing the forces exerted by London Clay. Behind the western retaining wall the clay had become saturated through inadequate drainage and sections of the wall had been thrust forward by up to 12 inches (300mm).

The solutions adopted involved varying combinations of improved drainage, large vaults behind some of the upper and weaker sections and using the east wall as an abutment for cast iron girders of large section spanning between the two walls (§5.15).

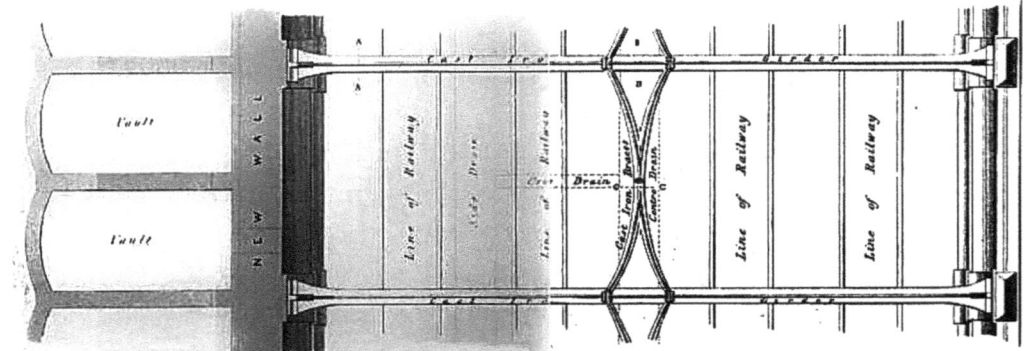

5.15 Vaults, beams and strutting to prevent further movement and ease pressure on retaining wall, from Dempsey (1855)

This last measure was supplemented by strong wooden struts running horizontally between the footings of the two walls to prevent movement of the lower part of the western wall once the upper part had been restrained.

Although the cast iron girders were removed when the railway was widened around 1900, one or two were still in evidence many years later (§5.16).

Drainage measures taken in 1843 involved drilling holes six to eight feet (1.8 to 2.4m) long and three inches (75mm) in diameter inclined upwards through the wall, with perforated cast iron tubes being introduced and fixed into the wall. The water thus drained from the clay was gathered in a large open drain by the side of the permanent way and near the foot of the western wall (§5.17).

The cutting between Chalk Farm Lane Bridge and Primrose Hill Tunnel is 400 yards (366m) in length and upwards of 60 feet (18.3m) in height, with higher ground behind. By 1844 it was in a very precarious state, with a tendency to slip, notably on the down side (south) bank, until trenches three to six feet (1.2 to 1.8m) deep had been excavated to receive perforated pipes.

5.16 Cast iron girder showing section of original retaining wall, close to Parkway Bridge, c1955 (left image)

5.17 Drainage of soil behind retaining wall (right image)

CHALK FARM RAILWAY LANDS: A GUIDED TOUR 1830 TO 2030

5.13 LNWR's first interchange operations

The L&BR was keen to take greater control of the goods trade and, following Pickford's lead, was determined to expand its interchange operations. The Company had acquired the lease of Semple's Wharf at Hampstead Road Locks and in 1841 laid two sidings to the wharf, the change in level being accommodated via a reversing spur (§5.18). Evidence of this remains in the form of the skewed arch under the North London Line in what is now Paddock Lane (#14.3).

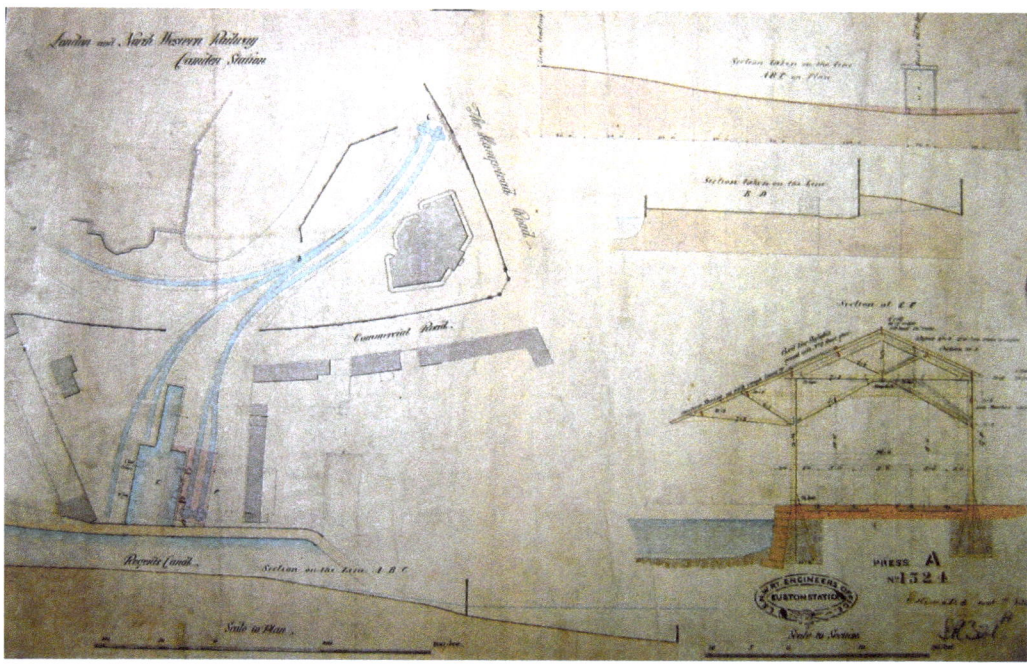

5.18 LNWR interchange basin with reversing spur, 1848

While the change in level could be accommodated without interfering with the towpath that continued to run along Commercial Place, the growth of canal-rail interchange must have disrupted towpath operations.

In March 1845, the Company purchased the freehold of Semple's Wharf and of the towing path between the wharf and the Company's land. Shortly thereafter the LNWR reached agreement with the Regent's Canal Company to relocate the towpath away from Commercial Place. The new towpath was to run on a bridge across the front of LNWR's interchange basin before switching to the south side of the canal via a diagonal bridge, the Roving Bridge, avoiding the need to bridge over entrances to the two docks on the north bank not in LNWR ownership.

By 1847 the LNWR was negotiating with the RCC to enlarge its dock and the railway communication with the dock. Wagons were ramped down to the basin via the reversing spur to a single-story wooden shed on the east side equipped with a number of cranes (§5.18).

5.14 Roving Bridge

A roving bridge is a bridge over a canal constructed to allow a horse towing a boat to cross the canal when the towpath changes sides.

Camden's Roving Bridge, built in 1846 immediately upstream of Hampstead Road Locks, is of cast-iron construction, effectively two arches, one above the

GROWTH OF TRAFFIC IN 1840s

5.19 The structure of the Roving Bridge

other, with the upper one constrained by tensioned rods. The bridge is formed as a distinctive cast iron arch cum vierendeel truss, a rare example of a cast iron arch bridge with wrought iron tie bars fixed at the top of the parapet (§5.19). No other cast iron towpath bridges with these have been identified. The tie bars carry the tensile loads and induce a state of permanent compression in the lower flanges in the same way as in a post-tensioned concrete beam.

5.20 Anchorage for tie bars

The clear span of the bridge is 79ft 6in (24.25m) with a rise of four feet (1.2m). The parapets are at 7ft 3in (2.2m) centres. It is cast in four pieces. Each side of the bridge consists of two halves, joined at the centre with two hexagonal bolts. At the ends of the bridge the top rails swell into massive blocks, with large cylindrical anchorage lugs cast integrally, each of which carries two 1¼ inch (32mm) diameter steel tie bars (§5.20). Originally of wrought iron they run from the top of the bridge, but the curvature carries them down to below the footpath at the centre.

The bridge was manufactured in Newport, Monmouthshire by Joseph Deeley's London and Newport Iron Works. As well as an iron founder, Deeley was an engineer and an inventor, having developed a patent foundry furnace that allowed iron to be smelted using a cleaner and less costly process, resulting in both a higher yield and a superior quality of iron.

The towpath bridge that crosses the entrance to the Interchange basin was erected by the RCC at the same time as the Roving Bridge, under the same contract.

5.15 Hampstead Road Locks

The RCC decided in mid-1846, after the Roving Bridge had been completed, to provide horses for towing. It divided the Regent's Canal into three post stops where horses would be changed. The stabling at Hampstead Road Locks, next to the Lock-keeper's Cottage, seen in §5.21, provided stalls for up to 18 horses in a single storey building between the Lock-keeper's Cottage and the stablemaster's cottage at each end.

Barges in the southern lock had to be towed across to the northern bank to continue their journey upstream. The rope would pass under the Roving Bridge on the upstream side to be attached to the horse, now on the bridge. The horse then pulled the barge across to the towpath (§5.22).

The cast iron handrail of the Roving Bridge and the stone parapet of the abutments are deeply scored, evidence of the forces required to turn the barge against the flow of canal water (§5.23). Cotton towropes are heavier than water, to allow boats to pass without entanglement. They pick up particles of sand and silt from the bed of the canal. The scarring is created by the abrasive action of the sand.

5.21 Stables at Hampstead Road Locks, 1947, *John Gay* (left image)

5.22 Towing a barge out of the southern lock (centre image)

5.23 Scarring of cast iron parapet of Roving Bridge (right image)

5.16 Housing the company's servants

The Locomotive Department was seeking housing for the accommodation of engine drivers as early as May 1840, before the auctions of Lord Southampton's estate later that year.

The minutes do not specify where in Camden the first cottages were built, but the Davies map of 1843 (§5.24) suggests that these were around Ferdinand and Harmood Streets. These streets are close to the service road that led from Camden Station to the Hampstead Road (§5.4).

Evidently the Phase 2 reconstruction, with its two engine sheds, created a need for further accommodation. In 1846 the trapezoidal offices, recently occupied by the Goods Department, were converted for use by engine drivers, presumably as temporary accommodation. A few years later this building was swept away by the creation of the North London Railway.

5.24 Extract from Davies map of 1843

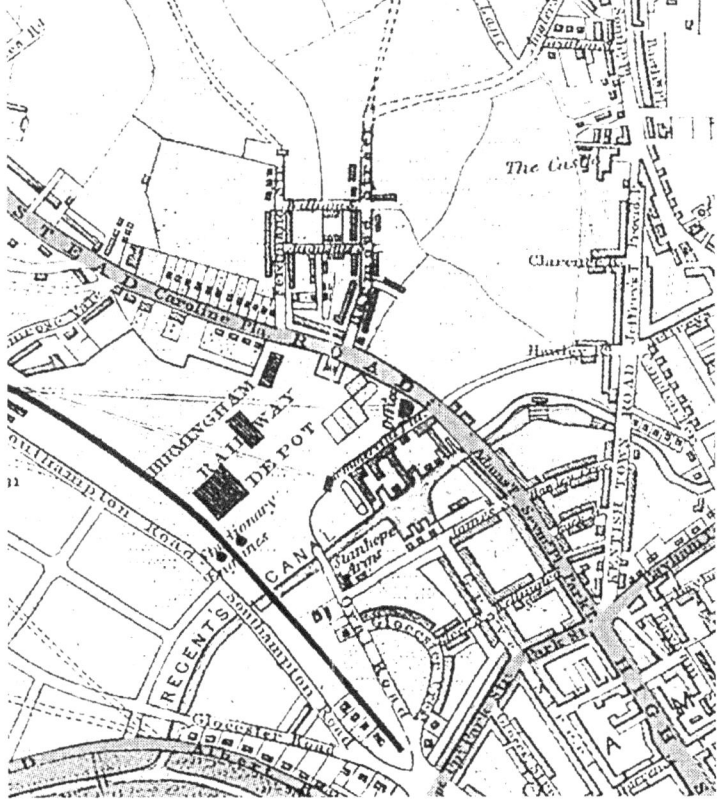

GROWTH OF TRAFFIC IN 1840s

Cottages were also built on the west side of the Roundhouse as seen in the Camden Station general plan for Phase 2 (§5.4).

As part of the Phase 2 restructuring, the Locomotive Department requested that 70 cottages be built for those working at the new Passenger Engine Shed. Access to the shed would have been via Fitzroy Road and its extension into what is now Dumpton Place (#11.7).

A suitable piece of land of 1¾ acres (0.7ha) was found on St. George's (now Chalcot) Road (§5.25). that had been Lot 262 in Lord Southampton's sale of August 1840. In September 1848 the Company reported they had entered into negotiations to purchase 1¼ acres (0.5ha) of this land for £2900. Evidently, the other half acre was retained for future better-quality houses fronting St. George's Road.

5.25 Daws map extract, 1849

5.26 Enlarged Daws map extract, 1849 (left image)

5.27 Railway Cottages, Manley Street, Primrose Hill, 1962 (right image)

The Company invited tenders for the erection of 42 cottages and accepted that of William Palmer of Kentish Town for £5859 or about £139 (£21,000 today) per cottage.

An enlarged Daws map extract (§5.26). shows that the railway cottage terraces were among the earliest housing built in what is now Primrose Hill and confirms the number of cottages. An early version of St. Mark's Church is also shown. The longest of the terraces, which had 16 cottages, is seen in the photograph (§5.27).

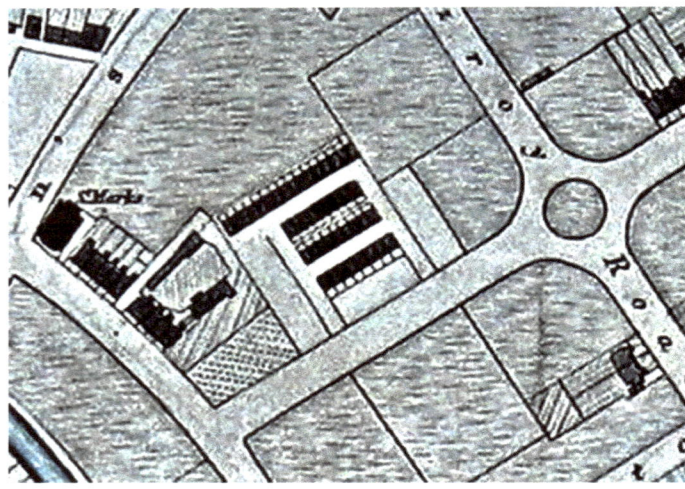

CHALK FARM RAILWAY LANDS: A GUIDED TOUR 1830 TO 2030

6 NLR and 1850s reconstruction

6.1 Connection to the Docks: the NLR
6.2 Hampstead Road station on NLR
6.3 NLR impact on Roundhouse
6.4 NLR impact on main line
6.5 Camden Station: the third phase
6.6 Coal supply
6.7 Water supply for locomotives
6.8 A succession of fires
6.9 The Electric Telegraph Works
6.10 Access to Eton's Chalcots Estate
6.11 Public perception of railway lands

6.1 Connection to the Docks: the NLR

The rail freight connection between Camden Station and the London docks was not made until the completion of the East and West India Docks and Birmingham Junction Railway (E&WIDL) in 1851. The name was changed to the North London Railway (NLR) in 1853. The tracks were aligned over the original goods sidings as shown in the 1852 plan (§6.1), requiring the construction of a viaduct and the demolition of the former railway offices as the line approached the bridge over the Hampstead Road.

The plan curiously omits the Construction Shop. The original locomotive shed has gone, apparently moved to Southampton in 1850. The building seen

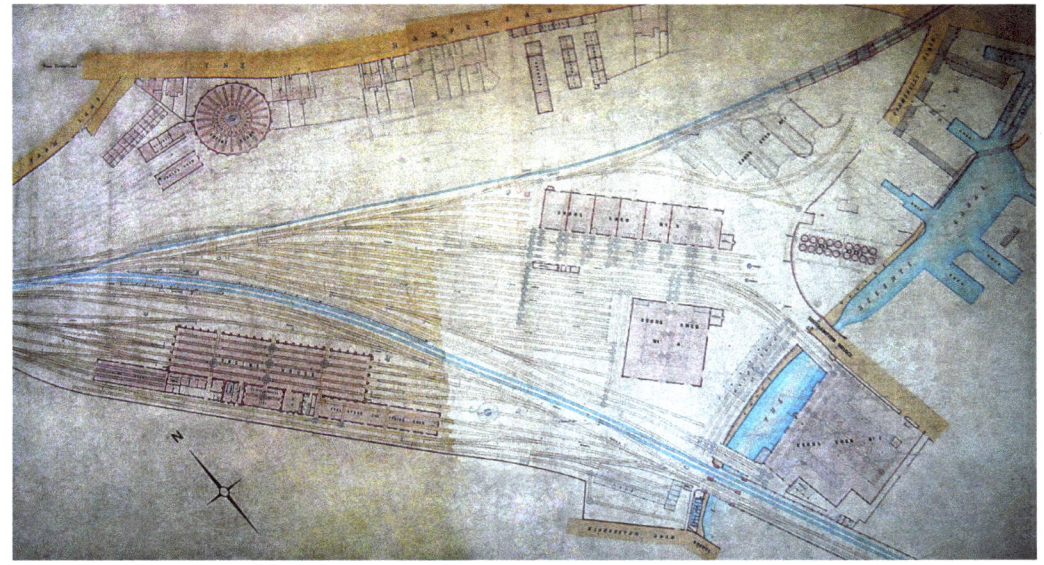

6.1 Plan of Camden Goods Station, 1852

6.2 Collapse of arches of E&WIDL, 1849, from *Illustrated London News*

rather faintly northeast of the coke ovens is believed to be the first warehouse provided for Allsopp, the Burton brewers (#8.6).

With the through line from Camden Station, goods could be moved directly to and from the London Docks, and the railway was a direct rival to the Regent's Canal at last. The line also proved very successful as a passenger line for city workers commuting from the suburbs to Broad Street.

Construction of the E&WIDL had not been straightforward. On Sunday 18 November 1849, no fewer than seven of the newly erected arches, those near the Kentish Town Road and crossing the Hawley Road at Camden Town, fell with a resounding crash (§6.2). The cause was never fully ascertained, but weak foundations, affected by the proximity of the Fleet River, were probably the main factor.

Instructions were given in May 1850 to authorise the removal of the trapezoidal building that was originally intended for the principal offices of the Company and later used as a lodging house for engine drivers.

The LNWR required that the E&WIDL erect their works and lay down lines on its land at the E&WIDL's expense, such works and lines to become, on their completion, the absolute property of the LNWR. Dockray specified in June 1850:

> the E&WIDL shall forthwith proceed to provide construct and complete to the satisfaction of … the Engineer of the LNWR company, a double line of railway with all proper works and appliances including the sidings sheds platforms points and turntables necessary at junctions

In the event, the permanent way was laid double only part of the way into Camden Station (§6.1), from which point it was laid single until Chalk Farm Lane Bridge. The Inspector for the Railway Commissioners required a signal where the line became single and a second signal where the LNWR siding serving the Construction Shop crossed the new permanent way. Here a pathway led from the goods depot into the Hampstead Road. This pathway needed to be protected by a pair of gates placed under the charge of the signalman, with the line between this point and the first signal post protected by close fencing on either side. Permission to open the line was obtained in June 1851.

Neither the Construction Shop nor the pathway are shown on the 1852 plan, but the exit onto the Hampstead Road, passing to the west of the 1840s stables, is evident. This pathway must have been one of the main entrances for those working in Camden Station.

The Hampstead Road station was designed and built by the LNWR. A meeting in March 1851 had before it a 'plan and estimate for a passenger station at Camden Town (sic) for the East and West India Dock traffic', at a cost of £2024 (£370,000 today). The work was to be:

executed forthwith by contract', on the basis that the LNWR would pay for the construction, 'the E&WID Co to pay all the expenses of the management and working of the station for a rent equal to the cost of the same'…..'the station in any case being under the control of the L&NW Co..

6.2 Hampstead Road station on NLR

The LNWR was a 'main line' railway and local traffic was largely left to the NLR. Hampstead Road station opened in 1851 with platforms on both the LNWR lines, serving commuters between Euston and Watford, and NLR lines. It was re-sited four years later, when the NLR moved northwards, was renamed Chalk Farm in 1862 and rebuilt in 1871. Chalk Farm Station had platforms on both the LNWR and NLR lines with a footbridge link between the two as shown in §6.3.

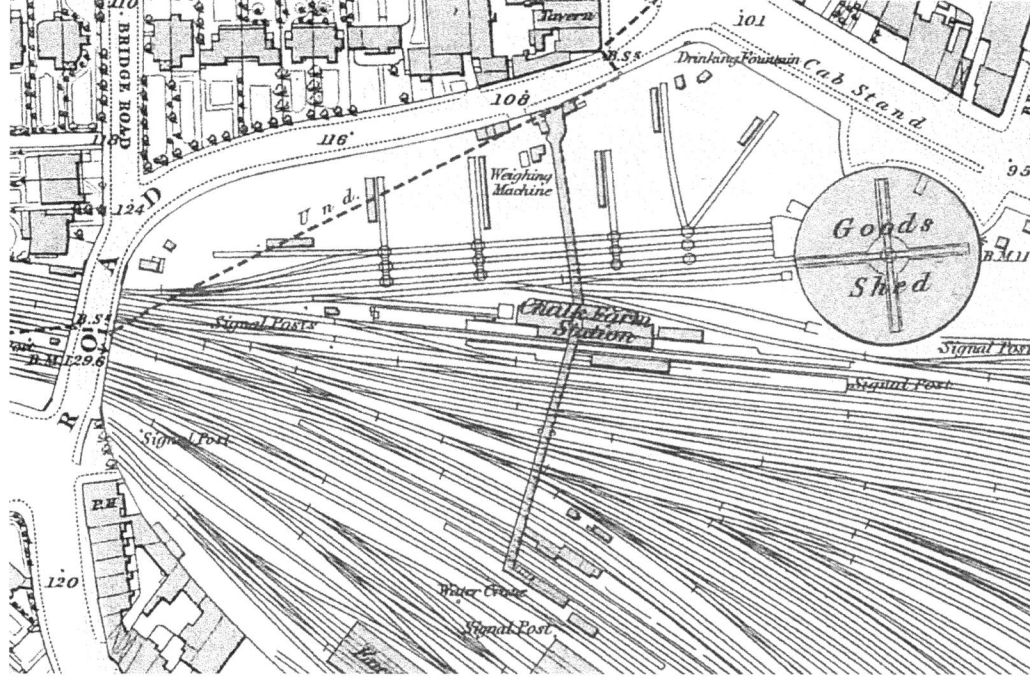

6.3 Chalk Farm Station 1870, extract from OS map

The NLR considered it obtained little benefit from the stoppage of a few main line up passenger trains at Hampstead Road. It proposed in April 1852 that all LNWR up traffic access NLR trains for the convenience to the public and the commercial advantage to both companies. LNWR agreed to remove their ticket taking platform and collect all tickets on the up journey immediately adjoining the Hampstead Road station, shown in §10.11.

6.3 NLR impact on Roundhouse

The Roundhouse had been awkwardly located from the outset in the Phase 2 expansion. The E&WIDL isolated the engine shed further from the central operations of the goods yard.

From the opening of the 'Dock line' the Roundhouse was used primarily for the LNWR engines working on the NLR, but also accommodated some engines 'for sale' and 'in store'. In January 1854 the NLR obtained temporary stabling for its new locomotives in the Roundhouse until its engine shed at Bow was completed later that year. By this time plans were in hand to move the NLR northwards, closer to the Roundhouse (#6.4). Together with the engine shed being under-utilised, this will have prompted consideration of how the Roundhouse could be put to better use. LNWR plans of 1854 show the Roundhouse to be converted into a goods warehouse. It is likely that this conversion had taken place by 1855.

Thus, after less than ten years' operation, the Roundhouse was abandoned as an engine shed to avoid conflicts of movements adjoining the NLR and free up more space for the goods yard. It was briefly a corn and potato store in the 1860s until in 1870 it became a bonded store for Gilbey's whisky in barrels, transported from their Highland distilleries (#9.5).

6.4 NLR impact on main line

The NLR's success as a passenger line for city workers commuting from the new estates caused an increase in traffic that aggravated congestion on the main line. Built to relieve it, Hampstead Junction Railway ran from the NLR at Camden Town to Willesden (§6.4), thus allowing NLR trains to bypass the main line. It opened in 1860 with stations at Kentish Town (Gospel Oak), Hampstead Heath, Finchley Road and Edgware Road (Brondesbury).

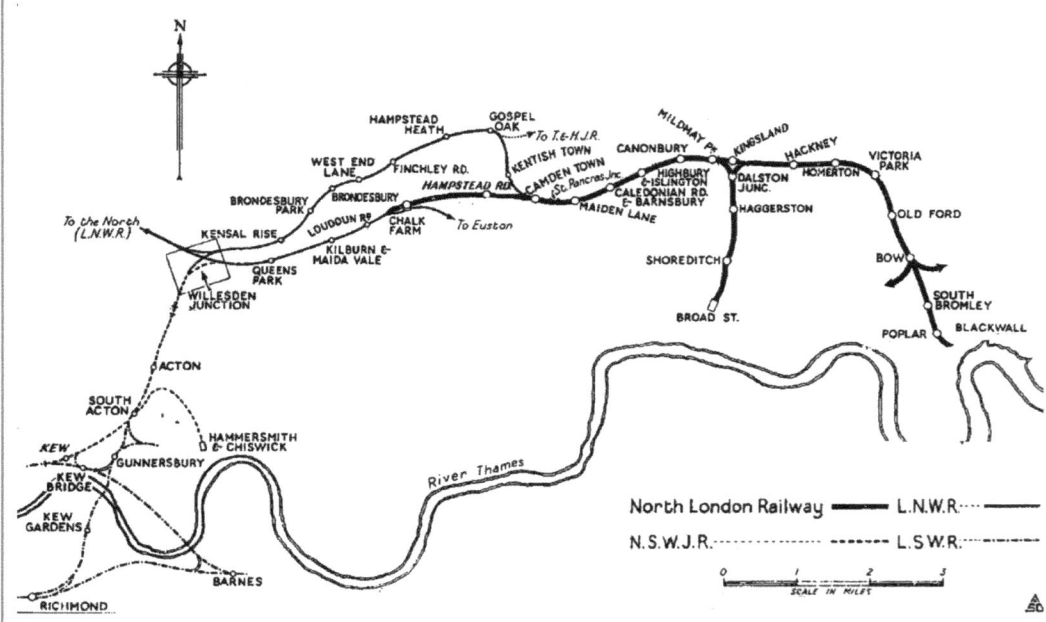

6.4 North London Railway and associated lines

6.5 Camden Station: the third phase

In spite of the remodelling of the Goods Depot in 1847, the major increase in traffic that followed the reduction in tariffs for goods carriage two years earlier required a larger marshalling area. A radical replanning of the goods yard started in 1852, following on from completion of the NLR, and was approved in June 1854.

Tenders for part of the work were received the following month. This included the removal of the Construction Shop to make way for repositioning of the NLR northwards. By this time the NLR track had been doubled over its Camden Station section. The major part of the Construction Shop was taken down in 1855 and re-erected as a carriage shed at Euston, but the 1847 vaults on which it was founded remained and were later extended to create coal drops.

The cattle pens were relocated to Maiden Lane on the NLR in time for the opening of the nearby Caledonian Cattle Market in 1855, thus providing a ready access to the City.

In July 1856, an estimate of the revised cost of the Camden Station enlargement amounting to £114,000 (about £16M today) was submitted. The Phase 3 arrangement, shown in the plan (§6.5), was built over 1856-57, apart from the stables on Gloucester Road, which were completed in 1858.

Houses alongside the Hampstead Road and ranges of stables that had been built only a few years previously (§6.1) were cleared away. The access track

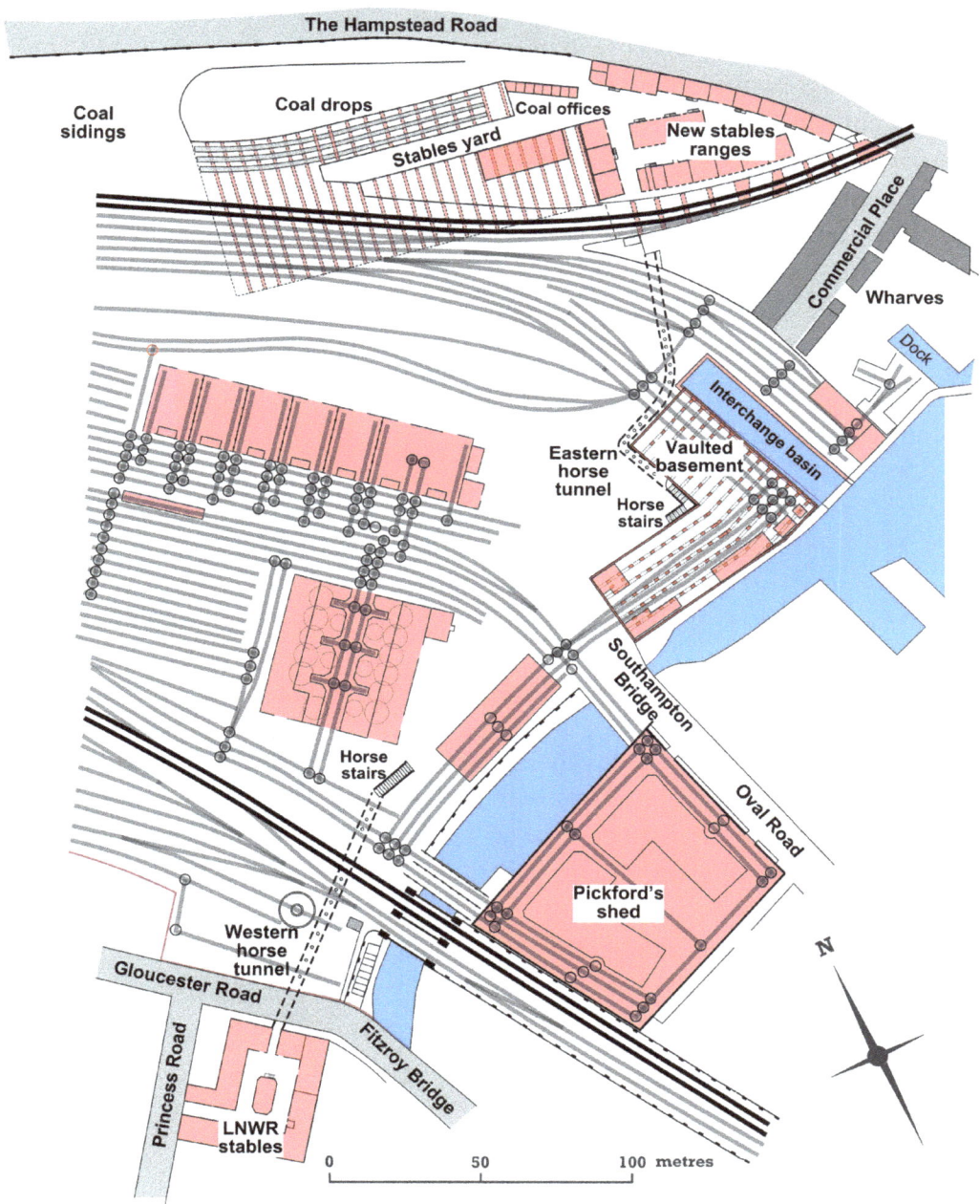

6.5 Reconstruction of Camden Goods Station, 1856, redrawn from plan in National Archives

from the Hampstead Road that had been used for almost 20 years was blocked by the Great Wall (#6.11).

The relocation of the NLR left an almond-shaped remnant of land between the road and the railway. Four new stables ranges were built there, at the eastern end. in what became Stables Yard. An entire and quite separate stables complex was built by LNWR for Pickford on Princess Road. Horse tunnels passing under the main line or under goods sidings connected these stables complexes to the goods yard, as shown in §6.5.

The interchange basin was realigned and enlarged to its present size. A new building substantially in wood with three roof trusses was built, the eastern span covering the basin while the other spans, including a smaller intermediate span, housed goods sheds on the western side. Five cranes were provided on each side of the dock. The railway approached this building from the east side while the west side was for road transport. A loading platform or 'bank' allowed goods to be moved across the building from rail to road and vice versa. The three-span building is essentially that shown in the schematic of Gilbey's premises, seen in §9.4.

The adjacent ground level was raised, partly on vaults, to the main level of the goods yard. Railway lines extended at this level towards the edge of the canal, supported on the east side by a retaining wall. The 'ale vaults' were built as a basement west of the Interchange Basin to attract and retain the important beer trade. Goods sheds that were open on their northwest side stood on these vaults (§6.6). Goods offices, which had temporarily been located on the other side of Oval Road, were built on two floors fronting Oval Road, with an opening for goods sidings (§6.7).

6.6 Goods shed built over ale vaults, from Drawing No. 7 Proposed Alterations and Enlargements, Camden Station, 1860 (left image)

6.7 Goods offices, Oval Road façade, from Drawing No. 6 Proposed Alterations and Enlargements, Camden Station, 1860 (right image)

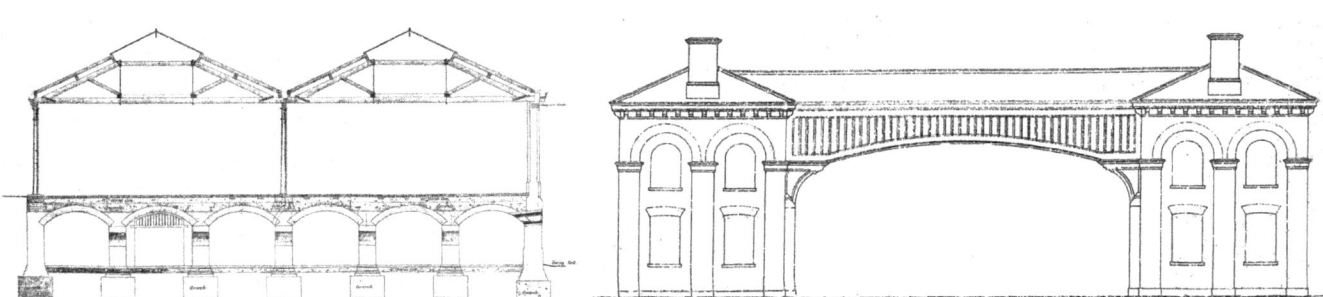

The development of goods offices after 1860 is described in #8.3.

Following arrangements made with the Regent's Canal Company, the LNWR proceeded with the construction of an additional railway bridge between the Goods Depot and the warehouse south of the canal that was now rented to Pickford by the LNWR.

As part of the remodelling, the coke ovens and chimney were finally swept away, new retaining walls being built along the canal to allow the railway level to be extended. David Stevenson observed in August 1854 (*op. cit.*):

> Years ago I climbed the coke-oven chimney shaft here. It was newly built and was esteemed a wonder. Three towering shafts marked Camden Station, from whatever point around London one viewed the prospect. Two of these long since sank into a heap of bricks. This week the last of our landmarks was hauled down, and a few minutes and a "hurrah!" restored the column of air it had so long displaced.

6.6 Coal supply

Since the first consignment of Clay Cross coal by rail to London arrived at Kilburn Station in July 1845, coal had become one of the most important commodities handled by the railway companies. For more than a hundred years after 1850 the movement of coal was the bread and butter of British railways, the tonnage carried being always well over half the total volume of freight traffic. In 1865, for instance, the quantity of coal carried by rail was 50 million tons compared with 13 million tons of other minerals (principally iron) and nearly 32 million tons of general merchandise.

The consortium of South Yorkshire coal mines, with which LNWR was in negotiation in 1854, made it a condition that coal drops should be provided. As part of the Phase 3 reconstruction, land up to the Hampstead Road east and west of the Roundhouse was raised to railway level behind a new retaining wall. The area created behind what is designated the 'Great Wall' provided space for coal sidings, a belated commercial response to the growing GNR trade in coal at King's Cross. To enable carts to reach the new coal sidings an access ramp or 'horse road' led up from the Stables Yard entrance to the east side of the Roundhouse, shown in 1870 on §8.1.

However, in contrast to most other goods depots, the LNWR considered that the entire space at Camden would ultimately be required for the Goods Department. It planned that Willesden was to become the principal depot for coal and would be provided with the means of transhipment to the canal for distribution in London. The arrangements being made to accommodate coal at Camden were to be regarded as temporary and made available through inexpensive alterations that accommodated the future purposes of the Goods Department. This may explain why the coal sidings were moved to a more constrained location west of the Roundhouse (see OS map of 1893 – §4). However, by 1921 they were back on the east side (§11.3).

While coal may have been secondary at Camden Station, it was not insignificant. In 1864 the Colliery Guardian noted, under the heading "*The Coal Yard at Camden*", that while LNWR in their enormous business had not made coal traffic such a speciality as the Great Northern, nevertheless in the previous year the Company had paid city dues (or coal duties) of 1s 1d per ton on 759,000 tons. At that time the coal traffic handled by King's Cross was closely similar (*Darley, 2018*).

6.7 Water supply for locomotives

In 1859 it was reported that the supply from deep wells sunk into the Chalk was failing. Twenty years of pumping from the chalk aquifer by rapidly growing industry in London had caused the decline. This drop in groundwater level continued until about 1950 when legislation and the decline or relocation of water-intensive industries reversed the situation: groundwater levels started to rise quite steeply from 1960.

The locomotive depot at Camden was one of the principal ones on the LNWR and the growth in engine numbers and size placed serious demands on the available water supply. To provide an inexpensive supply for the washing of locomotives and carriages, the Company appears to have adapted the winding vaults to a new role as a water reservoir (*PPIY, 2020*). As the LNWR was still sinking artesian wells in 1847, including one to supply the Passenger Locomotive Shed, this use would have started in about 1850, soon after the vaults were sealed in 1849. At this time the ventilation grills that are now a feature of the winding vaults would have been provided to avoid a build-up of humidity.

The supply from the vaults would have been pumped to a holding tank. Some evidence for this is seen in existing pipework in the vaults and further evidence in a series of what appear to be holding tanks seen in the 1852 plan (§6.1) between Fitzroy bridge and the mainline railway bridge, very close to the winding vaults and well placed for train washing. These tanks appear on the 1870 OS map and on a plan of 1885 (§6.8).

It is not clear why buffer storage was needed. All of this remains an intriguing hypothesis, and the tanks shown could equally have held water pumped from the Regent's Canal.

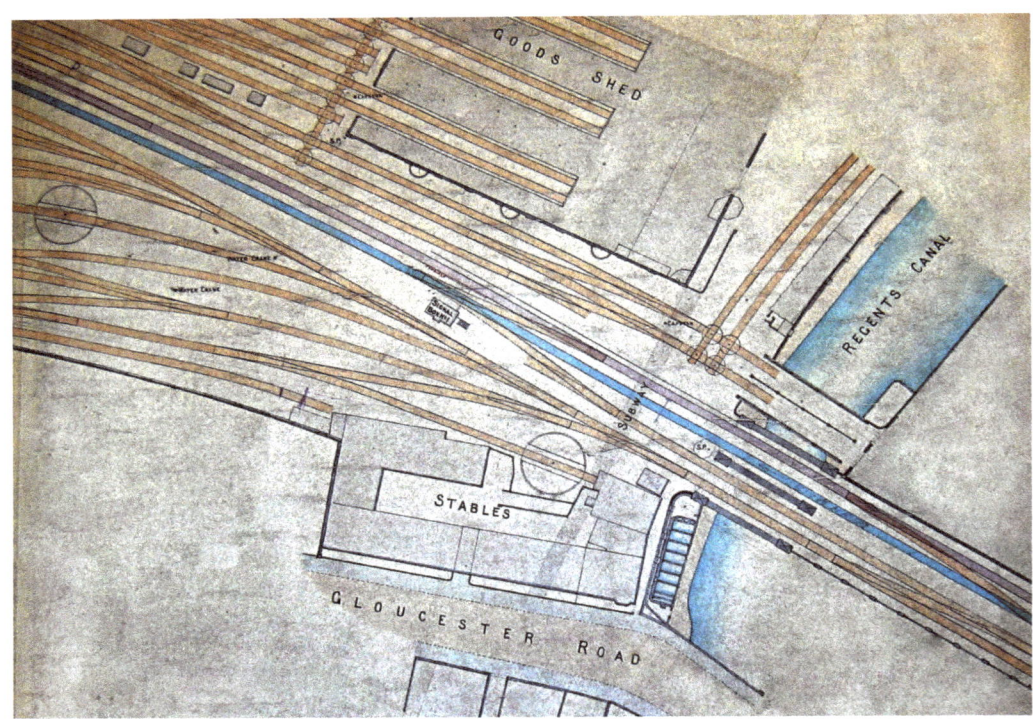

6.8 Evidence of a water supply for train washing in the siding, turntable and nearby storage tanks near Fitzroy Bridge, 1885

6.8 A succession of fires

In 1833, eight of the insurance companies that provided the bulk of the fire protection for London consolidated into the London Fire-engine Establishment. This organization would be incorporated into the metropolitan government in 1866 and become the London Fire Brigade.

James Braidwood, a pioneer of the scientific approach to firefighting and recognised as the father of the British fire service, with an international reputation from his leadership of the Edinburgh Fire Service, was invited to head up this precursor organization. He faced an early test, as the London Fire-engine Establishment, on 16 October 1834, fought a highly destructive blaze at the Palace of Westminster.

Oval Road suffered a succession of devastating fires in the middle of the 19th century. The first of these, that at the Rotunda piano factory in 1851, must have led to major increases in insurance costs and to recommendations from the insurers as to how to cut premiums by reducing risk. James Braidwood himself led the fire services on this occasion and wrote the ensuing report.

In consequence, in 1854, the Company resolved that measures be taken for the immediate removal of the hay and machinery from Pickford's warehouse into a separate building and that other changes be made to obtain insurance on more favourable terms.

Despite this worthy intention, the proposed rearrangement of Pickford's warehouse was dictated by a dramatic and devastating fire in June 1857, said to have been the most destructive in London for quarter of a century (§6.9). Over 100 horses released from their stables in the basement bolted in panic along Oval Road (§6.10). James Braidwood again superintended operations, but there was little he could do as the entire building was one mass of flames with loaded wagons and trucks dropping into the basement as the fire gained mastery. Flames were overlapping the roof of the Stanhope Arms and adjoining premises.

6.10 View along Oval Road towards Rotunda factory and Camden Goods Station, June 1857, from *Illustrated Times*

Pickford's new warehouse was rebuilt without stables. New stables were to be constructed on the opposite side of Gloucester Road to accommodate 270 horses. A second fire in November 1867 removed much of the roof of Pickford's new warehouse with its glass louvres. This caused Pickford to abandon its Camden shed.

James Braidwood led the municipal fire services in London for almost 30 years. Personally distinguished for his heroism, he would not ask anything of his men that he would not do himself. He was killed tragically on 22 June 1861 in the Tooley Street fire which took hold of a series of dockside warehouses at Cotton's Wharf near London Bridge station. Braidwood, although now 61 years old, led the firefighters personally, and was killed when a falling wall crushed him.

6.9 Fire at Pickford's warehouse from Primrose Hill, June 1857 from *Illustrated Times*

The Tooley Street fire spread throughout the wharfs along the Thames and took two weeks to extinguish. It caused damage equivalent to over £200M in today's money and led to the 1865 Metropolitan Fire Brigade Act, which established the London Fire Brigade as a municipal department. James Braidwood's funeral a week later, on 29 June, drew huge crowds, the funeral cortege stretching 1.5 miles (2.4km) behind the hearse. Queen Victoria sent her sympathies to his wife.

6.9 The electric telegraph works

The 24 July 1837 saw the first use of Cooke and Wheatstone's electric telegraph, only patented the previous month, when Robert Stephenson introduced it on a trial basis for the Camden Incline (#3.12).

6.11 Original 1858 factory buildings of electric telegraph works in Gloucester Road, now part of redevelopment called the Courtyard

In 1846 the Electric and International Telegraph Company, which owned the Cooke and Wheatstone patents, was incorporated for public telegraphic communications using railway routes as corridors for the overhead lines. Their Gloucester Road works (§6.11), built in 1858, housed an extensive factory carrying out a great variety of operations: both those relating to any apparatus in use in telegraph offices and those relating to line and construction work. The former were carried out by some 70 skilled mechanics and apprentices and the latter by about 100 trained workmen and labourers (*Scudamore, 1871*). The location of the telegraph works is shown on §4 and §8.1.

The two storey buildings at the rear (§6.11) housed the mechanics' and carpenters' shops, instrument stores, insulator, battery and wire-fitting shops and packing shed. The re-winding of coils with copper wire was one of the most important operations. Fronting Gloucester Road, a one-storey building housed the lacquering shop, testing room, tool store and general offices.

The company was nationalised and taken over by the Post Office in 1870, the single storey building on Gloucester Road being replaced by the present three-storey building the following year. The buildings are now part of The Courtyard redevelopment.

6.10 Access to Eton's Chalcots Estate

David Stevenson, by now a senior employee in the Goods Department, resided in Montrose House, a villa west of Bianca Lodge (§1.10), originally on Primrose Vale but later accessed from Chalk Farm Lane on what subsequently became Regent's Park Road. He observed in October 1853 that:

> The ball-room at Chalk Farm Tavern is no more. It has been taken down to make way for some new houses. And so farewell thou scene of gents and dirty muslin! At one time, I suppose, greater swells frequented the place – white kids, cravats, and well-cut coats, and fair forms charmingly arrayed; but they all went their way, and of late years 'sixpenny hops' have made night hideous there - soldiers and servant maids, dirty drabs, and dangerous 'young fellers' in curious clothing, with short pipes and wonderfully unclean hands, - such a set! And they, too, are all gone!

Montrose House was located at the corner where The Chesterfields, a residential block converted from the former Boys Home, now stands. Stevenson sold his property in Chalk Farm Lane for £1300 (about £180,000 today) in 1856 to his employer, LNWR, to afford a right of way to Eton's Chalcots Estate. This was the start of King Henry's Road.

6.11 Public perception of railway lands

The Great Wall of Camden symbolised the separation of the Goods Station from the public domain. The massive wall ran along the Hampstead Road (now Chalk Farm Road) from just north of the canal bridge to beyond the Roundhouse (§6.12). It retained the railway lands up to 15 feet (4.6m) above street level. David Thomson (1963) described it as '..higher and blacker than the wall of Manchester's gaol.'

The barrier was mental as much as physical, to which the dearth of text and images about the activities behind the wall bears witness. The goods depot was strictly out of bounds to the general public. The world behind the retaining walls, both those along Chalk Farm Road and the Regent's Canal towpath, therefore remained secretive, undiscovered and unappreciated until the goods traffic retreated in the mid 20th century.

When seen at night the Camden Station, from the immense number of gas lamps – between 200 and 300 distributed in all directions – had the appearance of a large township.

It is to be regretted that very little oral history has been gathered for what was the largest goods yard in London.

6.12 The Great Wall seen here at its highest, from *Fay Godwin*, 1982

7 Stables complex

    7.1   The railway horse
    7.2   Development of stables complex
    7.3   The Stables
    7.4   Long Stable
    7.5   Provender Stores
    7.6   Tack Room
    7.7   Horse Hospital
    7.8   Horse tunnels
    7.9   Pickford's stables

7.1 The railway horse

Victorian London was a 'horse-drawn society', with many thousands of stables. London depended on horses for the transport of goods and people, just as today we depend on motor vehicles. Horses were everywhere and a whole world of support services was needed, again just as for motor vehicles today. The rapid growth of the metropolis and of horse numbers and the vehicles they drew could cause congestion on a major scale (§7.1).

7.1 Crossing London Bridge at noonday, 1872, from *Illustrated London News*

The movement of higher value goods both to national destinations and to and from the ports was largely in the hands of the railway companies: railways were the major users of horses prior to WWI, a carrying trade largely subcontracted to agents. The two largest such agents, Pickford and Carter Paterson, had some 4,000 and 2,000 horses respectively at the turn of the century.

Railway companies required as much space for stables as for engine sheds. In 1864 about 90 horses were dedicated to shunting and sorting at Camden Goods Depot, about 15% of the total, typically undertaken by Shire horses and Clydesdales. However, the great majority of horses in railway company stables were used for collection and delivery of goods and passenger luggage. Goods cartage mainly used heavy horses while faster parcels and passenger luggage duties were by half-heavies or 'vanners'.

As a source of power, the Victorian horse had to compete with both man and machine. At the beginning of the 19th century, the cost of keeping a horse was two to three times the hire of a day labourer, while the daily work of a horse was equal to that of five or six men. The cost of horse power was therefore about half that of manpower. It was reduced further over the next century, while the cost of manpower increased modestly.

The horse's advantage over the machine started with low cost and flexibility, but as machines became more powerful, the horse had to work harder to compete, leading to an increase in the size of horses, an increase in the horse's workload, a reduced working life and more rapid depreciation. Favoured animals were those that best turned food into money, fodder being the major operations cost and representing 10% of agricultural output by the end of the 19th century, with London by far the largest market.

The provision and care for working horses in the early industrial era was poor. Horses were generally kept at ground level or 'below grade' until about 1870. Stabling of horses on well-aired and lit upper floors accessible by ramps appeared in London from about that date, Pickford's stables (#7.9) being a remarkable forerunner.

The treatment of horses gradually became a greater issue through the later 19th century. A number of breeding societies were formed in the 1870s and the London Cart Horse Parade was started at this time to encourage and reward better care of horses. Sir Walter Gilbey, who features in Ch. 9, was a central figure in this movement, which also influenced the stabling of horses in terms of improved lighting, ventilation and drainage.

The role of the horse continued to be important well into the 20th century, despite attempts by horseless carriages to drive it off the congested roads. The message of §7.2 is that motor vehicles and horse vans both had an important role for goods transport in the mid 1930s.

The London Midland and Scottish Railway (LMS), which succeeded the LNWR in 1923, had some 2000 horses employed in the London area in 1938. With the largest 'stud' in the UK, at about 8000 horses, the LMS owned two thirds of all horses employed by the railways.

Funds for replacement of horses and carts competed with other uses. The costs of maintaining horse-drawn vehicles were low in comparison to motor

7.2 Convoys of horse and motor vans emerging onto Oval Road from Camden Goods Station in 1934

vehicles in the 1930s. The low top speed of the horse was less of a disadvantage in urban areas with traffic congestion. In 1938 motor lorries were restricted to 30mph (48km/h), or 20mph (32km/h) if articulated or over 2.5 tons loaded.

The internal combustion engine finally signed the death warrant of the working horse after WWII. In 1947-8 more than 200,000 horses were put down, 40% under three years old.

The last shunting horse, 'Charlie' a Clydesdale (§7.3), was sold into railway service as a six-year-old and worked in Camden Goods Station in the 1950s. Charlie was withdrawn from duty at Newmarket in March 1967 at age 24. The presence of a horse for shunting rail wagons containing nervous racehorses had evidently been a reassurance to those in the wagons.

7.3 The last shunting horse *Charlie* in action

7.2 Development of stables complex

The third phase of development of Camden Station in 1856 saw the goods yard extended north to the Hampstead Road, requiring demolition of the 1846 stables ranges and building of four new stables ranges. The 1856 stables complex included two horse tunnels, a feature unique to Camden. They were provided on operational and safety grounds to facilitate the movement of horses from stables to their place of work, passing under the mainline railway and goods sidings. The overall plan of stables and the alignment of the horse tunnels is shown in §6.5. This chapter describes these features in greater detail.

The stables complex at Camden Goods Station is a more complete example of Victorian industrial stables than any other in the country, illustrating the development of stabling over the second half of the nineteenth century. This remains the case despite the finest part of the complex – Pickford's Stables – having been lost (#7.9).

Given how little infrastructure remains as evidence of the major impact horses had on the Victorian industrial scene, the Camden complex assumes an increased importance. The key features of Stables Yard are shown in the location plan (§7.4).

The four 1856 stable ranges were built of plain yellow stock brick as single storey stables with hay lofts above, as shown on the original drawing of the four stables ranges (§7.5). They provided bays for 162 horses. Wooden stairs gave access to the pitching holes of the hay lofts. Windows with high sills and round-headed openings to the ground floor provided light and ventilation to the stalls from above. The original 1856 stable bay configuration can still be seen in the western bays of The Stables (§7.6). All other stables/bays have had storeys added.

Typically stall dividers were of the hanging type ('swing bales' – see §7.34 and §7.35). However, little remains of the former stable fittings.

7.4 Camden stables complex schematic

7.5 Stables ranges, from Drawing No. 8 Proposed Alterations & Enlargement at Camden Station, 1856 (left image)

7.6 Original stable bay configuration, 1975 (right image)

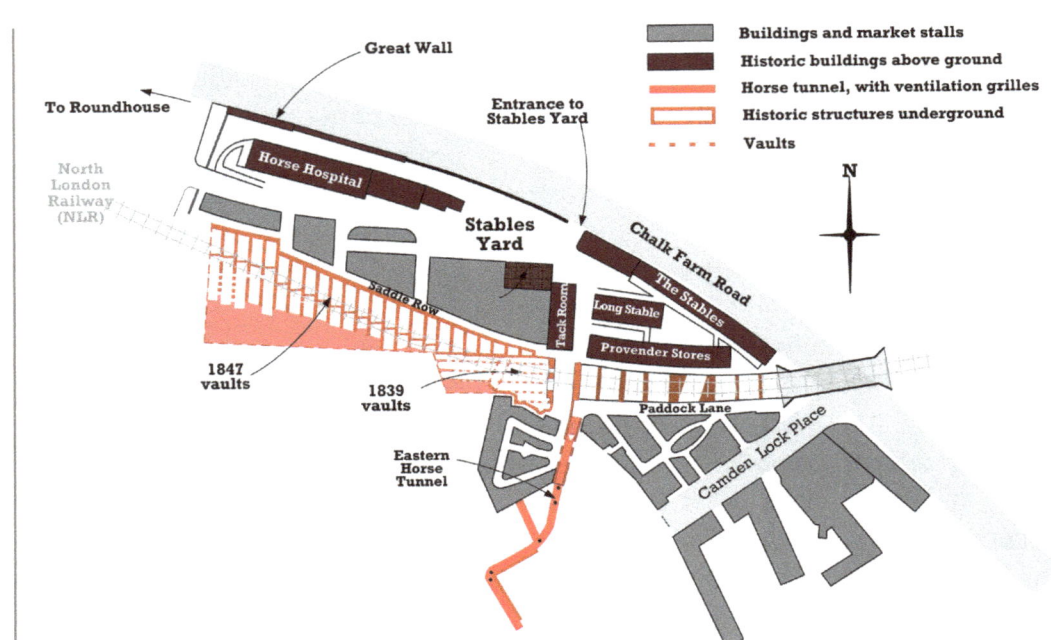

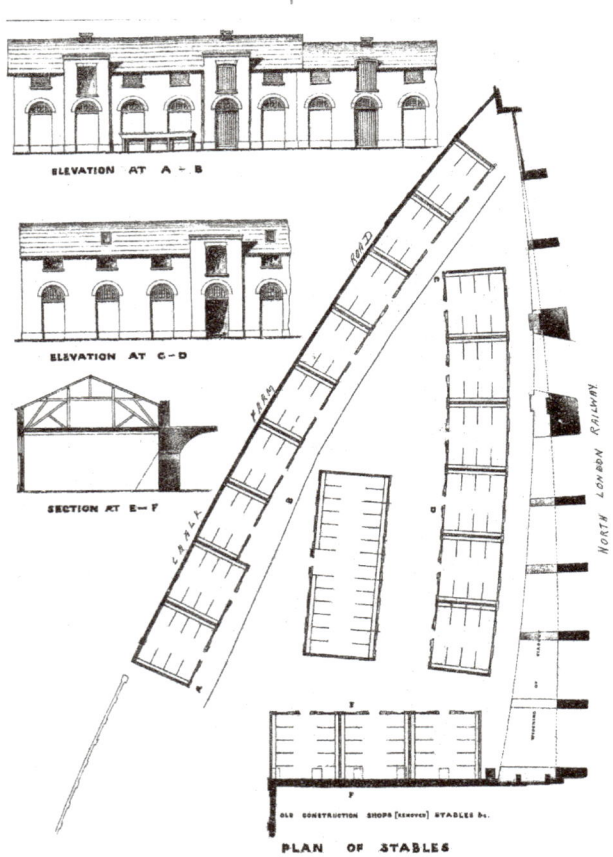

The 1857 fire in Pickford's Oval Road warehouse had destroyed the basement with its 216 stalls and 15 loose boxes (#6.8). Their new stables were intended for an estimated 270 horses but ultimately provided for about 240. They formed six ranges around a central services building, creating not only the largest stables complex of its day but one that was exceptionally sophisticated.

CHALK FARM RAILWAY LANDS: A GUIDED TOUR 1830 TO 2030

The next significant stables complex was built by LNWR for Allsopp in 1876. Located opposite Pickford's stables in Gloucester Road, it provided for 72 horses and was, like Pickford's, connected to the Western Horse Tunnel. This tunnel provided safe access under the Euston mainline to the main goods shed, where Allsopp leased the basement for storage of ales.

The construction of Gilbey's No. 2 Bond in 1875 (#9.5) displaced most of the horses stabled in the vaults behind, which now became part of the bonded store. This may explain the 1881/1883 phase of stable building in Stables Yard. Floors were added in 1881 to all stable ranges except The Stables. In 1883 a new two-storey range, now known as the 'Horse Hospital', was built west of the existing four stable ranges in Stables Yard. This new range, which provided loose boxes on the upper floor for sick and injured horses (hence the name) was extended to the southeast in 1897.

The last major addition in Stables Yard was in 1900 when stalls for an additional 42 horses were provided in The Stables on an upper floor with a gallery for access.

Two stables for 17 horses were provided beneath the NLR viaduct and four stalls in 1887 in a lean-to stable. A further 54 horses could later be stabled beneath the former coal drops. Stables Yard had stabling for about 420 horses in 1925, while the two ranges on Gloucester Road added a further 310 horses.

W & A Gilbey maintained stables behind the gin distillery in Oval Road, with access from Upper James Street, for around 70 horses until 1894 when their stables moved under the arches of the NLR at Camden Road station. The new stables, which opened onto Bonny Street, could accommodate about 100 horses that worked on Gilbey's collection and delivery operations, many between Camden and the Docks.

At the peak, therefore, some 800 horses worked in Camden Goods Depot moving goods to and from the yard with some residual shunting, although hydraulic power had by then largely taken over the shunting operations. This total does not include parcels and passenger luggage operations, for which the LNWR had additional stables at Euston and Broad Street.

From the bridge connecting Long Stable to Provender Stores, the views to west (§7.7) and east (§7.8), taken in 2007 before the recent upgrade, create a strong impression of an industrial past.

7.7 Looking west to the Tack Room, with Provender Stores (left) and Long Stable (right), 2007 (left image)

7.8 Looking east to The Stables, with Long Stable (near left), The Stables (far left) and Provender Stores (right), 2007

If the next sections describing the architectural form of each stable block prove a little dry, turn to a Pathé news clip of 1949 made on the occasion of a flu epidemic. It gives a vivid reminder of the activities in Stables Yard about 75 years ago in what appears to be a wholly different world, a throwback to the previous century.

https://www.youtube.com/watch?v=ZYx47Z-p2EE

7.3 The Stables

The Stables was built in 1856 as a 1½ storey range 28 bays long in plain yellow stock bricks. The eastern 21 bays, which step back slightly to the south, were raised in 1900 to provide an upper storey of stabling.

Along Chalk Farm Road, the ground floor façade has high-level semi-round windows, some retaining timber small-pane casements. A change in the brickwork is evident on the raised section, where the windows are segmental-headed (§7.9).

The western seven bays of The Stables are the only surviving part of the four 1856 ranges to retain the original single storey and loft arrangement (§7.6). This section has two stabling units of three bays and, at the west end, a two-storey bay under a hipped roof with a chimney stack that must have been the gatehouse (§7.10). The south-west corner of the building has its corner cut at 45 degrees to provide better turning space for horses and wagons. The former gatehouse has been much altered internally.

7.9 The Stables: view from Chalk Farm Road, 2007

Further east the ground floor is in seven three-bay units, with the addition of piers to support a cantilevered steel and brick jack-arch gallery with concrete floor, by which the upper stables were reached (§7.11). Access to the

7.10 The former gatehouse at the Chalk Farm Road entrance to Stables Yard, 2012 (left image)

7.11 View east along gallery providing access to upper floor of The Stables, 2012 (right image)

CHALK FARM RAILWAY LANDS: A GUIDED TOUR 1830 TO 2030

gallery is via a ramp attached to the north side of Long Stable (§7.13). The floor to the upper storey is of steel and brick jack-arch construction contiguous with that of the gallery. A wooden bridge formerly connected The Stables and Provender Stores, since removed. The gallery retains its precast concrete drinking troughs.

Internally, the stable units were each about 19 feet (5.8m) by 28 feet (8.5m) with three stalls on each side of a central passage. The original west section retains timber internal construction with the 1856 hay loft roof.

7.4 Long Stable

Although the shortest of the four 1856 stable blocks, the 28 stalls in a single undivided space on the ground floor explain the name. Long Stable (known earlier as 'Middle Block') is seven bays long. It was raised in 1881 to provide an upper level of stabling for a further 24 horses reached by a ramp on the south side (§7.12).

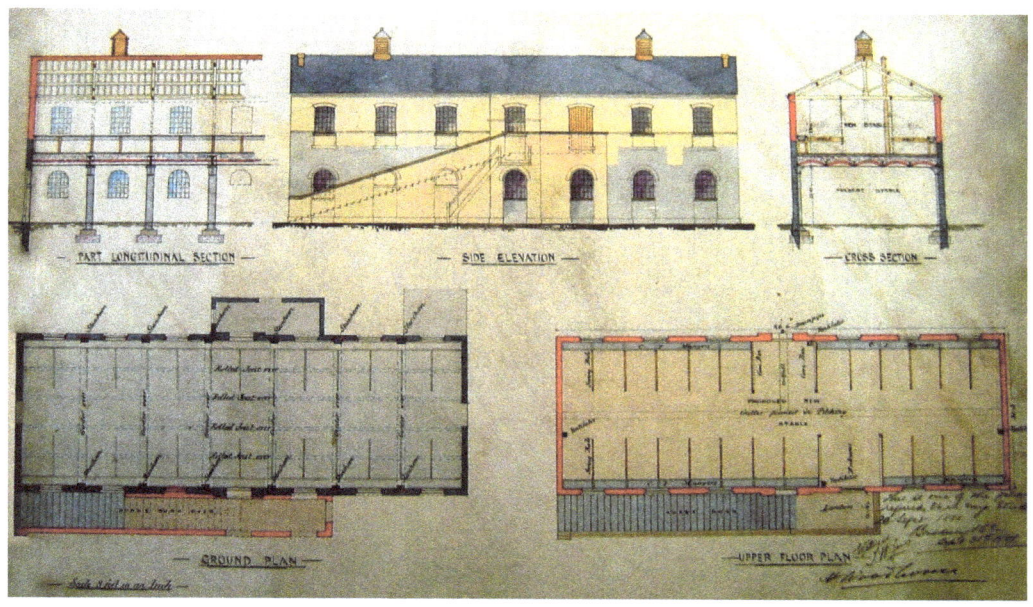

7.12 From Drawing No. 1 Proposed Stable over Middle Block, 1881

On the ground floor round-headed openings with high level sills light and ventilate the stalls from above. The later first floor openings have segmental heads, as shown. The east gable end has a small upper-storey hatch over a widened ground floor opening. The west gable end has had its upper-storey opening enlarged as a goods hatch.

The 1881 'horse road' to the south had steps with 4½ inch (114mm) risers made of cast iron. Its position is evident on the south wall. The ramp to the north was brick built with concrete-paved surfaces and an intermediate landing.

A second ramp was added to the north in 1900 to provide access to the gallery on the upper storey of The Stables (§7.13). Only this latter ramp now survives.

The ground floor is shown in §7.14, which also reveals the structure. The upper floor rests on cast-iron stanchions that support wrought-iron I-section

7.13 Horse ramp for access to upper storey of The Stables, 2007 (left image)

7.14 View east through ground floor of Long Stable showing structural elements, including stanchions, girders and jack arches, 2013 (right image)

girders carrying rolled joists to brick jack-arches and supports timber king-post roof trusses.

7.5 Provender Stores

Provender Stores backs onto the curved line of the NLR, though narrowly separated from it. An 18-bay range it was raised in 1881 by two storeys to provide provender processing and storage (§7.15).

The ground floor stabling is typical, the bays being grouped in threes with central entrances, upper loophole openings, and round-arch arcading with high-silled windows for small pane pivoting casements. The first floor has round-headed windows (§7.16), the second-floor segmental heads. Many of the loophole openings, which were extended to both upper storeys, have been enlarged. All but one of the timber hoist jibs at eaves level have either been removed or replaced by steel beams.

The east gable end wall has been rebuilt in blue brick. The west gable end has a bridge to the Tack Room at first floor level, recreated in 2015 to match the original which had been removed.

Internally the range comprised six stable units each with eight stalls. The floors inserted in 1881 were of iron construction with trussed beams. Timber roof trusses were used. The upper floor and roof appear to have been replaced in concrete and steel.

7.15 From Proposed Alterations to Provender Stores, 1880 (top left image)

7.16 Round-headed windows to first floor of Provender Stores (top right image)

7.6 Tack Room

This range differs from other ranges at the eastern end with flat-headed windows and 12-paned sashes. It was raised in 1881 as part of the expansion of the Provender Stores, when the ranges were linked by a bridge. The first floor was later used as a tack room, hence the name. The west side is abutted by the 1875 former bonded warehouse.

The slate roof is in two parts: gabled to the south and hipped to the north. The three bays of the ground floor originally stabled 27 horses (§7.5).

The east elevation has the same arrangement to the ground floor as other 1856 stabling. Each of the three stables has three arched bays with a central projecting entrance bay and the flanking bays closed up to the round-headed windows, many of which still retain their original wooden frames. The northern loading bay retains a simple hoist over the head of the door (§7.17).

7.17 The Tack Room showing new bridge from Provender Stores (left) 2021 (left image)

7.18 Stairs to horse-keeper's dwelling, 2010 (right image)

Next to the northern stable is a door opening for access to the first floor horse-keeper's dwelling (§7.18), formed from the three northernmost bays. These retain three 12-pane sash windows and three brick chimney stacks to both the east and north sides.

7.19 Bridge from Provender Stores to Tack Room before its removal, 1975

The bridge to the Provender Stores extended from the southernmost loading bay (§7.19). Demolished sometime after 1975, a replacement recreating the original was erected in 2015 (§7.17).

The interior of the building has three bays to both floors. It was originally built of timber-framed construction, still surviving to the northern stable bay. In 1881 the southern bays were altered; cast-iron columns and girders were inserted,

STABLES COMPLEX

and the wooden floor was renewed. Wooden roof trusses and timber benching, partition and harness hooks survive from its later use as a tack room.

7.7 Horse Hospital

When this range of stables was first planned its narrow sloping site was already embanked on the north side for the inclined roadway that led to a coal yard and had been enclosed to the south by coal drops. The two-storey range was built in two phases. The western and larger part, built in 1883, comprises the five western bays and accommodated 92 horses (§7.20).

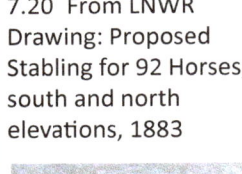

7.20 From LNWR Drawing: Proposed Stabling for 92 Horses, south and north elevations, 1883

The eastern part, added in 1897, includes three bays of two storey stabling and a single-storey office bay, providing stabling for around 40 horses and a store-room. The south elevation steps back (see §13.4), marking the building phases, whilst the north side has a continuous building line except for the later addition of a single-storey store and men's mess room at the east end.

7.21 West end of Horse Hospital with curved ramp, 2007

At the west end is a small lean-to, formerly the boiler house, and a curved horse ramp (§7.21). The upper storey of the west end has a landing for the semi-circular horse ramp with an opening to its balustrade, originally for a wooden chute to the manure pit below.

The upper part of the ramp has a store-room below; the lower, straighter part was added as part of the 1897 extension. The curved ramp is uncommon, ramps usually being built against the side of a stables building for economy of space.

Its shape and position were evidently dictated by the site. In the first phase it had a steep gradient of about 1 in 6 that was flattened when the ramp was extended in the second phase.

The ground floor of the 1883 building with its five bays divided by thick brick walls (§7.22) has cast-iron classically finished columns to central openings, flanked by large wooden-framed windows all under iron lintels, supporting brick jack-arching to the upper floor. It is accessible only from the south side. This open-fronted arrangement suggests that the ground floor was probably intended for cart sheds, the design later being changed to stables under pressures of growing horse numbers.

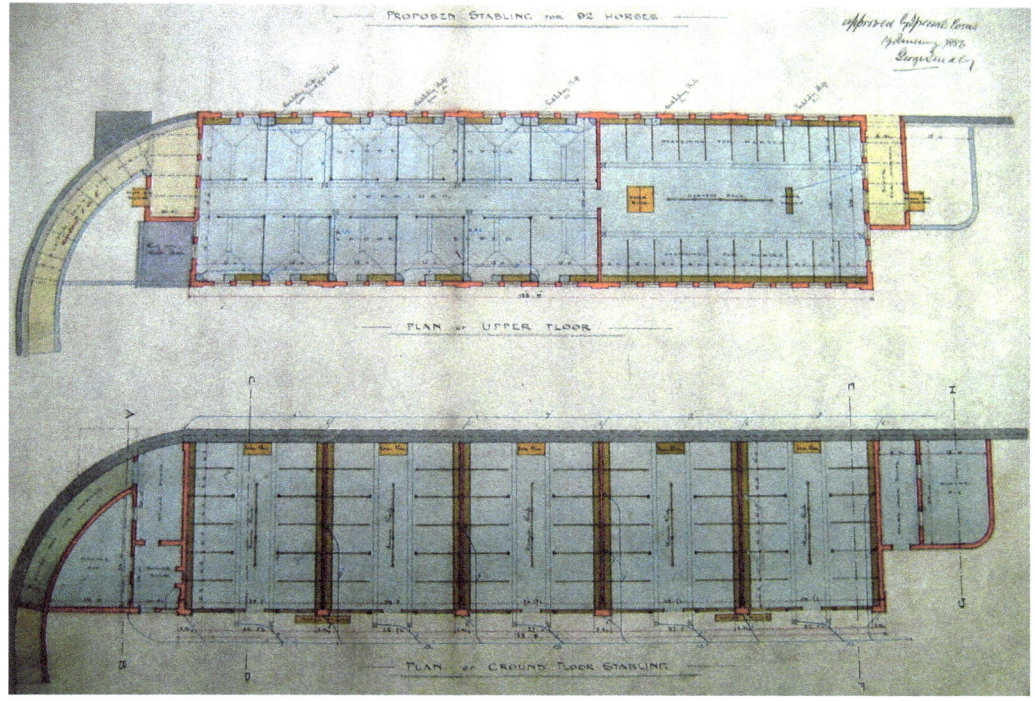

7.22 From LNWR Drawing: Proposed Stabling for 92 Horses, plan of ground and first floor, 1883

There were six stalls to both sides of each room, making 60 stalls on the ground floor. Originally there were harness racks to the centre of each bay and corn bins against the north wall. The original brick-paved floor survives. It has a slight camber and is incised with gulleys for drainage. The eastern part of the range, designated as standings for 20 horses, was built with wooden bales suspended from joists between the roof beams. Some tethering hooks and a solitary trough are now the only surviving fittings.

The first floor of the 1883 range is divided into two unequal parts. The larger western part retains twelve loose boxes with cast iron door posts, cast as a piece with the columns that are bolted to tie-beams, and timber boarding below the iron grilles and rails (§7.23).

7.23 Western end of upper floor of Horse Hospital with former loose boxes, 2008

STABLES COMPLEX 95

7.24 Horse road leading along north face of Horse Hospital, formerly up to coal yard, 2007

These retain the most substantial surviving stable fittings in the stables complex, including mangers and hayracks and remains of the wooden ventilation shafts that originally ran from the floor to the roof.

The north elevation abuts the horse road (§7.24), an embanked roadway, its angle of incline reducing the 1883 range to a single storey on this side (§7.20). The elevations of both parts have recessed panels, divided by pilaster strips, each with four high-level segmental-headed stable windows. In recent years two of the window openings have been extended to form doorways. The stable ranges are linked by another horse ramp originally built against the east end of the first phase and retained after the extension was added, although partly remade into steps after the closure of the stables.

The ground floor of the 1897 stable extension is in two parts and has a plainer construction, with I-section stanchions supporting brick jack-arching. In the western part the stalls were against the north and south walls with dividers suspended from hooks in the ceiling beams. The narrowest eastern part had stabling on the north side only. No stable fittings survive from the 1897 stable range.

All parts are built of yellow stock brick with red brick floor bands, dentilled cornices and segmental window heads, although with poorer quality detailing to the later range. The first phase has oculi to the end gables, although obscured to the east by the later building. The slate pitched roof on wooden roof trusses, gabled to the stable ranges and hipped to the former store-room, has a long louvred vent to the ridge of the earlier range and a small vent to the extension. In addition, the original stable range had five ventilation stacks to the north side of the roof but no evidence of these now survives externally.

Ventilation to the north side of the stables was through the openings, two to each bay, at the junction of the wall and ceiling, with wooden shafts carrying up to vents on the roof. A single-storey store-room to the east, set back from the stable range but part of the original phase of construction, retains the brick jack arching of the former horse ramp above.

The last horses to be stabled in the Horse Hospital were those of W & A Gilbey from the mid 1950s until 1967, as described in #9.12. The six horses and coach were part of their well-known four-in-hand, the horses all Irish Hunter type bay geldings. They were looked after by five Gilbey stable staff, including a head coachman and his assistant. The coach was housed on the ground floor, while the horses would have been stabled in the loose boxes on the first floor to give them the space to lie down. This may explain the survival of the stable fittings on the first floor, which form such a vital element in the Horse Hospital becoming the Grade II* listed jewel in the stables complex.

7.8 Horse tunnels

Two horse tunnels were built in 1856 to provide safe passages for horses under the railway tracks and sidings, referred to as the Eastern Horse Tunnel and the Western Horse Tunnel.

The tunnels, of round-arched brick construction with concrete footings, are ten feet (3.0m) wide by nine feet (2.7m) to the crown, formerly with random Rowley Rag paving six inches (15cm) thick on six inches (15cm) of hardcore (§7.25). They are kept dry by asphalt over the top of the tunnel and damp-proofing cavities within the walls, draining to four inch (10cm) lateral drains and a six inch (15cm) longitudinal drain-pipe below the centre of the tunnel – a quite sophisticated construction.

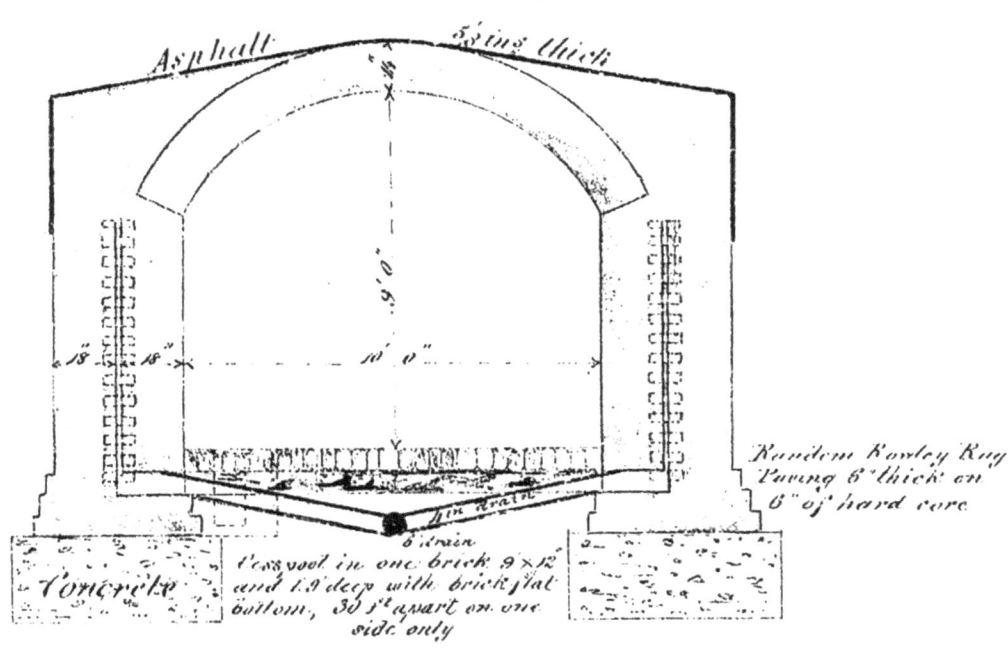

7.25 Cross-section of Tunnel, Drawing No. 3 Horse Tunnel – Camden Station, 1854

Sometime between 1856 and 1866, when many of the vaults were used by Bass and Allsopp for storing beer and ale, a branch tunnel was made from the Eastern Horse Tunnel to the 1839 vaults, the remnant of former goods sidings. This may have been used for trundling beer barrels by barrow or trolley as the passages were too narrow for use by horse-drawn vehicles (§8 on page xvi). In 1866, following the construction of the main LNWR goods shed in 1864, a branch was made from the Eastern Horse Tunnel to the basement of the shed. Both these branches are shown in §8.13.

The Eastern Horse Tunnel has its northern end in Stables Yard. From there it circumnavigates the Interchange canal dock and the extensive system of Wine and Beer Vaults, built at the same time as the tunnel, passing under the goods

7.26 Eastern Horse Tunnel looking towards foot of stairs up to 30 Oval Road 2011 (left image)

7.27 Eastern Horse Tunnel: ventilation grilles seen in forecourt of Interchange, leading to 30 Oval Road 2010 (right both images)

sidings leading to the dock. At its southern end it emerges via horse stairs (§7.26) at 30 Oval Road, formerly the forecourt of the goods offices. Its alignment may be discerned from the cast iron roof lights and ventilation grilles placed regularly about ten feet (3.0m) apart in the paving of the Interchange forecourt (§7.27).

The Western Horse Tunnel served to connect the major new stables built by LNWR for Pickford on the west side of Gloucester Road with the goods yard, passing under the mainline to Euston. It emerged via horse stairs at a location that became the south corner of the LNWR goods shed when built eight years later. It was relocated southwards when the main goods shed was enlarged in 1931.

In 1876 the LNWR built stables for Allsopp on the east side of Gloucester Road and connected these to the Western Horse Tunnel via horse stairs.

7.9 Pickford's stables

Pickford's main London warehouse off Oval Road, built in 1841 and enlarged in 1845, accommodated up to 230 horses in the basement. It was subject to a dramatic and devastating fire (#6.8) in June 1857. By then it was owned by LNWR who leased it to Pickford. It was rebuilt by LNWR the same year on a larger footprint but without stables. At the same time a new set of stables was constructed by LNWR just off Princess Road, a site where once Calvert had intended a brewery but had built only *The Engineer* public house in 1849. New stabling was needed for some 270 horses with all the requisite smiths' shops, harness rooms and machinery.

Pickford's stables were served by the Western Horse Tunnel that ran under Gloucester Road. The tunnel was built in 1856, apparently in anticipation of the need for additional stables.

No drawings and almost no photographs exist for the Pickford's Stables complex that operated over the 85 years from 1857 to 1942, before sustaining major damage in WWII. Recreating this original complex has had to rely on very limited and poor-quality sources. The only photograph is one of the Engineer public house (§7.28), which shows a little of two sides of Pickford's Stables.

The photograph is believed to date from the 1870s. By this time, the business of Felix Calvert and Co., who had built the Engineer and sold the site to LNWR, had been liquidated. A joint-stock company, the City of London Brewery

Company, had been formed in December 1859 to purchase and carry on Calvert's business.

Pickford's new stables were rebuilt over 1857-58 on well aired and lit ground and first floors to accommodate some 240 horses, the first floor accessible by a ramp, all arranged around a central services building. Two decades ahead of their time, this innovative solution created for Pickford by LNWR's architect was barely remarked on then or since. They were far in advance of the stables built in Stables Yard at the same time, described above, both in size and sophistication. The much-admired Great Western Railway's Mint Stables at Paddington (*Russell, 1995*) were built from 1877 and only raised to three stable floors served by ramps towards the end of the century.

Pickford's Stables ranges were three storeys with stabling on the basement and first floor and fodder storage and chaff cutting on the second floor. The central service block was four floors. The ground floor housed the steam engine, boiler and flue, with coal storage to supply the boilers. On the first floor were the farriery and harness makers' shops. The second floor housed machinery for making horse feed and provided storage for such provender. Their previous stables had steam hay-cutters which could prepare 50 trusses of hay an hour. There was further storage on the third floor.

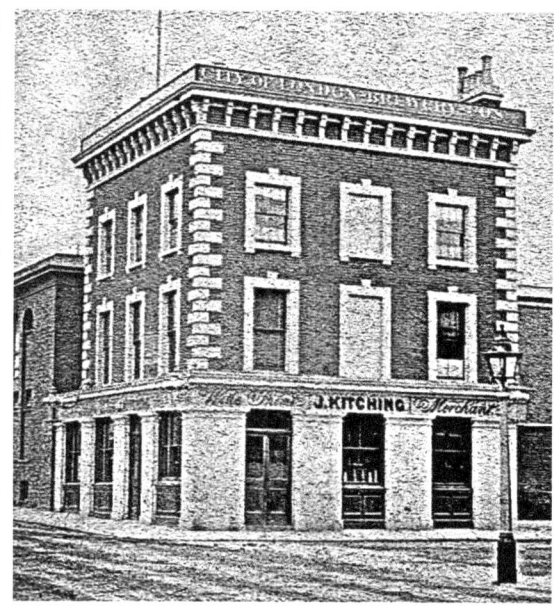

7.28 The Engineer showing part of Gloucester Road and Princess Road frontages of Pickford's Stables

The farriery would have been busy providing new sets of horseshoes for the stud, as each set lasted only three to four weeks. Typical tools used in the farriery are shown in §7.29, although the image was taken in the former farriery in Stables Yard, housed in one of the arches under the NLR.

7.29 Farriers' tools, Stables Yard c1975

The next two plans show the arrangement of the stables on the ground (§7.30) and first floors (§7.31) and the author's categorization of the six stables ranges on §7.31.

The brick-built walls were one and a half bricks thick, with recesses a single brick thick for window reveals and for visual effect. First and second floors were supported on circular cast iron columns and longitudinal main joists, with wrought iron cross-joisting to support brick jack arches. Floors were laid in asphalt to a fall for drainage.

Hay and other feed was offloaded from barges moored alongside the stables on the Regent's Canal and raised by hoist to the second floor to be transferred to the central services building via one of the wooden bridges (§7.32, §7.38). From here, after processing, feed was distributed to the storage areas on the second floor of each of the stables ranges via the four wooden bridges (§7.39).

7.30 Pickford's stables: ground floor plan

7.31 Pickford's stables: first floor plan

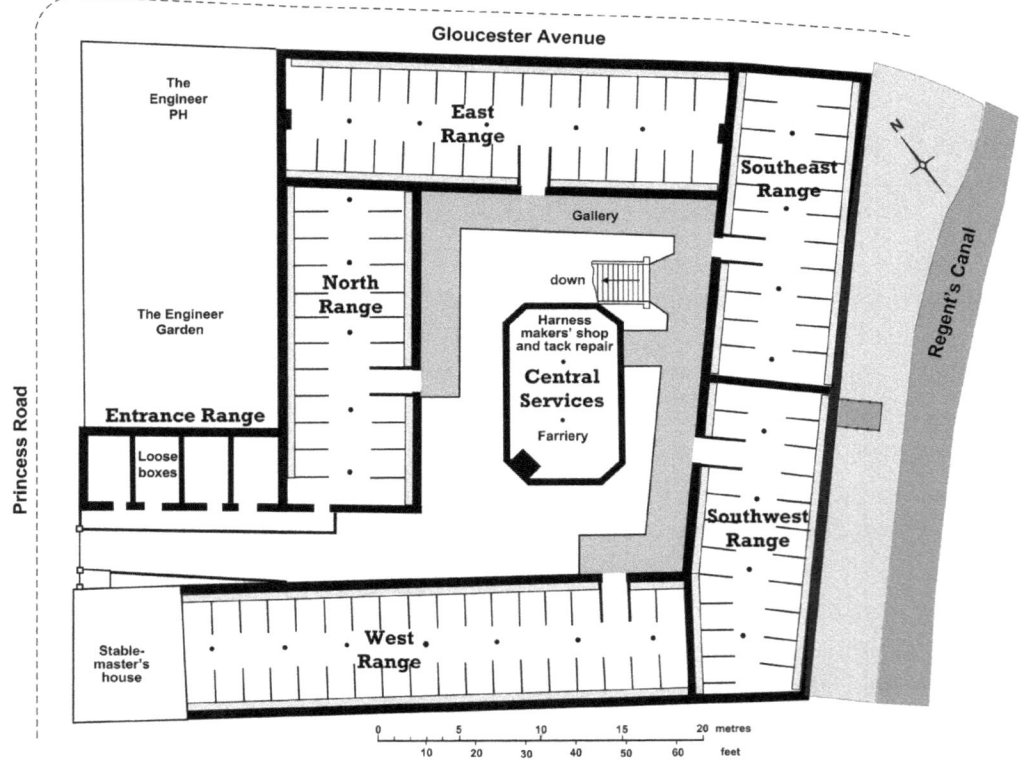

Much of the barged supply would have come from Cumberland Market, at the end of the Cumberland Branch of the Regent's Canal.

The yard was served by the horse tunnel that ran from the goods depot under the busy main line railway, providing a safe passage to the stables (§7.39). This can be seen in the recreated Gloucester Avenue elevation.

7.32 Pickford's stables: second floor plan

showing both the yard level and the street level (§7.33). It is assumed that the window arrangement followed a similar pattern for all ranges, but that the lower windows facing the street were blind.

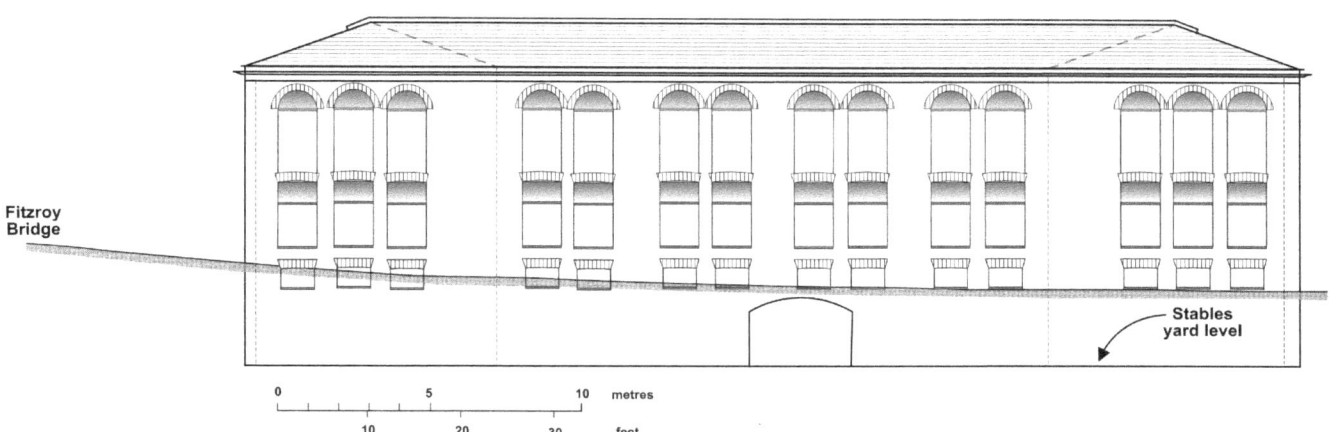

7.33 East Range: elevation to Gloucester Avenue

Stalls were separated by swing bales, as shown in §7.34, without the alternating panel partitions seen in another typical stable arrangement (§7.35), which shows the hooks and pegs required for harnesses, collars and tackle that were singular to each horse.

The gated street entrance on Princess Road led via a steep cobbled slope down to the stables yard, which lay well below the road level. The daily manure cart required a third horse at the front to pull the cart up the slope "with sparks flying off the horses' hooves" (*Friends of Chalk Farm Library, 2001*).

STABLES COMPLEX   101

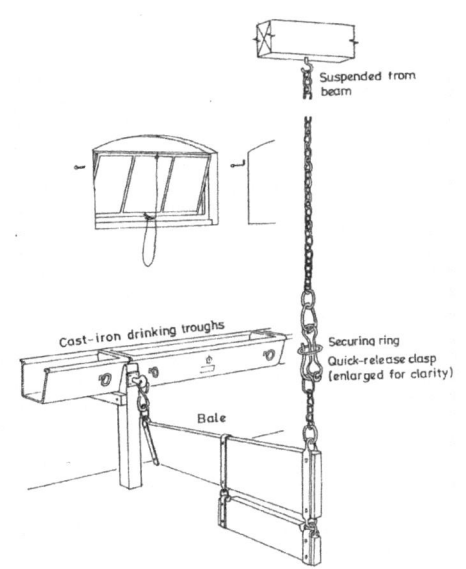

7.34 Swing bale and means of attachment (left image)

7.35 Stables with partitions and swing bales, 1900 (right image)

7.36 Entrance Range and services building: south elevation to entrance ramp and stables yard. Recreated from Drawing: Princess Road Stables, Dangerous Structure Notice, Partial Rebuilding, 1931 in CLSAC

The entrance stable range (§7.36) housed loose boxes, and there would have been a room for veterinary services. Also shown are the gallery that served all the stables ranges at first floor level and the wooden bridges linking with the central block at second floor level.

In 1942, the stables suffered major war damage from an incendiary bomb. "News came down to us one night (in the shelter in Primrose Hill) that stables nearby had been hit and the horses were running wild through the streets" (*Friends of Chalk Farm Library, 2001*). The target would have been Camden Goods Station. The horses were safely released before being rounded up later. Stable hands could shelter in the basement of the stablemaster's house, converted under Air Raid Protection (ARP) measures.

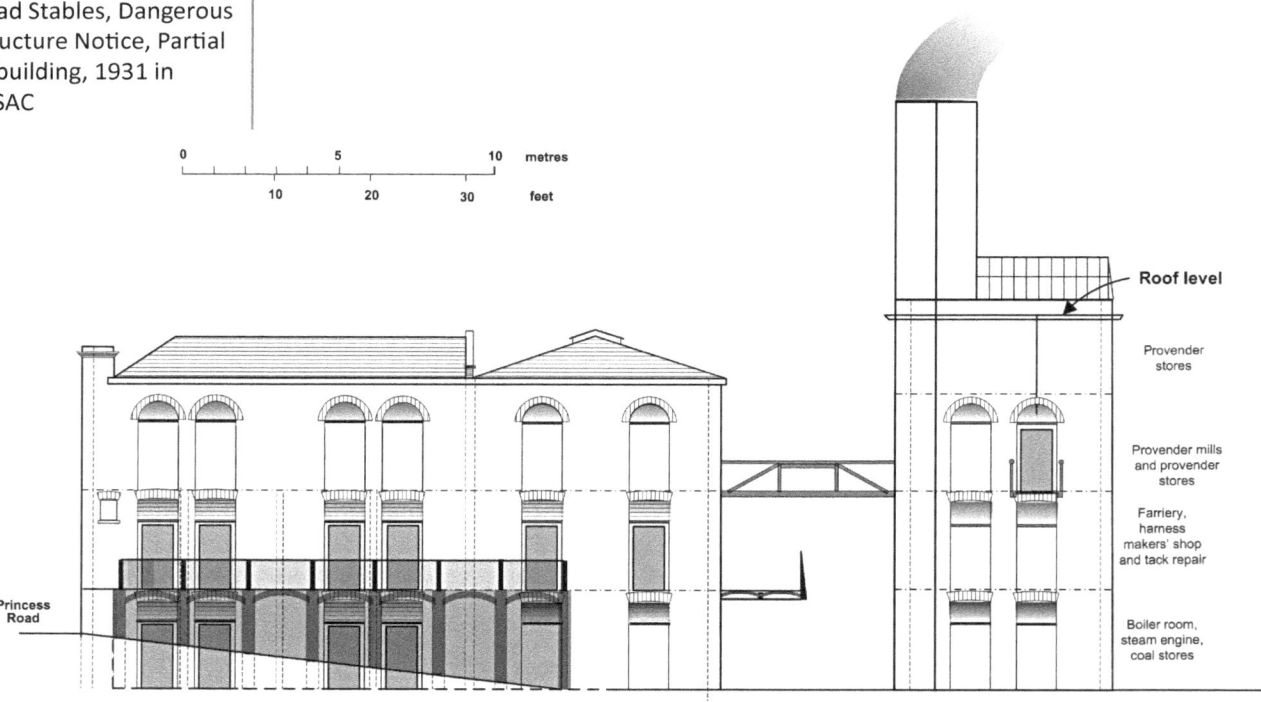

The fire resulted in Pickford's stables being reduced from three to one or two storeys, a pale reflection of their former size and architectural significance. While primarily a response to war damage, this would also have served the drastically reduced demand for horse-drawn haulage.

An oblique aerial photograph of 1946 (§7.37) shows the repaired and reduced stable ranges. On the nearside is Primrose Hill School, while *The Engineer* public house lies on the corner of Gloucester Avenue and Princess Road. On the other side of Gloucester Avenue, the stables formerly occupied by Allsopp, with their two storeys, appear to have survived the war intact, complete with wooden stairs to the pitching hole of the hayloft. The horse stairs that connected them to the Western Horse Tunnel remain in the 42 Gloucester Avenue building complex. Beyond lies the covered footbridge that crossed the main line railway to carry workers from Camden Goods Station to messing facilities - a 'people tunnel'.

Some anecdotal evidence came from Peter Toms, the son of a former stablemaster, born in 1938, who described to the author how he grew up in the stablemaster's house at No. 44 Princess Road *(Primrose Hill remembered, 2001)*. As a boy in the late 1940s, he used to meet horses emerging from the horse tunnel to give them a rub down and guide them to their stalls, a reminder that the past described here is not so distant.

This first account of these remarkable stables merits more than architects' plans and elevations. Alison Kemp, a local resident, has created three animated scenes, as shown in §7.38 to §7.40.

7.37 Oblique aerial view to northeast showing reduced stables ranges, 1946

7.38 Southwest and southeast ranges facing Regent's Canal, showing fodder supply being offloaded from narrowboat, viewed from St Mark's Crescent with Fitzroy Bridge on right, *Alison Kemp*, 2023

STABLES COMPLEX

7.39 East Range showing opening to Western Horse Tunnel (inset), ramp to first floor gallery of Southeast Range and wooden bridge from Central Services to second floor fodder storage, *Alison Kemp*, 2023

7.40 Princess Road entrance to stables yard showing team of horses for manure removal, loose boxes in Entrance Range, Central Services building, gatekeeper's shed and stablemaster's house, *Alison Kemp*, 2023

8 Camden Station from 1860s to 1900

8.1 Layout of goods yard
8.2 Oval Road entrance
8.3 Goods offices
8.4 Main goods shed
8.5 Hydraulic systems
8.6 Capturing the beer trade
8.7 Ale Vaults
8.8 Goods interchange
8.9 The goods business
8.10 The workforce

8.1 Layout of goods yard

The third quarter of the nineteenth century saw yet more major changes to the buildings, if not the configuration, of the Goods Depot which are treated as Phase 4 in the evolution of Camden Station. The layout in 1870 is shown on the OS map (§8.1).

By this time the former Pickford's warehouse had become the "A" Shed and had just been rebuilt for W & A Gilbey, while the Roundhouse was being converted into a bonded store for Gilbey's highland whisky. Both had briefly been potato markets or grain stores.

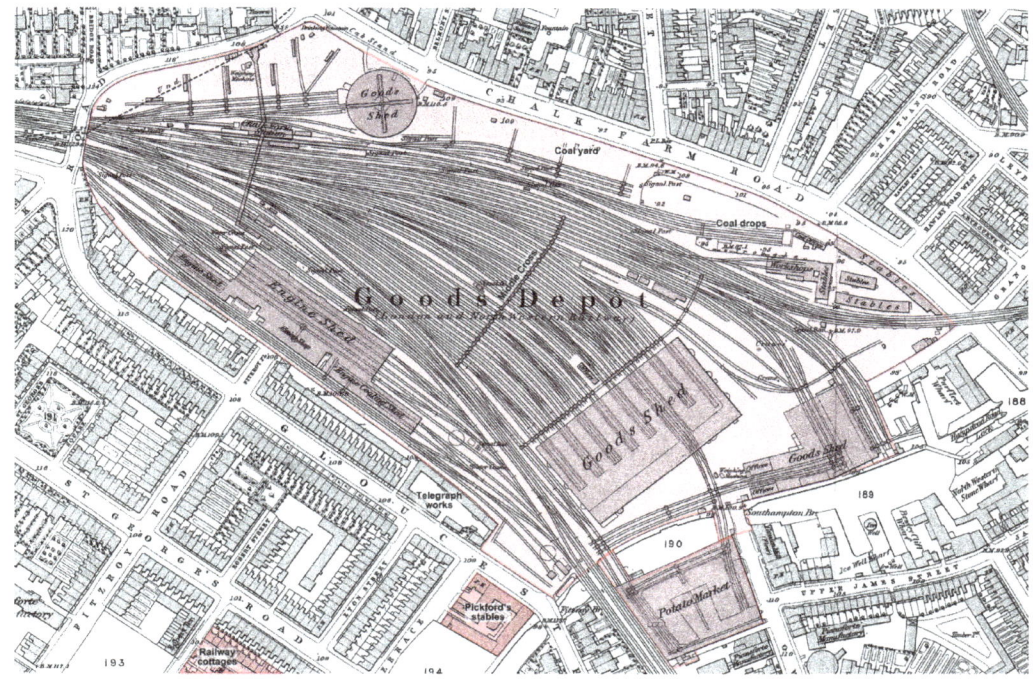

8.1 Camden Goods Station, 1870 from OS London Large Scale Series

The density of goods yard sidings, which accounted for some 20 miles (32km) of track, is striking. Two lines of wagon turntables and capstans ran across these sidings, one immediately alongside the main goods shed and the other more westerly. The latter, used for marshalling arriving trains into their appropriate sidings, was known as 'Middle Cross' (§8.1). Both arrays of sidings enabled the reordering of goods wagons as the trains were assembled.

In October 1866 there were 100 locomotives operating at Camden: 33 passenger, four banking, 46 main line goods, 15 shunting, and two ballast engines. The goods yard handled the outward despatch of 27 trains each night and in the early hours received a similar amount of inward traffic from the 'country'.

8.2 Oval Road entrance

8.2 Three speaker tubes embedded in 1866 façade of the goods offices

8.3 View east along Regent's Canal to Southampton Bridge, from W N Beal's 'Through London on a Monkey Boat' 1906-8

Oval Road led to Southampton Bridge over the Regent's Canal and provided road access to Camden Goods Station via a granite-setted yard that extended to the forecourt of the major goods warehouses: the main LNWR goods shed, the Interchange Warehouse (and its precursors) and the "A" shed. Here the horses that worked the goods station could be coupled to drays and wagons that had already been loaded for distributing by road the goods that had arrived by rail. Or horses would be uncoupled from drays so that the goods delivered by road could be prepared for onward carriage by rail.

Drays and wagons moving into Camden Goods Station would pass over the weighbridge alongside the weighing office at the Oval Road entrance (§11.13). Those draymen who were uncertain where to deliver their load could draw up alongside the Enquiry Office located at the corner of the goods offices and speak with the clerks inside via the speaker tubes in the wall (§8.2).

A view of the Oval Road entrance at Southampton Bridge in the early 1900s is seen in §8.3, looking east from the towpath of the Regent's Canal. It is partly obscured by the bridge carrying two rail sidings to the "A" Shed and by the covered loading bank between rail and road bridges. Two goods wagons can be observed on the rail bridge.

Features shown have been numbered and their present status is described:

1. Gilbey's "A" Shed with loading bank (demolished).
2. Rail bridge with two sidings connecting main goods shed with "A" Shed (demolished).
3. Gilbey gin distillery (part of Hucks' Bottle Stores and, later, Gilbey House).

4. Hucks' Bottle Stores (now Gilbey House).
5. Main railway offices; accessed from Oval Road via enclosed external wooden stairs to upper floors (largely demolished, but façade retained as part of The Henson).
6. Hydraulic accumulator tower (demolished).
7. Towpath with ramp for horses to be led out of water if train whistle from nearby mainline bridge caused them to take fright (extant).
8. Barge beyond bridge with towing horse approaching Hampstead Road Locks.

8.3 Goods offices

At the start of operations in 1839 the goods offices had been moved to the trapezoidal building adjoining Commercial Place (#3.6). They appear to have remained there for only about five years as, in 1844, tenders were issued for erection of new offices for the Goods Department. The trapezoidal building was converted to accommodate the Locomotive Department in 1846 and was demolished in 1850 to make way for the NLR.

The approved tender of £512 (£85,000 today) for the new offices suggests that these were not very substantial and may have been intended to be temporary. Their location is not known but is believed to have been close to the Oval Road entrance. Given that the east side of Oval Road had yet to be raised to railway level, the goods offices must have been on the west side, at the head of the embankment that sloped down to the Regent's Canal towpath.

After demolishing the coke ovens and raising the land to railway level in Phase 3, the goods offices were relocated on the east side of Oval Road in 1860, as described in #6.5.

These offices were enlarged for the Goods Department in 1866 with the addition of two floors spanning three rail sidings that ran through the building from the Interchange basin (§8.4). A goods shed, open to the goods yard, had already been built ((#6.5) behind the goods offices (§8.5). The goods shed was supported on the 1856 Ale Vaults.

8.4 Front elevation of goods offices facing Oval Road, bridging the opening for rail sidings. From Drawing No. 4 Proposed New Offices for Goods Department, 1866 (left image)

8.5 Side elevation of goods offices showing goods shed on the eastern side (left). From Drawing No. 4 Proposed New Offices for Goods Department, 1866 (right image)

In 1874 the Goods Superintendent, Mr Woodhouse, prepared plans for an additional storey to the goods offices. This can be seen in §8.7. In 1880, a plan and estimate for enlarging the offices and covering over part of the goods shed was prepared.

The goods shed/offices were further enlarged in 1900 by a second floor along the towpath extending to the Interchange forecourt. On the ground floor Maples, the furniture retailers in Tottenham Court Road, had a bedstead store. An external staircase was built at that time from Oval Road to the first and second floors.

8.6 From Drawing No. 1, New Delivery and Cartage Offices etc., General Plan, 1903

8.7 From Drawing No. 3, New Delivery and Cartage Offices, etc., Front Elevation (part), 1903

In 1903 the opening for sidings was filled by new Delivery and Cartage Offices. The plan (§8.6) and the part elevation to Oval Road (§8.7) show how the Delivery and Cartage Offices were accommodated. The 1866 symmetry of the Oval Road façade was compromised by a single storey addition next to Southampton Bridge, seen in the plan and in §9.37. Under the new arrangement this was to house part of the Cash Office, the new Time Office and a police post.

The goods offices continued to undergo a series of expansions to reflect the nature and size of the business and the personnel employed. Later changes to the goods offices are described in Ch. 11.

8.4 Main goods shed

In 1864 the LNWR built a goods shed to replace several smaller scattered goods facilities. This had a plan area of 100,000 square feet (9289 sq. m) and was the largest at that time in the country. It could hold 135 wagons. About 750 wagons containing some 1500 tons of goods could be loaded and despatched a night. Goods arriving were marshalled in the forecourt that extended across all the bays of the shed. The nine platforms or 'banks' were divided into 'country' destinations, as seen in the plan (§8.8).

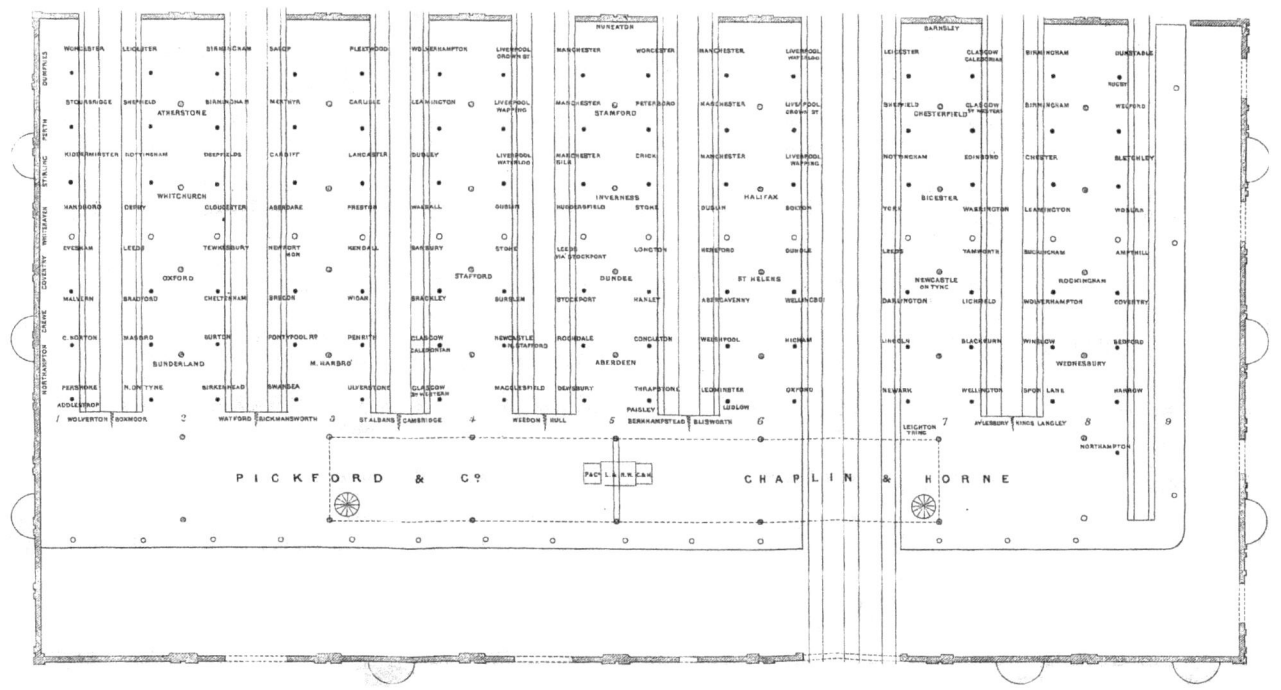

8.8 Plan of main goods shed from Humber (1866)

The plan of the new goods shed shows that offices were provided for both Pickford and Chaplin & Horne in an elevated section of the main goods shed (seen in §11.3), reached by spiral staircases. Soon after, the two railway agents had to abandon their joint warehouse on the opposite bank of the canal, formerly Pickford's warehouse, after it was destroyed by the 1867 fire (#6.7).

The goods shed was raised on vaults extending over the whole area of the shed (§8.9). These were leased to Allsopp for the storage of ales after Bass had declined the offer to base their storage there. The vaults were connected to the Eastern Horse Tunnel by a spur (§8.10).

Beer barrels would have been lowered by hoist to the basement and moved from there via the horse tunnel for further distribution. Later a lift allowing loaded wagons to access the basement vaults was installed, but onward distribution remained a manual task.

CAMDEN STATION FROM 1860s TO 1900

8.9 Basement of goods shed, 1987 (left image)

8.10 Entrance to basement from Eastern Horse Tunnel, 1987 (right image)

8.5 Hydraulic systems

The development of hydraulic power was led professionally by William Armstrong (*1850*) and was still in its infancy. There is no record of exactly when the LNWR installed the first hydraulic system at Camden Goods Station. It was already being considered in 1853, but the Phase 3 works do not appear to have included any provision for hydraulic power. By contrast, the GNR at King's Cross commissioned a hydraulic power system as early as 1851, as part of the initial development of their goods station.

It was claimed in 1864 (*Railway News)* that four locomotives and about 90 horses were exclusively dedicated to shunting and sorting at Camden. The associated cost would have prompted the introduction of hydraulic power and the timing was probably associated with the Phase 4 expansion in 1864, which included provision of hydraulically operated turntables, capstans and cranes for the new goods shed and associated sidings. In support of this date is the fact that, in 1866, soon after the main goods shed had been constructed, the LNWR upgraded operations at its "A" Shed, the warehouse formerly occupied by Pickford, but now shared by Pickford with Chaplin & Horne.

The first hydraulic accumulator tower (seen in §8.3 and §12.3) was built in about 1865 on the north bank of the Regent's Canal, immediately west of the Oval Road entrance. This was well placed to serve both the main goods shed and the "A" Shed, and later the hydraulic lifts and cranes in the Interchange Warehouse.

The accumulator would have consisted of a vertical cylinder, standing in the centre of the tower, with a ram which supported a crosshead. The crosshead ran between guides on two sides of the tower. From the crosshead was hung a weight-case, which provided an annular space around the cylinder that could be filled with anything cheap and heavy, in London usually Thames ballast. The load on the accumulator depended on the diameter of the ram and the pressure for which the hydraulic network was designed but could be 80 tons or more.

In operation, the accumulator rose and fell in the tower according to the demand for power.

An 'Additional Accumulator House' was built in 1866 just off Gloucester Road and alongside the Western Horse Tunnel (§8.11). This location allowed the two accumulator towers to be connected hydraulically via pipework that ran through the Western Horse Tunnel, supported on brackets mounted on the tunnel wall. This pipework was diverted to the towpath retaining wall (it can be seen in §12.3) via the deviated section of horse tunnel in the early 1930s. The support brackets to pipework long removed now present an archaeological curiosity.

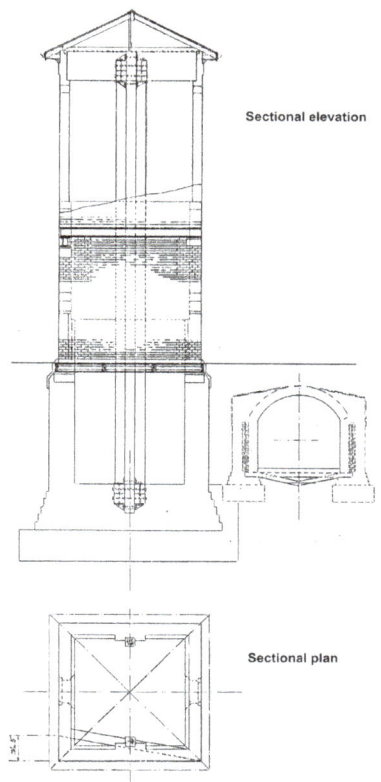

8.11 Additional Accumulator House, 1866, extract from LMS, Camden MPD, Alterations to Accumulator House 1931 (left image)

8.12 Additional Accumulator House, 2013 (right image)

This hydraulic accumulator tower is believed to be the oldest of a handful of LNWR accumulator towers to survive (§8.12). The lower part of the tower was altered to accommodate new rail tracks when the line was widened in 1931.

The original location of the steam engine, boilers and pump that powered the hydraulic system in the mid 1860s is not evident. Following the construction of Allsopp's Stables by LNWR in 1876, these facilities were provided in the northern part of the stables complex. Electric pumps replaced the steam driven pumps in 1923, but it is likely that the accumulator towers would have continued in service. The pumping station buildings were demolished in 2000. It is not known when the equipment was removed from the Gloucester Avenue tower. It now houses a lift as part of the 42 Gloucester Avenue complex.

8.6 Capturing the beer trade

For much of the population of London in the first half of the 19th century, beer was considered a safer drink than water, as well as more pleasurable.

Burton on Trent was already a major beer brewing town. When Burton brewers succeeded in replicating the pale ale produced in London, the quality of Burton water allowed the development of Burton India Pale Ale, or IPA, Britain's leading export beer in the 19th century, brewed to keep during the long sea voyage to India. Burton became the world's most important beer town.

Beer from Burton on Trent was also one of the major commodities transported to London by canal and railway. Capturing this trade was important to the LNWR. Bass was the largest and Samuel Allsopp and Sons the second largest of the famous nine Burton brewers. They already had warehouses on the Regent's Canal to serve the London market. The railways extended sidings into the Burton breweries which allowed their share of the London market and other regional markets to grow quickly.

By the 1870s, beer was the major commodity shipped by rail other than coal. Bass alone transported almost 300,000 barrels to London in 1874, some 80 million pints. Its base at St. Pancras had stables with up to 100 horses to distribute its barrels around the capital. Beer was so important to the Midland Railway that a Bass director sat on its board.

Allsopp was the first enterprise attracted to Camden goods depot. Allsopp started transporting beer to London by railway in 1845, and in 1848 signed a seven-year lease with LNWR for warehouse accommodation. Allsopp's first warehouse was built as a series of vaults in 1849 on a site just to the north of the coke ovens (§6.1). Trade with London was stimulated by the sidings that LNWR constructed into Allsopp's breweries in Burton on Trent.

Allsopp's 1849 warehouse was swept away with the coke ovens in the Phase 3 reconstruction and they moved their storage facilities to the Ale Vaults.

8.7 Ale Vaults

The Interchange Basin was rebuilt in Phase 3 with the same canal frontage but a different alignment. It was increased in size to 210 feet (64m) by 45 feet (14m) to take six barges, and this basin remains.

The plan (§8.13) shows what was then termed the 'Ale Vaults' with a view to capturing the valuable beer trade. Their location can be seen in a broader frame in #6.5.

At that time, in 1866, they were leased variously to both Bass and Allsopp. The plan shows how the Eastern Horse Tunnel was to be extended by a branch into the basement of the new main goods shed that had been built in 1864, effectively a massive enlargement of the Ale Vaults.

At the time of the plan, the L-shaped 1856 vaults at bottom left were occupied by Bass, for whom they had originally been built for storage of ales and beers.

These vaults connected on their east side with the Interchange Basin. Barges could tie up alongside the vaults and barrels could be lifted into the vaults via their openings to the dock. All the 1856 vaults remained open until Gilbey took them over for wine storage in bond, when they were bricked up, as described in #9.5.

As can be seen in the plan, the three northern vault openings formed part of Allsopp's premises, a small area securely walled off from Bass' warehouse.

These connected with the dock and allowed the landing of beer from barges for Allsopp. After landing, Allsopp's barrels would be moved via an underground passage that connected with the substantial remnants of the 1839 vaults, built under the sidings and engine lane of the original goods depot (§8 on page xvi). Allsopp had first taken these facilities over in 1859 on a 21-year lease. Allsopp also occupied the arches, seen at the top of the plan, that had supported the 1846 wagon construction shop. Those arches that are omitted from the plan were also leased by Allsopp (and perhaps others) as stabling. Bass would also have had a large need for stabling, probably leasing a substantial part of the four ranges in Stables Yard.

The major vaults run east-west and are 12 feet (3.7m) wide, about nine feet six inches (2.9m) high from the floor to the crown of the vault and have three foot (0.9m) wide footings. The transverse openings in these vaults are only about six feet (1.8m) in height and vary in width from 11 to 13 feet (3.4-4.0m), with 4½ feet (1.4m) footings.

The environment of the vaults was well suited to the storage of beer. The means of moving beer (or wine) barrels around the vaults can be appreciated in the 1987 photograph (§8.14), where the wooden sleepers used for barrel runs were still evident many years after such work had ceased. The photograph is looking west along one of the major vaults and shows the intersecting minor vaults on each side. Labour costs in moving barrels around the complex of Ale Vaults must have been high.

When the main goods shed was being planned, Bass was invited to occupy the basement, which extended under the whole area of the shed (§8.8 and §8.9). This would have released the 1856 Ale Vaults for Allsopp. Negotiations in 1863 revealed that Bass already had an agreement with the Midland Railway, extending to 1865, for all their rail traffic except that for London. Bass was keeping its options open in the expectation that the Midland Railway would soon construct substantial facilities that Bass could occupy for their large and growing traffic into London.

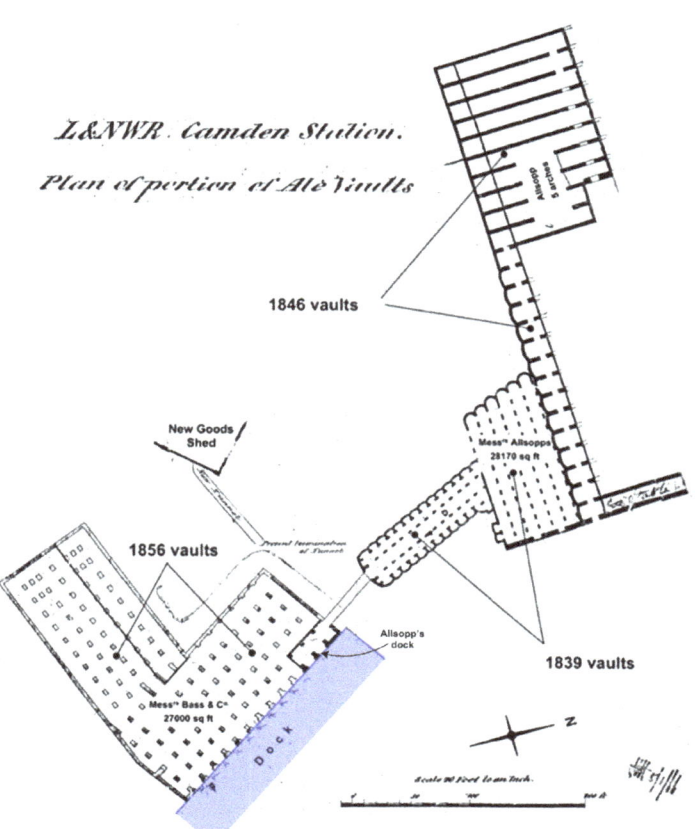

8.13 Plan of portion of Ale Vaults, 1866

8.14 Looking west along major arch showing former barrel runs, 1987

CAMDEN STATION FROM 1860s TO 1900

Soon after, the Midland Railway built the St. Pancras Goods Depot by clearing away what was then Agar Town and Bass elected to move there, building a warehouse on the southern side of the Regent's Canal and a bridge across to the goods depot. Bass' commitment to St Pancras and the Midland Railway grew when St Pancras Station was built, its undercroft famously designed around the dimensions of Bass beer barrels.

Allsopp remained committed to Camden Goods Station and took over the 1856 vaults when Bass left. When W & A Gilbey, the wine and spirits merchants, became LNWR's major tenant in the late 1860s (#9.1), Allsopp moved into the basement of the main goods shed. This released the 1856 vaults for Gilbey. which leased all three sets of vaults shown in §8.14, among other major facilities, for storage of wine in barrels. Their involvement is described in the next chapter.

8.8 Goods interchange

The first LNWR interchange facilities were developed in the 1840s and are described in #5.13. They were further expanded in Phase 3 as described in #6.5. The three-span interchange warehouse was essentially maintained until the 1890s. The layout at rail level is shown in the plan (§8.15).

A new and stronger loading platform was built in 1890, but the next major change was the addition of a new span in 1896 that carried the warehouse to the eastern boundary, where it met the retaining wall and Gilbey's Triangular Bottle Stores. The rail handling side now operated under cover. Yet the improvements of the 1890s were short-lived as by the turn of the century plans were being drawn up for a substantial new interchange warehouse (#11.2).

8.9 The goods business

The railways were originally built primarily for freight. The goods business, the reception and onward delivery of the inward traffic and the loading and despatch of the outward traffic, took place out of public gaze in its own private world, one that operated 24 hours a day.

This new mode of travel had also opened opportunities for passengers, such as the weekend move of the social elite to their country houses to take part in the local hunt.

Lack of data prevents direct comparison of receipts for passenger and goods traffic but their relative importance may be related to national trends. In 1845, passenger receipts were twice goods traffic receipts. By 1852 the value of goods traffic was almost that of passenger traffic and five years later had overtaken passenger traffic in value. Between 1860 and the end of the century, goods receipts increased by about 350%, whereas passenger receipts increased by only 40% (*Wade, 1900*). In revenue terms, growth in passenger traffic, notably commuters, was largely offset by pressure on fares from competition with bus and tram services.

The railways were considered to be common carriers and thus subject to the Carriers Act 1830, but the Railway and Canal Traffic Act 1854 placed

8.15 Interchange facilities as provided in Phase 3

additional obligations on the railways due to their monopoly status. Each railway company was now required to take all trade offered and to set and publish the same levels of fares to all in respect of any particular service.

However limited the data, the strong growth of the goods business from the 1850s to the 1870s and the increasing importance of goods traffic in the second half of the nineteenth century appear undeniable. Growth at Camden Station was probably below national averages as the LNWR started decentralising its goods handling operations from the 1860s onwards. Nevertheless, by the 1880s Camden Station was the principal goods yard among many LNWR yards in the metropolis, receiving wagons from subsidiary depots for marshalling into larger trains serving the country.

By 1850, the trade in coal imported into London had reached about 3.5 million tons. Almost all was seaborne. Twenty years later, in 1871, this trade had doubled to over seven million tons, with railways having captured

CAMDEN STATION FROM 1860s TO 1900

over 60% (*Simmons, 1986*). A further 15 years later, Firth (*1886*), in a letter to The Times, referred to over 11 million tons coming into the London coal tax area yearly, of which nearly seven million came by railway. The rail-borne quantity did not change greatly over the next 20 years.

The Company had paid coal duties on 759,000 tons of coal in 1863. This volume of traffic may have been sustained for a few more years, before falling away as coal was increasingly moved to other LNWR depots to supply local markets. The nearest such depot was in Leybourne Street, just outside the CFRL, where Thomas Wood had leased the area between the canal and the viaduct from the NLR in 1850 as a coal wharf. On the north side coal stacks were built in 1860 for loading wagons using three of the railway arches. Evidence of this remains in the form of granite sets, kerbs and bollards. Another nearby depot was at Maiden Lane, also on the NLR.

The two major Burton brewers transported their beers and ales to Camden Station in the early 1860s. By the 1870s, the larger of these, Bass, had moved to St Pancras, while Allsopp developed correspondingly large operations at Camden. If we allow Allsopp half the volume of Bass, then in the mid 1870s it would have moved 150,000 barrels annually to London by rail, equivalent to about 30,000 tons, perhaps 40,000 tons after allowing for other materials used and for onward transport by rail to the Docks and further afield.

Gilbey was selling almost two million gallons (9 million litres) of wines and spirits annually by 1880. Allowing 50% of a packing case to be liquid, this would be equivalent to about 18,000 tons when packaged into cases, of which perhaps 5,000 would be distributed by horse drawn drays in London. The wines and spirits that arrived in barrels would have constituted another 12,000 tons, and the wood for packing cases, bottles, cork and other materials used in their operations at least another 5,000 tons, suggesting about 35,000 tons in total travelled annually by rail.

The beer and wine volume might therefore have amounted to 10-15% of the total Camden traffic in the mid 1870s, with coal perhaps 40%. General merchandise continued to represent about half the volume. Incoming bulk goods would have included hay and other horse feed, cement, iron, building materials, cotton cloth as well as manufactured goods and agricultural produce. Some of the incoming goods were transhipped for onward transport to the Docks. Much of the outgoing merchandise would have originated in the various parts of the empire and passed through the Docks such as imported fruits, wool, timber, silk and cotton fibre, spices, hops, wheat and other cereals. One of the largest outgoing consignments would have been newsprint for daily and weekly newspapers and journals.

Rail freight volumes increased up to the early years of the 20th century. After WWI there was a decline, prompted by organisational change and industrial unrest before relative stability returned until the mid-1950s (§8.16). It then fell swiftly to about 20% of the peak volume. Not only were more and more deliveries being made by road, but the Clean Air Act and the development of North Sea gas each had a major impact, with activity in the Railway Lands reflecting this.

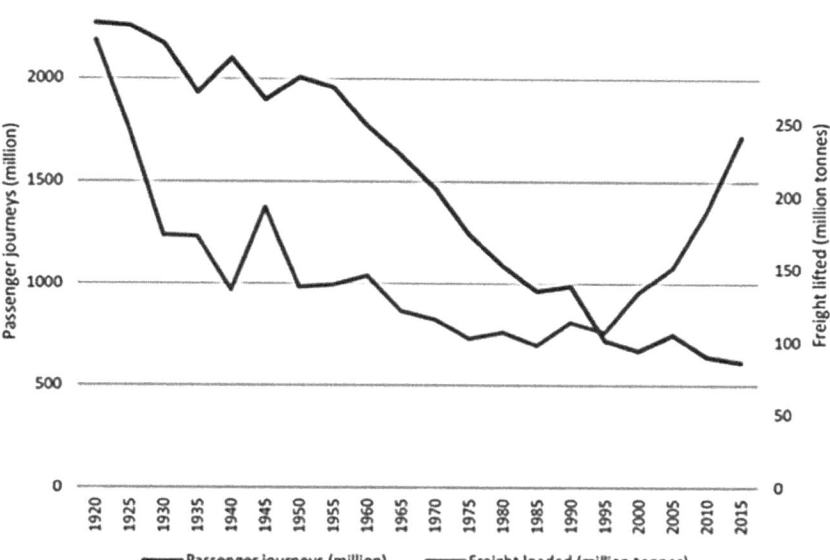

8.16 Passengers and freight carried by rail 1920 to 2015, from Railnatter, 2021

8.10 The workforce

The movement of goods demanded a small army of labourers, clerical staff for administration, weighbridges to measure what moved, and tight security to avoid loss. Goods depots have always been barred to the public, with the result that images and information about their operation have been sparse.

Camden Passenger Engine House or Motive Power Depot stretched for more than 700 feet (215m) from the turntable behind the Pembroke Castle to well beyond the Lansdowne. Many rail workers lived nearby and used the footbridge in Dumpton Place to get to the engine shed. The Lansdowne was open when they came off shift in the early hours.

Besides some six pubs on the west side of the tracks, including The Engineer, many others clustered along Chalk Farm Road and Jamestown Road. Camden also boasted a Windsor Castle, an Edinburgh Castle, a Carnarvon (sic) Castle and a Dublin Castle to meet the thirst of workers from all parts of the realm.

Separating drinking establishments for the four home nations was a prudent move as well as a welcoming signal. During the Phase 2 enlargement of Camden Station, ill feeling grew between the English 'navigators' and Irish labourers, employed in similar numbers. A furious and ultimately deadly battle started, and police had great difficulty in quelling the fight, reinforcements having to be dragged from the funeral of a colleague in Somers Town. More about the navvies role in the construction of the railway is given in #3.8.

In 1900 LNWR employed some 60 office staff in a variety of duties from ledgers and invoices to journals and printing. The range of annual salaries was from £30 to £570, with a mean of £160. This compares with the cost of labour which, when determining the savings in operating costs from construction of the new bottle stores in 1896, was estimated by William Hucks as 'not less than £70 per head per annum'.

It was not until the 1880s that female staff were employed in the goods offices in numbers but, once accepted, their administrative roles rapidly expanded, a tell-tale feature being the expansion of the lavatory provision.

9 W & A Gilbey: the Camden story

9.1 The move to Camden
9.2 Movement of wines and spirits
9.3 Camden premises
9.4 Import/export and excise
9.5 Bonded warehouses
9.6 Camden workforce
9.7 "A" Shed
9.8 Distillery
9.9 Triangular Bottle Stores
9.10 Hucks' Bottle Stores
9.11 Interchange Basement Warehouse
9.12 Stables and horses
9.13 Gilbey House

9.1 The move to Camden

The firm of W & A Gilbey was created in 1857 as an importer of inexpensive wine. It established its warehouses and business in London's West End and moved into prestigious head offices at the Pantheon in Oxford Street (site of the present Marks & Spencer) in 1867.

It was not long before its premises in Oxford Street became inadequate. In early 1869, Gilbey was persuaded by George Findlay, the General Goods Manager of LNWR, to move its bottling and warehousing to Camden. Gilbey offered LNWR the inducement of an annual traffic amounting to some £20,000 (over £3M today).

The two major premises that were offered to Gilbey initially were the "A" Shed (formerly Pickford's Warehouse) and the Roundhouse, both now operating as potato markets and grain warehouses. The "A" shed was to be Gilbey's main bottling and storage warehouse, while the Roundhouse was intended for storage of whisky and other spirits in bond. Both buildings needed substantial investment before they could be used, although the basement of the Roundhouse could receive whisky immediately. Provision was to be made elsewhere at Camden for the potato and flour and grain businesses that were displaced.

Gilbey wanted vacant possession of the Roundhouse and of the whole of the "A" Shed together with its basement vaults. This was approved on the understanding that the LNWR reserve the agent's office in the "A" shed. Some £10,000 (£1.5M today) was spent by LNWR converting the "A" shed into a useful warehouse of four floors each of 1¼ acres (0.5ha) with an acre (0.4ha) of glazing. A lease of 21 years was granted in September 1869, by which time rebuilding the "A" shed to Gilbey's requirements was almost complete.

Warehousing, bonded storage, bottling and forwarding progressively moved to Camden from the West End. These operations were to be based in Camden for almost the next 100 years.

Gilbey took over much of the extensive vaulting under the goods station, which provided an excellent environment for storage of wine. Its premises in Camden covered a floor area of 20 acres (8ha) with the various warehouses capable of storing 880,000 gallons (4 million litres). W & A Gilbey was the start of the modern wine and spirit business and the first to establish overseas. It became the largest drinks firm in the world and the major employer in the Camden area.

Gilbey's Camden operations had none of the glamour of their French chateau, their Bordeaux vineyards, or their Highland distilleries, and were not used to promote Gilbey's wines and spirits to the general public – not even the London gin that was distilled in Camden. The extensive above and below ground premises were only revealed to those in the trade, who could hardly fail to be impressed by a tour of the operations, followed by lunch in the wine vaults or bonded stores that had been laid out especially for the occasion.

The deaths of two brothers, Alfred (1879) and Henry (1892) created significant liabilities for death duties, which led in 1893 to conversion of the partnership into a private limited company. Sir Walter Gilbey, who in the same year was created a baronet, became chairman.

9.2 Movement of wines and spirits

Gilbey's wines, fortified wines, and spirits other than gin and whisky were imported through London Docks. Whisky was delivered by train from Gilbey's Highland distilleries while gin was distilled on the premises in Camden. All wines and spirits destined for the domestic market were moved to bonded storage until excise had been paid. For export, special consignments were securely dispatched by rail to the Docks under the supervision of the Inland Revenue.

The workflow at Camden involved many stages, as explained further in these pages. The work flow for the domestic market is illustrated in §9.1. The export market differed in not having to pay excise duty after release from bonded storage.

9.3 Camden premises

From 1869 Gilbey started to take on the lease of a number of railway facilities. The date of their first occupation of these varied as shown (§9.2), as did the length of lease which was arranged so that the leases of all premises expired on the same date in December 1890. The plan of these facilities is shown in §9.3.

Premises required adaptation to Gilbey's requirements. The major task was to rebuild the former Pickford's Warehouse which from 1870 became Gilbey's "A" Shed and the centre of its wine operations.

The use of the alphabet to designate Gilbey's premises appears to have been initiated for the first lease and may have been an LNWR initiative. It is shown in the plan (§9.3) that became part of the lease renewed in 1891, each

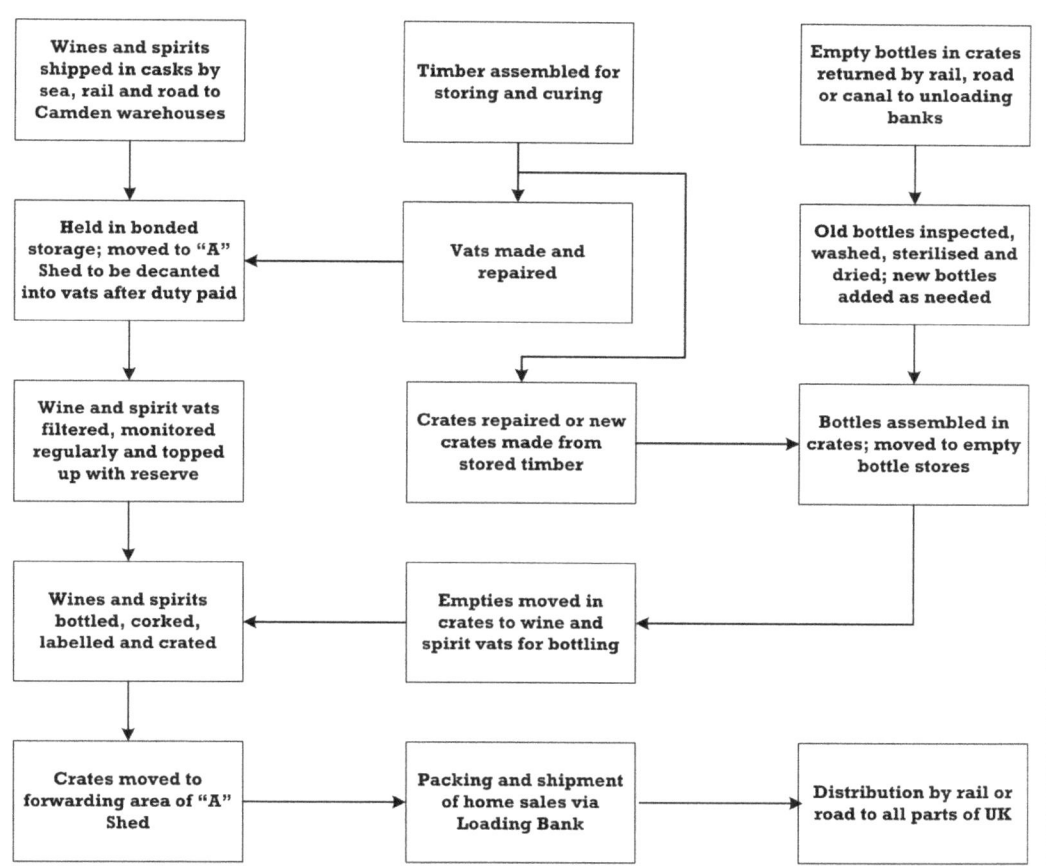

9.1 Work flow of Gilbey's Camden operations serving domestic market

No.	Gilbey premises and date of first occupation	Former use	Date of lease	Current status
1	**"A" Shed (1869)** Upgraded by LNWR. Opened 1870	Pickford's warehouse (1841); flour, grain & potato store (1867); Thomas Salt, Burton brewers in basement	25.9.1869	Demolished for Lock House
2	**Gin Distillery and four arches under NLR (1870)** Opened 1872, stables behind	John Taylor's Wharf (1848), Taylor's Steam Flour Mills (c1850), destroyed by fire (1870), LNWR	16.3.1874 (option to purchase)	Rebuilt as part of Gilbey House
3	**Round House and Arches 2, 3, 4 & 5 (1871)**	Goods engine shed (1847); corn & potato store (c1865)	28.9.1876	Music venue and media centre
4	**No. 2 Bond (1875), No. 4 Bond & Construction Shop (part) (Export Warehouse)** Purpose built by WAG	Construction Shop for goods wagons (1847);	3.2.1877	Demolished. Only 'Gin House' survives
5	**Triangular Bottle Warehouse (1875)** Purpose built by LNER for WAG, later Export Warehouse		1877	Gutted by fire (1980), demolished
6	**No. 1 Bond and Catacombs below Nos. 2 & 4 Bonds (1877)**	No 1 Bond built for Bass (1856); later became Allsopp's beer vaults and stables (c1864); Catacombs used by Allsopp	1877	Stables Market, Part demolished

9.2 Schedule of main premises at Camden included in leases with LNWR and forming basis of new lease in 1891

letter from A to K, apart from I, representing one of the premises. Essentially the same premises are depicted in the schematic (§9.4), a view from the north showing the situation in 1894. As may be seen, bonded warehouses were given numbers as well as letters. How these numbers were sequenced is not clear: it does not appear to be by date of first occupation.

9.3 Main premises at Camden included in leases with LNWR and forming basis of new lease in 1891

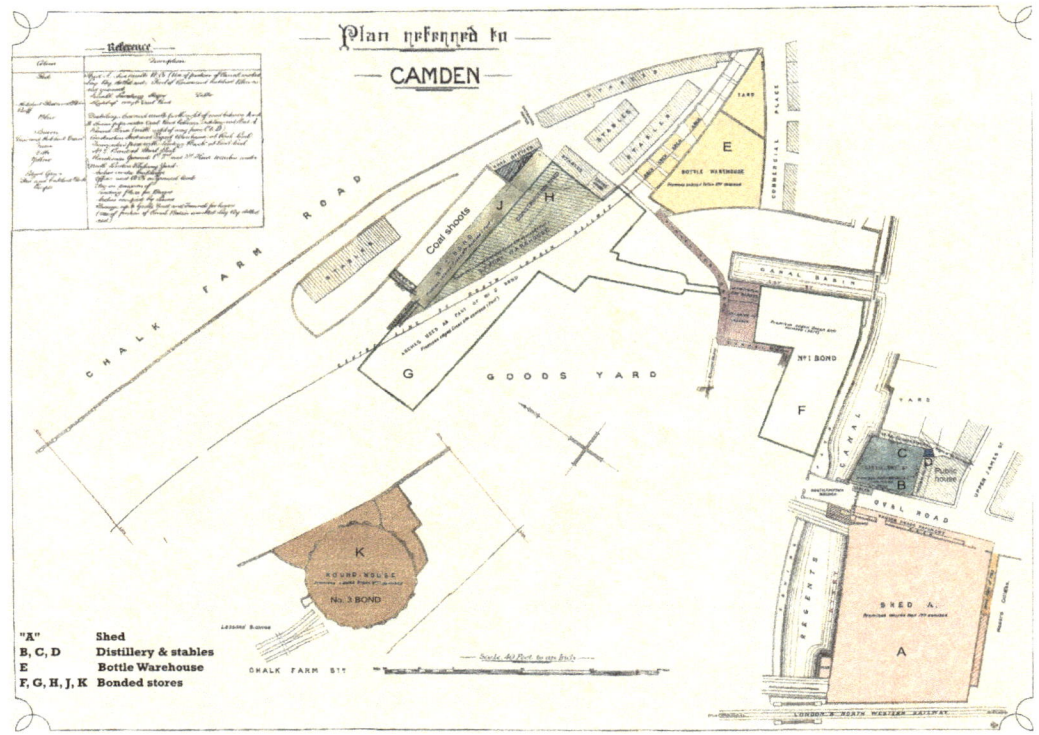

9.4 Gilbey's premises at Camden Goods Station, 1894, engraving from Gilbey Book of Wines (unpub.), 1896

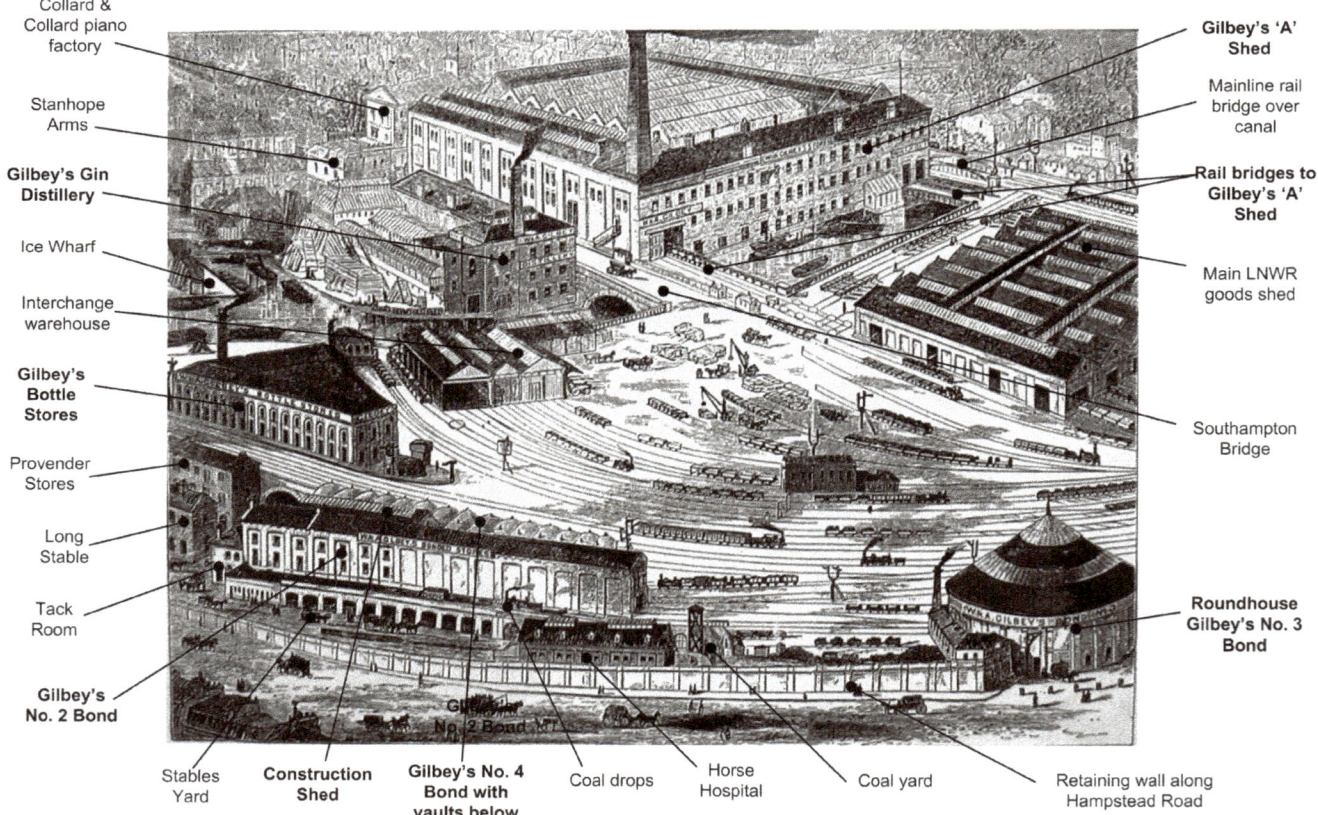

Not shown on the plan is Gilbey's No. 1 Bond, which lay below ground west of the Interchange Warehouse, and No. 5 Bond, which was located under the arches of the North London Railway at Camden Town station and leased from the Marquis of Camden.

CHALK FARM RAILWAY LANDS: A GUIDED TOUR 1830 TO 2030

These and other storage areas could hold 8000 butts of wine, equivalent to 4000 tuns or 16,000 hogsheads to use some of the strange volumetric units employed in the wine trade (§9.6). Almost half the storage was in the "A" Shed, with 10-15% in each of four other storage areas: the Roundhouse, No. 1 Bond, No. 2 Bond and the Catacombs.

9.4 Import/export and excise

The Wine Vaults of London Docks held 18 miles (29km) of casks, extending under the Wine Quay and the basement of adjacent warehouses.

Casks were lifted from the ship's hold by hydraulic cranes that were housed in the turrets of transit sheds. They were landed on the quay and placed in long rows. In the foreground of §9.5 is part of a consignment of Tarragona wine shipped by W & A Gilbey Ltd.

9.5 Gilbey's casks on Wine Quay at London Docks awaiting transport to Camden Station

After being landed, shives (wooden bungs) were taken out to enable customs officers to gauge casks and sample their contents.

Gilbey's wines were then carried directly to their bonded warehouses in Camden, by rail, road and sometimes canal, where more than 20 Excise Officers were employed to ensure the interests of Her Majesty's Revenue. Movement around and between bonded warehouses was severely restricted and openings blocked in order to secure the tax revenue.

These peculiar circumstances related to Gilbey's importance to the tax authorities. Gilbey was paying £1 million in excise duty (about £150M today) when the tax revenue of the whole country was £85 million.

Inevitably with casks in storage there was some loss of content through the outside of the cask, a loss known as 'ullage'. A cask of 100 gallons (454 litres) of

W & A GILBEY: THE CAMDEN STORY

spirits was allowed one gallon (4.5 litres) of ullage by the Inland Revenue, duty being due on 99 gallons (449 litres). But vatting of the cask left, perhaps, a further two gallons (9 litres) absorbed in the wood of the cask. Unless this was recovered by 'grogging', in other words adding water, Gilbey vatted only 97 gallons (440 litres). A major dispute arose with the Inland Revenue because Gilbey considered these regulations severely penalised the merchant.

In principle, Gilbey could only recover the two gallons by using the same casks over and over again. This created its own logistical problems, as many casks were sent to Highland distilleries or returned to their country of origin. It also created a need for coopers to repair casks promptly.

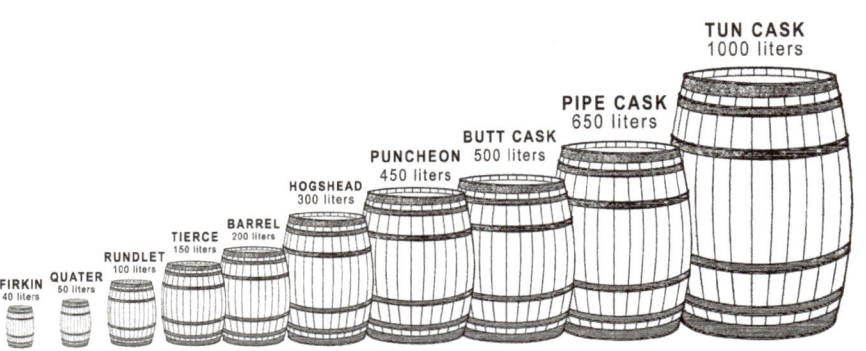

The extraordinary units of measurement used for barrels of wines and spirits are shown in §9.6.

9.6 Measures of wine in barrels

9.5 Bonded warehouses

Roundhouse – No. 3 Bond

Gilbey adapted the Roundhouse by first building a new mezzanine floor of 15,000 sq. ft. (1393 sq. m) in 1870, seen in the engraving (§9.7). It also built a new entrance from Hampstead Road, just out of sight in §9.8, a view of the building from Chalk Farm Road.

The Roundhouse held 15 major vats and some 6000 casks of whisky, brandy and rum in bond, amounting to about 150,000 gallons (682,000 litres).

Under the supervision of the excise authority, about 500 casks were released from bond daily and sent to the "A" Shed for bottling.

The Roundhouse had a major disadvantage as a warehouse for whisky, temperature fluctuations causing heavy evaporation losses of about 1000 gallons (about 4500 litres) per year. As already seen, these evaporation losses caused serious conflict with the Excise, which only recognised losses of 1% through evaporation.

9.7 Barrels of whisky and other spirits in the Roundhouse, 1875, from *Illustrated London News* (left image)

9.8 Gilbey's No. 3 Bond 1871-1964 (right image)

Gilbey planned to reduce evaporation losses by converting the Roundhouse to a cellared three to four storey warehouse with a roof that provided better insulation. These plans were, fortunately, not realised, and alterations were confined to the formation of a ceiling to secure uniformity of temperature.

In 1947 Gilbey ordered 12 large hermetically sealed vats to remedy loss by evaporation.

Wine and Beer Vaults: No. 1 Bond

9.9 Wine and Beer Vaults, 1987

The Ale Vaults, which will now be referred to as the Wine and Beer Vaults, were built on the west side of the Interchange Basin in 1856 for Bass as described in #8.7. Gilbey took over the Wine and Beer Vaults as its No. 1 Bond. Also known as Gilbey's Cask Bond, with a storage capacity of 6000 casks and with blending vats holding over 60,000 gallons (273,000 litres), the Wine and Beer Vaults (§9.9) were admirably suited for the storage of wine on account of their constant temperature.

They also had access to the canal. Goods arriving in London Docks could be barged along the Regent's Canal to the Interchange Dock (§9.10), where they were unloaded at the wharf that Gilbey shared with the LNWR. From the landing point goods could be moved to Gilbey's No. 2 and No. 4 Bonds via the Eastern Horse Tunnel (§8 on page xvi).

For Gilbey, as for other traders, the essential attraction of Camden Town was its access to the Docks by road, rail and canal. Although the Regent's Canal was predominantly used to transport lower value materials such as timber, cork and empty bottles, it also carried wines and spirits from the Docks to be offloaded into the No. 1 Bond (§9.11).

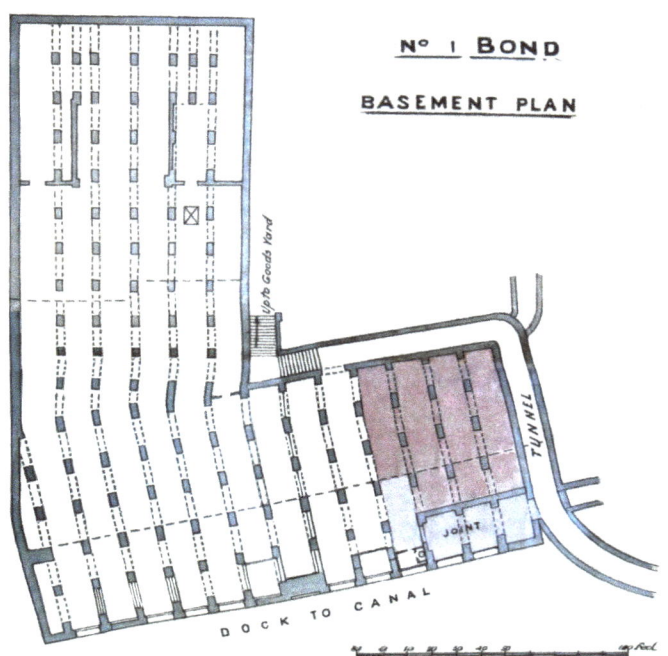

9.10 Plan of Wine and Beer Vaults, showing barge landing stage and Inland Revenue inspection area in mauve and area occupied by LNWR in red. The Eastern Horse Tunnel winds around two sides and leads via the 1839 vaults to the 1847 vaults

9.11 View across Interchange Basin to west. Most of the openings created for the Ale Vaults have been bricked in for wine in bond (top left image)

9.12 Pipes of wines in the Catacombs awaiting processing and bottling (top right image)

No. 2 and No. 4 Bonds and Catacombs

It was Gilbey that christened the 1847 vaults, which earlier supported the Construction Shop for wagon building and repair (#5.10), the 'Catacombs'. This designation has been extended into the older 1839 vaults and into the 1856 vaults that were their No. 1 Bond, including the Eastern Horse Tunnel.

The 1847 buildings created an area of 0.7 acres (0.3ha), ideal for wine storage with no daylight intruding and an even temperature (§9.12). The vaults were later extended further into Stables Yard to support coal drops.

These vaults were closely associated with No. 2 and No. 4 Bonds but were not part of bonded storage. No. 2 Bond was built for Gilbey by LNWR in 1875 to act, in combination with No. 4 Bond, as its Export Warehouse handling mostly Indian and colonial preferences. Its long narrow form (§9.13), squeezed between the 1847 vaults and coal drops, held up to 200,000 gallons (909,000 litres) in 17 large vats.

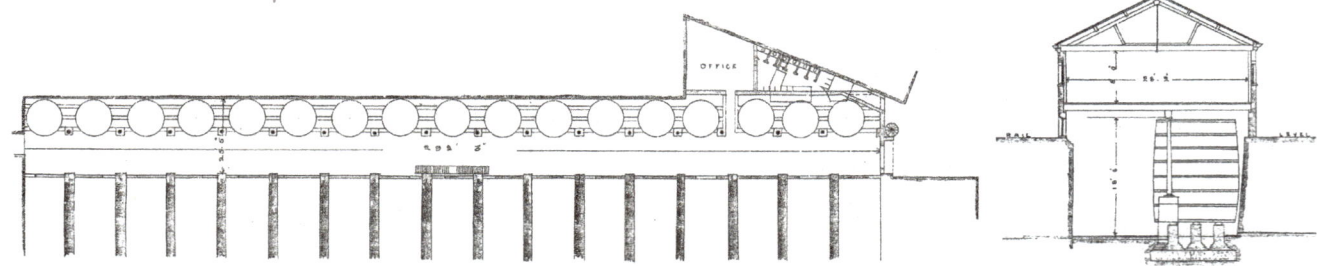

9.13 Plan at ground level and cross-section of No. 2 bond showing 12,000 gallon (55,000 litre) vats, with bottling/packing for export and hoist to storage above

Trains to London Docks, known as the 'Gilbey Special', were loaded at the northern end of No. 2 Bond (§9.14). In 1896 this activity moved to the Triangular Bottle Stores, when they became the Export Warehouse.

The Catacombs, comprising the 1847 vaults and their extensions, the remnants of the 1839 vaults and the 1856 Wine and Beer Vaults, together with the Eastern Horse Tunnel, created a complex that few can comprehend. Understanding is not helped by the confusing redevelopments in Camden Markets, notably Horse Tunnel Market. That this warren was already a puzzle to earlier observers may be appreciated from the story published in *The Restaurant* of December 1910:

> So vast is the cellarage that when our representative, in company with several other guests, was being shown around by a gentleman who has been associated with the firm for about a quarter of a century, he had a narrow escape from spending the night wandering amongst the alleys of casks, for the guide lost his way and only the friendly offices of a cellarman saved the position.

Gilbey's No. 2 and No. 4 Bonds are shown in the schematic of 1894 (§9.4). The galvanized corrugated roof of No. 4 Bond, seen in the schematic and in the 1921 aerial photo (§11.3), was replaced around 1930. The scars of the earlier corrugated roof are clearly seen on the wall of No. 2 Bond in the panorama (§9.15).

9.14 No. 2 bond with coal drops alongside, December 1976. Earlier there had been a rail siding off the NLR to a loading bank at this end

No. 5 Bond

Gilbey leased nine railway arches for No. 5 Bond from the Marquis of Camden in 1876. These were located on Bonny Street, adjoining the west side of Camden Road Station, and carried the NLR. Given their distance from Gilbey's main operations, they would have been inefficient to manage. They were converted to stables in 1896.

9.15 From left: No. 2 Bond showing scars of former roof, remnant of Construction Shed, roof of No. 4 Bond (former Export Warehouse), Triangular Bottle Stores behind NLR signal box and Interchange Warehouse, 1976

9.6 Camden workforce

Gilbey's workforce was variously engaged in offices; in bottle washing; crate making; wine and spirits operations; bottling, corking and labelling; vat and cask repair and maintenance; loading and unloading gangs; carting; horse husbandry, etc. It comprised about 800 at the peak in around 1900.

Almost everyone living in Camden would have known someone working for Gilbey. Many families had members working for Gilbey over several generations. People in Camden Town strove for the recommendations that helped them find work for Gilbey as it was a job for life, an important consideration at that time. It was said you could only get sacked if you stole or hit a director.

One of the largest set of records in the Diageo Archive is the collection of Gilbey Conduct Books. They create a distorted impression of the conduct of employees, as they predominantly record the theft of alcohol, either through illicit drinking on the premises or attempts to smuggle it from the premises. The ingenuity workers used to secrete alcohol on their person is manifested in the many devices displayed in the Diageo Archive. However, apart from the Conduct Books, there is little information about how Gilbey treated its employees, or what facilities were provided for their social welfare or entertainment.

A small selection of these conduct records is given in §9.16. Drinking on the premises during working hours was treated very strictly but did not prevent the firm later giving a good character reference. Miscreants caught abusing the strict rules about alcohol were, on a first occasion, often assigned to bottle washing, work that had low prestige and provided little opportunity for misdemeanour.

9.16 Excerpts from Gilbey Conduct Books in Diageo Archive

Name	Age	Service (years)	Misdemeanor	Consequence
Frederick Mead	23	4 (1879)	Damaging horse and harness by careless driving	Discharged
Birmingham (one of foremen interviewed)	-	1884	Stated he had a glass now & then but drank little – replies vague and almost incoherent – evidently his brain is seriously affected	Objected to emigration because of wife's health. Received £25 to give him a new start
Walter Challis	27	10 (1889)	Had been drinking, Champagne Grand with foil removed and strings cut found	Discharged
Frederick Cox	26	9 (1890)	Strongly suspected of taking three bottles of 1887 Port from the Bins or Wine Floor to the Claret Floor	Seen by Mr Newman Gilbey and discharged
William Hutchinson	36	17 (1895)	In charge of wines being carted from No. 2 Bond, allowed Facer to open cask and drink through india rubber tube	Severely reprimanded. Wages reduced 2/- per week for 16 weeks
Harry Crawford	36	18 (1897)	Found under vats on spirit floor unable to give satisfactory account	Transferred to bottle washing for four months
Charles Martindale	47-9	27-9 1901-3	1901 Had been drinking 1902 Hid flagon of Rubicon for drinking 1903 The worse for drink	Removed from piecework Bonus (19/6) stopped Discharged
William Vine	35	15 (1905)	Left Round House with pint flask of whisky in his pocket	Discharged

With a non-unionised workforce, the power in any negotiations in the 19th century lay with the employer. A petition on behalf of the Camden workforce in 1890 declared that:

- During depressed trading from 1877 to 1880 the Firm reduced pay for piece-work and weekly wages of day-workers. Trade has now revived and the Firm is flourishing.
- The men employed at Camden Town are looking forward to a speedy fulfilment of the promise to restore to the men that which had been taken away.
- The Firm should consider giving every man in their employ less than five years (stable men and carmen included) one week's paid holiday, in addition to the ordinary Bank Holidays.

Gilbey, in response accepted most of the request and added an annual bonus, to be assessed by the Company. Based on 1889 sales of 918,430 dozens, the bonus shared was almost £1000 (£160,000 today), employees receiving up to four weeks' wages; the higher the weekly wage, the greater the bonus. Some 400 to 500 employees benefitted from this arrangement.

9.17 Some fifty of the workforce, probably foremen

Up to 1900, almost all workers were men (§9.17). The first female employee at Camden was Annie Salter in May 1890, working in Export. Until 1914 there was a rule that no married woman was allowed to work for the firm, and those that married had to leave. This changed markedly during both world wars, and most markedly after WWII.

The following images (§9.18 and §9.19) show some of the activities of the workforce:

In 1923, the Management Committee recommended a grant to the Camden Social Club at a rate not exceeding one penny per head (£0.80 today) for each female and two pence per head (£1.60 today) for each male member per week.

9.18 Bottling, corking and capping Triple Crown Port (formerly Invalid Port) at 240 cases of 12 bottles/hour (left image)

9.19 Coopers remaking barrels (right image)

9.7 "A" Shed

The "A" Shed was where bottling was carried out for the home trade. Casks of wines and spirits that had been released from bonded storage were moved by steam powered lifts to the top floor, which formed a receiving quay. There hogsheads of brandy, puncheons of rum and other casks awaited transfer into the vats below. Upwards of 100 vats were arranged on stages, varying from 1500 to 9000 gallons (7000 to 40,000 litres), into which the casks were decanted. The vats, made of seasoned oak, stored some 450,000 gallons (2 million litres) and enabled 10 million bottles to be filled each year. A cross-section of the "A" Shed is given in §9.20 and a plan in §9.21.

Empty bottles had first to be inspected before they were washed. Bottle washing was at a rate of about 40,000 per day in the brick arched basement.

9.20 Cross-section of "A" Shed from Goad plan of 1891

9.21 Plan of "A" Shed

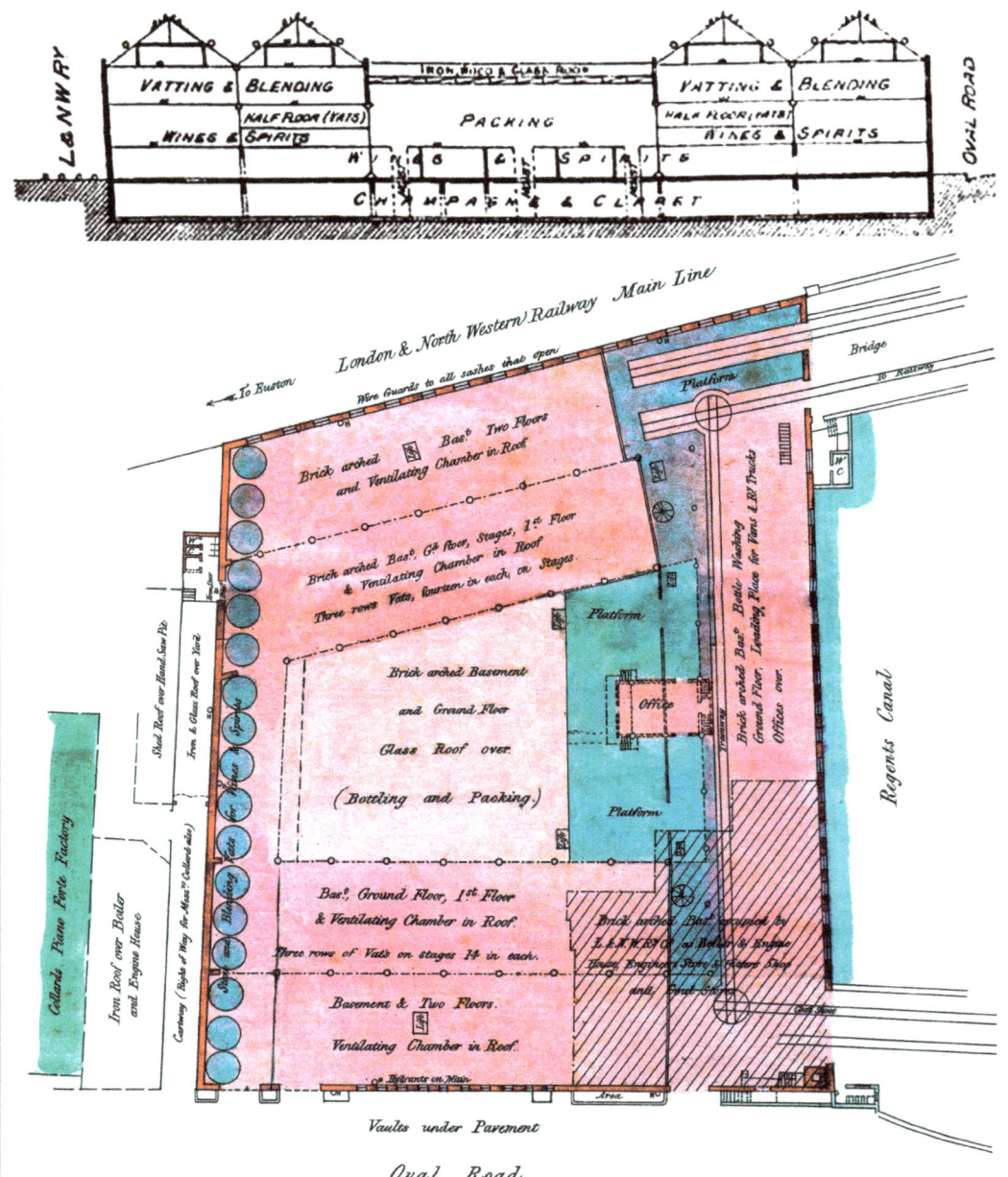

Crates had to be inspected for damage and repaired, if necessary, before moving the crates full of clean bottles to the vats for bottling.

Bottling was carried out on the ground floor below the vat storage floors and on either side of a central packing and forwarding area to which the full bottles were moved in their crates.

The "A" Shed was also where Gilbey had its production offices for many years, before new purpose-built offices were created at Gilbey House (now Academic House) in the 1930s.

The champagne and claret floor provided storage as close as possible to a French 'cave du vin'. Claret is shown maturing in the basement in §9.22 and §9.23.

Other operations are shown in a group of images (§9.24). About 350 hands were employed in the building.

Rail bridges communicated with the goods yard on both the north-western and north-eastern corners of the shed (§9.25).

9.22 Claret in cask, 1875, from *Illustrated London News* (top left image)

9.23 Claret in bottle, 1875, from *Illustrated London News* (top right image)

9.24 Spirit vatting floor (upper left image); bottling floor (upper right image); and sherry vault (lower image). Bottling was carried out on the ground floor by bottom filling using funnels and tubes to reduce oxygen pick-up.

9.25 Rail to road interchange: loading bank with rail siding communicating with Goods Yard via the western bridge

W & A GILBEY: THE CAMDEN STORY

Activities on the General Forwarding Floor are shown in §9.26. Casks awaiting vatting can be seen alongside the offices and lifts at the far end. Vats surround the packing and forwarding floor at every level. Bottles that have been filled are moved in their crates for packing and forwarding by road or rail. The loading banks with rail sidings alongside are just beyond the far wall. Beyond the loading bank is the Regent's Canal and the wharf alongside which barges were moored.

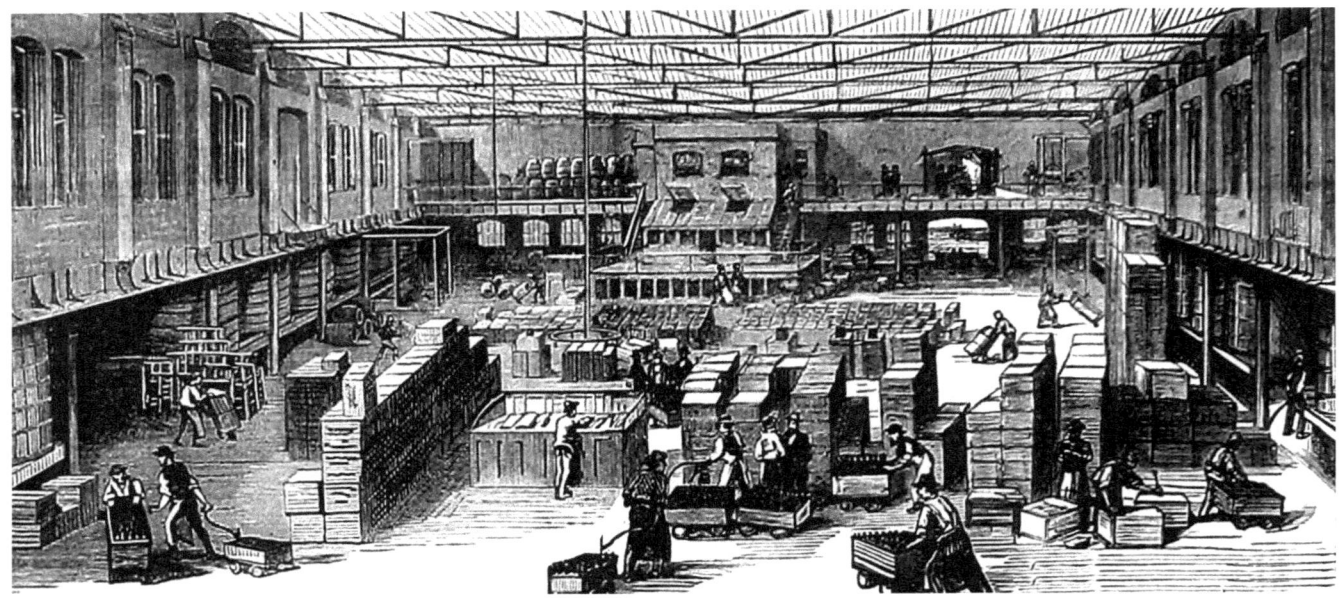

9.26 General Forwarding Floor of "A" Shed, view north, 1875

9.8 Distillery

LNWR acquired the building opposite the "A" Shed in Oval Road that had been Taylor's Flour Mills, built in about 1839 on ground raised by fill (#3.7) and damaged by fire in 1870. This became Gilbey's London Gin distillery (§9.27). The Distillery opened in 1872, providing 50 years' experience of distilling Gilbey's Gin before the boom of the cocktail era in the 1920s.

The site included engineering workshops which were taken over by William Hucks, who was appointed manager of the Distillery in addition to his role as Engineer. It also included stabling for 73 horses in a building at the rear adjoining the timber yard. Steam from the boilers in the Distillery was fed under Oval Road to power the "A" Shed lifts and machinery.

The freehold of the site was purchased by Gilbey from LNWR in 1894 for £6300 (about £1 million today) under a clause in the lease, just one element in assembling the jigsaw of property that was to be transformed into Hucks' Bottle Stores (#9.10).

9.27 Gin distillery, 1875

Gin was cheap and easy to produce. The 'botanicals' that flavoured the gin were carefully measured: juniper berries, coriander seeds, angelica, orris root and dried orange peel. The group of images (§9.28 to §9.30) shows some of the processes.

During prohibition large amounts of Gilbey Gin were bootlegged into America. Consequently, following the repeal of prohibition, Gilbey Gin became the leading brand in the USA.

9.9 Triangular Bottle Stores

The Triangular Bottle Stores was built for Gilbey by LNWR in 1875 for £16,000 (about £2.4M today). It had a ground floor and three shallow floors above, a total of 60,000 sq. feet (5574 sq. m). The major sides of the triangle were

9.28 Raking trays of maturing juniper. This room held eight tons of berries, taking six months to mature, 1961 (left image)

9.29 Still for introducing special flavours, 1961 (centre image)

9.30 Pouring juniper into pot stills. loaded with rectified spirit, 1961 (right image)

9.31 From Proposed Warehouse for Messrs W & A Gilbey, 1875. Elevation to yard; Commercial Place on left and NLR on right

formed along the north side of Commercial Place (now Camden Lock Place) and abutting the arches of the North London Railway. The short side was the elevation to the yard seen in §9.31.

Bottle washing was transferred from the "A" Shed to the new building, some 50 hands washing more than 50,000 bottles a day (§9.32). Carting the clean bottles to the "A" Shed for bottling was a major operation with many breakages caused by the uneven paving, as can be appreciated even today.

9.32 Bottle washing (left image)

9.33 Bottling Empire Red, 1963 (right image)

The building was converted into an Export and General Bond following the construction of Hucks' Bottle Stores in 1896 (#9.10). It took over the export function from No. 2 and No. 4 Bonds. Bottling for the export market was part of the function of what was now the Export Warehouse (§9.33). The Inland Revenue had officers on permanent duty at the warehouse. They required that the four arches under the NLR (in what is now called 'Paddock Lane') be sealed and approached only from the Stables Yard side.

The Export Warehouse had a siding directly off the NLR, where wagons were loaded with casks and assembled using capstan and ropes to form the 'Gilbey Special' (§9.34). This ran daily to London Docks with as many as 70 wagons being dispatched.

However, Gilbey evidently preferred to do as much of its own cartage as possible to and from the Docks, using its own vans to take goods from the Export Warehouse and to collect from the Docks on their way back for delivery at Bond. It was recommended in 1896 that four new vans should be purchased and five heavy horses, to work mostly as singles between Camden and the Docks, as they could then also be employed for the ordinary business of delivery.

Later in the 20th century, motorised vans or 'mechanical horses' took goods to London Docks from the Export Warehouse (§9.35), collecting from the Docks on the return journey for delivery at Bond.

The building is shown in §9.36 shortly before being destroyed by fire in 1980, well after Gilbey had left. It has been replaced by Building C, part of what is now Stables Market.

9.34 'Gilbey Special' being assembled at Export Warehouse siding (left image)

9.36 View up Commercial Place, c1976 (right image)

9.35 Scammell Mechanical Horses being loaded and exiting Commercial Place for the Docks c1940

9.10 Hucks' Bottle Stores

In 1892 Gilbey started to plan a new warehouse to be built on a site assembled from a variety of buildings and plots including: the Distillery; the engineering shop behind the Distillery; the stables; Leftwich's Wharf; and No.38 to No.46 James Street. It purchased the freeholds of the Distillery, the shops in Upper James Street and the Stanhope Arms with associated cottage and stabling. The lease to the wharf was purchased from Leftwich with a right to buy the freehold. This assembly of sites, apart from the Stanhope Arms, which continued as a public house, became Hucks' Bottle Stores.

The plan was part of a wider reorganisation to:

- duplicate bottling floors in case of fire;
- enlarge the export trade premises;
- transfer the Export Bond to the Triangular Warehouse from Bond No. 4, gaining warehouse room;
- give up No. 5 Bond in Bonny Street and convert the arches to stables;
- convey bottles and crates between the new Bottle Stores and the "A" Shed mechanically through tunnels under Oval Road, thereby reducing breakages.

The Bottle Stores were the brainchild of William Hucks, Gilbey's chief engineer, who had also been engaged to manage the Distillery. Without professional qualifications, he produced few plans. Large cost overruns resulted, partly from poor ground conditions that were almost certainly related to the fill deposited in 1838 (#3.7), and partly to major changes to the layout and number of floors. The Distillery had to be largely rebuilt on account of the poor subsoil, with its walls reconstructed on strong concrete foundations.

The schematic (§9.37) shows Gilbey's premises, including the major new bottle stores, around the turn of the century, viewed from the south. No. 2 Bond and the corrugated roof of No. 4 Bond lie beyond the Triangular Bottle Stores. The Stanhope Arms, once such an impressive feature in the landscape (§3.4 and §3.18), and now rather diminished by the new building, seems a reluctant survivor.

9.37 Schematic of Gilbey's premises c1900

One of the first ferro-concrete buildings in London, with immensely thick walls, the new bottle stores were built over six floors. They were used for storing empty bottles, bottle washing, and case making and repair. Some 25,000 cases were made and 40,000 cases repaired each year. The roof was used for seasoning timber and housed saw-mills and other machinery for making cases (§9.38).

Subways were built under Oval Road to connect with "A" Shed and bottles were then conveyed mechanically, reducing breakages of bottles and crates (§9.39).

The cork department moved into the bottle stores from the Pantheon in 1897.

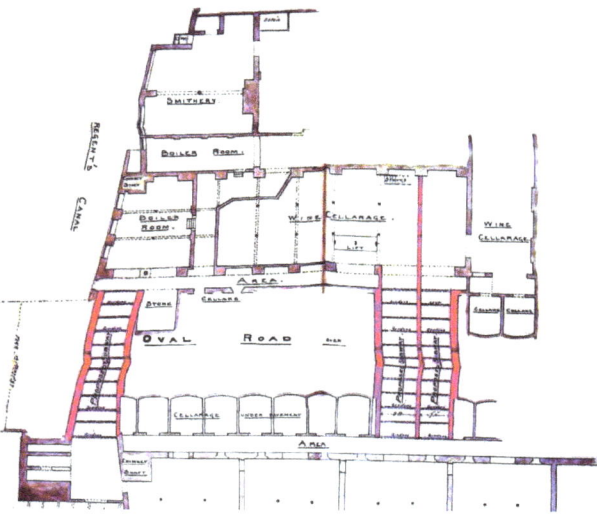

9.11 Interchange basement warehouse

The Interchange Warehouse, completed in 1905 was the third or fourth generation building on the site and was known by LNWR as the New Warehouse (#11.2). On the east side of the Interchange Basin, supporting the rail platforms and sidings, was the basement warehouse which occupies an area of 1467 sq. yd. (1226 sq. m). The basement warehouse (§9.40) was leased to Gilbey, initially for seven years from June 1905. This became Gilbey's Empty Bottle Stores, the bottles being stored in bins. It operated in conjunction with the Export Warehouse on the opposite side of Commercial Place.

9.38 Hucks Bottle Stores showing roof timber workshop, extract from 1921 aerial photo (§11.3) (top left image)

9.39 Plan of Distillery showing subways under Oval Road, c1896 (top right image)

9.40 Interchange basement warehouse, 2010 (bottom right image)

9.12 Stables and horses

Gilbey's stables had been located at the rear of the Distillery, backing onto a timber yard, with stabling for some 73 horses. They can be seen in the schematic of the 1890s (§9.4).

As this site was needed for the new bottle stores, new premises had to be found and the Bonny Street No. 5 Bond was converted in 1893 to provide 100 stalls as seen in the plan (§9.41).

Until WWI Gilbey operated a fleet of one and two horse drays pulled by heavy vanners for town deliveries and increasingly to provide cartage to and from the Docks (§9.42). Drivers wore Gilbey's special livery.

Gilbey's horses were of interest to the War Office during periods of conflict. The Company placed 50 horses at the disposal of the War Office in 1900 for a year for the Boer War. In August 1914 the War Office commandeered 17 horses, paying £45 (£6800 today) for each.

W & A GILBEY: THE CAMDEN STORY

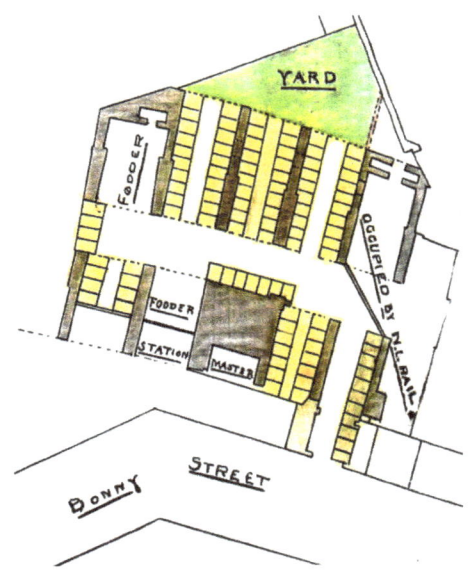

9.41 Plan of Bonny Street stables, c1896 (left image)

9.42 Two horse dray outside Bonny Street stables c1910 (right image)

Horses were not replaced after WWI, and Gilbey did not purchase any more horses until the early 1950s. The fine Irish hunter type bay geldings acquired were mainly used for advertising, but also for special deliveries such as to Buckingham Palace. Captain Frank Gilbey drove a pair of Gilbey horses for Princess Elizabeth's coronation, drawing the carriage in which Winston Churchill was riding.

Gilbey horses and the Gilbey coach were stabled in the Horse Hospital. Their four-in-hand became a common sight in the neighbourhood, seen here with Sebastian ('Bassie') Gilbey at the reins, passing the "A" Shed on his way to the new offices in Gilbey House, his preferred means of commuting to the Oval Road office (§9.43).

9.43 Four-in-Hand, with four chestnut bay horses passing the "A" Shed

In 1967 the company, which by then had merged with United Wine Traders to form International Distillers and Vintners, decided the coach and horses were no longer commercially viable and Walter Gilbey, the founder's grandson, took charge of them. They were much shown around Britain and used for ceremonial occasions. In 1974 they were transferred to Douglas on the Isle of Man where he now lives. They became part of the tourist scene in the summer months.

9.13 Gilbey House

Gilbey's head office had been at the Pantheon in Oxford Street since 1867. William Hucks had long urged Gilbey to move their head office to Camden, maintaining that the Pantheon was outdated, too far from their centre of operations, and "no longer influences the minds of the present generation".

Relocation of the head office became urgent in the 1930s. Marks and Spencer had made a substantial offer for the freehold in 1936 and Gilbey finally, reluctantly, sold the Pantheon.

It was decided to build on the corner site occupied since the 1830s by the Stanhope Arms. Gilbey had acquired the freehold in 1892, extending the lease of the public house. It had therefore not been incorporated into Hucks' Bottle Stores.

Serge Chermayeff, an architect with rooms in the Pantheon, was commissioned to prepare plans against a challenging environmental specification. This required wine to be protected from vibrations, for the building to be insulated from noise, and for special lighting to be installed in the sampling room (§9.44) so that colour could be judged.

Among the innovations adopted, cork footings protected the wine from vibrations, and acoustic absorbent plaster kept the noise down. Erich Mendelsohn, an eminent progressive architect who had fled Nazi Germany in 1933, provided advice and assistance with what became a notable building (§9.45).

The basement housed records and a strongroom; the ground floor – canteens; the 1st floor – the purchasing department; the 2nd floor – sales and advertising; the 3rd floor – export; the 4th and 5th floors – finance; and the top floor accommodated the directors, the boardroom and the committee room.

During the Troubles in the 1960s, with the Gilbey carriage parked alongside the offices, the IRA set fire to the adjoining bottling plant and badly damaged the carriage. The IRA later wrote to Gilbey apologising for their 'mistake'.

Gilbey's later moves are described in #12.2.

9.44 Sampling room, Purchasing Department, first floor, Gilbey House (left image)

9.45 Gilbey House, their head office from 1937 to 1964 (right image)

10 Railway from 1870s to end of steam

10.1 Overview
10.2 Primrose Hill Tunnel
10.3 New DC electric lines
10.4 Complex of underpasses
10.5 Up Empty Carriage Tunnel
10.6 Station evolution
10.7 Railways grouping
10.8 On Camden Bank
10.9 Wider impacts
10.10 Recollections of another world

10.1 Overview

The growth of the LNWR, both in the areas it served and in the volume of traffic, created the largest joint stock company in the world in the last quarter of the 19th century. The developments described here span from then to the British Rail (BR) era in the 1960s, although there was little change to the main line in the last 30 years of this period.

After the opening of Willesden sheds, which housed all the freight locomotives and many of those required for suburban services, Camden Shed or Motive Power Depot (MPD) had only to cope with some 50-60 engines. These were predominantly express types apart from some tanks for pilot work, and for shunting and ferrying empty carriage. The allocation under LMS and BR tended to consist entirely of the largest and newest locomotives.

The four-track line on Camden Incline, that had survived from 1837, was widened over 1898-1904 to reduce congestion of trains and allow movements of empty carriages in and out of Euston on separate tracks. This required the demolition of the eastern side of Park Village East.

Storage of coaches at Euston had proved inadequate and new carriage sheds and sidings were opened on the Incline in 1905 with paths for empty trains to run to and from sheds at Willesden. A new tunnel was constructed under Park Street (now Parkway) on the down side. The Up Empty Carriage Line (UECL) was constructed to enable empty trains from the up side to reach this tunnel.

10.2 Primrose Hill Tunnel

The two original tracks from Camden Station to Primrose Hill Tunnel had been augmented by two additional tracks on the south side, as part of the Phase 2

10.1 Southern portal, built 1879, entrance to the 'fast' tunnel, 2013 (left image)

10.2 The 'fast' tunnel vent shaft in rear garden of villa in Wadham Gardens, 2007 (right image)

expansion. These became the down side lines, the tracks being merged to go through the tunnel. This situation continued until a second tunnel was constructed south of the first tunnel to serve the main line, the original tunnel then serving the 'slow' lines. The new tunnel came into use on 1 June 1879, built by William Baker, Engineer-in-Chief of the LNWR.

The southern portal faithfully replicated the design of the original portal, down to decorative detail such as the lion masks, but is a little taller as the ground rises to the south (§10.1). It is the entrance to the 'fast' tunnel now used by West Coast Main Line (WCML) trains.

The fast tunnel forms an arc south of the original tunnel. Midway the vent shaft rises dramatically from a private garden in Wadham Gardens (§10.2). The property owner described to the author how railway personnel would appear from time to time, climb the vent shaft and disappear down the mouth of the shaft. This was presumably part of the six-yearly structural audit of the tunnel.

The remaining vent shaft for the northern tunnel is behind louvres, accessed from the Marriott Hotel car park.

10.3 New DC electric lines

The next stage of major expansion was essentially for suburban services. It was based on the broad concept of an electrified system embracing all the North London lines west of Broad Street, the electrified line to Watford, and the extension of the Hampstead services by electric trains to Kew Bridge.

The main lines from Euston to the north were already far too crowded to permit an intense electric service being superimposed on them. The decision was therefore taken to build a "New Line" on which the suburban electric services, designed for four-rail DC electric trains, would be almost entirely independent of the main lines. At Willesden Junction and eastwards to Chalk Farm widening could be done most conveniently on the up side of the line. Power for LNWR suburban electrification was generated at the Stonebridge Generating Station at Tokyngton Avenue, Wembley, built in 1916.

The New Line was opened in stages from 1912. Various stages of the New Line within Camden were completed over 1915-17, including two single track tube-type tunnels just north of the original Primrose Hill Tunnel. However, the entire project was held up pending the complete track-remodelling scheme at Chalk Farm, which was to create an elaborate system of burrowing junctions enabling electric trains to reach the tunnels from the Euston line or from the North London Line without interfering with other traffic. The up and down fast lines were on the south side, but on the Euston side of the tunnel they divided and down Camden Bank they straddled the slow lines.

Work was suspended in 1917 – the part-completed tunnels being used as air raid shelters in WWI – and the new layout was not commissioned until 1922. The new bores at Primrose Hill Tunnel, and new tracks from there to Queen's Park, were the final portion of the New Line to be opened.

The lines from Euston, the exit from Camden Goods Yard, and the newly electrified link from Camden Town all now led to the new non-conflicting junctions controlled by Camden No. 2 box. Here they were sorted out to enter the fast (southern) and slow (northern) Primrose Hill Tunnels and the twin electrified bores.

10.4 Complex of underpasses

The section of railway between Regent's Park Road Bridge and Primrose Hill Tunnel, the Primrose Hill cutting, features one of the most complex layouts of tracks in the entire railway system. Created to allow the new suburban electrified slow lines to pass under the main lines without conflicting movements, it involved a series of flyunders or burrowing junctions.

Work on the approach cutting in 1917, shortly before work was suspended, is shown in §10.3 and §10.4, viewed from each end of the cutting.

The track layout and burrowing junctions are shown being completed in 1922 (§10.5), as part of the extensive works involved in the Chalk Farm to Kensal Green track widening for the inauguration of electric suburban services.

The burrowing junctions were drawn by L. Ashwell Wood in the centre pages of the *Eagle,* the seminal British comic weekly, in the 1950s. Ashwell Wood treated young readers to vibrantly illustrated technical cutaways of modern mechanical wonders.

10.3 Construction of burrowing junctions, view NW from Regent's Park Road Bridge, 1917 (left image)

10.4 Construction of burrowing junctions, view from Primrose Hill Tunnel East Portals, 1917 (right image)

10.5 Construction of burrowing junctions near completion in 1922

10.6 "Amazing burrowing junctions, Chalk Farm to Primrose Hill Tunnels", *L Ashwell Wood*, 1947

Here he turns to a cutaway diagram of the burrowing junctions (*Allen, 1962*), looking southwest from an elevated location above the terrace of houses on the south side of Adelaide Road (§10.6).

A cross-section of the complex of tracks is given in §10.7.

The layout of the various lines in the approach cutting is shown in plan In §10.8. Flyunders and underground sections are shown hatched. The view is in the same sense as that of Ashwell Wood.

Twin HS2 tunnels to Euston are planned to cross the area with a vent shaft in the woodland between Adelaide Road and the tracks.

10.7 The complex of rail tracks shown in section

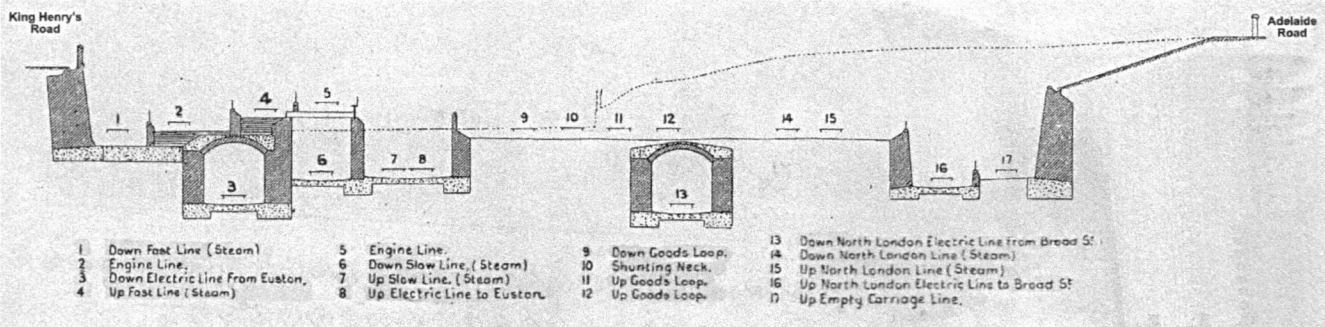

CHALK FARM RAILWAY LANDS: A GUIDED TOUR 1830 TO 2030

10.8 Plan of rail tracks in Primrose Hill Tunnel approach cutting, map data Google Bluesky, 2013

10.5 Up Empty Carriage Tunnel

The last significant addition at Camden was the Up Empty Carriage Tunnel, completed in 1922 as part of the prolonged scheme of improvements to the approaches to Euston station.

The 'Rat Hole' – as it was known to train drivers – permitted empty coaching stock from Willesden carriage sidings to cross from the up side of the railway to the down, without interfering with any of the running lines. Although it now carries EHV cable, it was never electrified (§10.9). Train crews went to great lengths to avoid stalling in its fume-laden close confines.

It runs from just east of Primrose Hill Tunnel, crossing under the mainline and former winding vaults to emerge just north of Parkway. Limited clearance restricted the tunnel to empty coaching stock as carriage doors would not open in an emergency. An 80 foot (24m) shaft located in the Western Horse Tunnel provides access (§10.10).

10.9 Up Empty Carriage Tunnel, 2012 (left image)

10.10 Shaft in Western Horse Tunnel providing access to UECL, 2008 (right image)

RAILWAY FROM 1870s TO END OF STEAM

10.6 Station evolution

The LNWR was a 'main line' railway and local traffic was largely left to the NLR. Chalk Farm Station, rebuilt in 1871, had platforms on both the LNWR and NLR lines with a footbridge link between the two after 1872. The North London Company was responsible for porters and other employees at Chalk Farm Station that were required for the interchange of passenger traffic with LNWR's trains.

10.11 Chalk Farm Station with bridge across to LNWR platforms, c1913

Until the 20th century the LNWR proper had no suburban services to speak of, except those associated with the NLR. After 1907, traffic was lost to Chalk Farm tube station, but the LNWR platforms lingered mainly for ticket collection purposes (§10.11). There was an additional exit onto Regent's Park Road to the left of §10.11. The NLR became part of the LNWR in 1922 as part of the consolidation of rail companies ahead of incorporation into the LMS under the Grouping the following year.

Ticket collecting from platforms declined, however, and this, together with the need for space for the new system of sub-surface tracks, led to demolition of the LNWR Chalk Farm station in 1915. No traces of the old LNWR platforms remain today, but the new Regent's Park Road Bridge, built in 1919, is shown in the image of that date (§10.12).

10.12 Chalk Farm Station with new bridge 1919

On 10 July 1922, Chalk Farm station, long closed to passenger traffic, was reopened, although with platforms only on the line to Broad Street.

10.7 Railways grouping

During WW!, when the railways were taken over by the Railways Executive Committee, more traffic was carried with less rolling stock, despite the reduction in railway personnel. As Michael Bonavia (*1980*) observed:

> The lesson that substantial economies could be obtained by getting away from traditional independence and operating railways more or less as a single system, was learned by both railway managers and outside observers.

The pressure placed on the railway network during WWI, combined with little opportunity or resource for proper maintenance, left it in poor condition; when peace returned it was losing money. The government's remedy was to impose a merger on most of the 120 railway companies then existing ....

With a view to the reorganisation and more efficient and economical working of the railway system Great Britain railways shall be formed into groups in accordance with the provisions of this Act, and the principal railway companies in each group shall be amalgamated, and other companies absorbed in a manner provided by this Act.

The Railways Act came into effect on 1st January 1923 to give rise to four large railway companies, in what became known as the 'grouping'. The London Midland and Scottish Railway (LMS), formed from the LNWR, the Midland Railway, the Caledonian Railway and several smaller railways, was the largest of the four and the largest joint stock company in the land.

The alternative was nationalisation, but it needed another world war and the proven efficiency of a single system to persuade the authorities.

The LMS assumed the management and operation of Chalk Farm Railway Lands, including Camden Goods Depot and Camden Shed, the former passenger locomotive shed. These are described in #11.5, with a focus on the 1930s as investment for many years after both world wars was limited. After nationalisation in 1948, the London Midland Region of British Railways administered Camden Goods Depot.

10.8 On Camden Bank

Nearly 600 trains ran daily in and out of Euston. Locomotives had blown up to a hundredweight (51kg) of soot from their chimneys before they reached Primrose Hill Tunnel (§10.13 and §10.14).

Here on the climb up Camden Bank, at the start of its epic 401.5-mile (646km) non-stop run from London to Glasgow in 5hrs 53mins 38secs on 16 November 1936, is the *Princess Elizabeth,* Princess Royal Pacific No.6201 (§10.15). The following day, it made the return run in 5hrs 44mins 15secs. Peter Green's oil painting was produced to coincide with the diamond jubilee of No 6201's construction in November 1933.

10.13 Coronation Scot behind blue streamlined Coronation 4-6-2 No. 6221 Queen Elizabeth passing up side carriage shed in 1938. Jubilee 4-6-0 No. 5563 Australia is backing out of Euston on down empty carriage line (left image)

10.14 Princess Coronation 8P Pacific No 46250 City of Lichfield and Black Five 4-6-0 No 44771 both slog up Camden Bank on 7 November 1958, hauling the 'Red Rose' express for Liverpool and empty coaching stock for Willesden respectively (right image)

RAILWAY FROM 1870s TO END OF STEAM

10.15 Princess Elizabeth on Camden Bank, 1933, at the start of her epic run, *G Peter M Green*, 1993

10.9 Wider impacts

As the railway grew in size, the intrusion of noise and pollution destroyed the pleasant nature of the area and was responsible for urban and social decay in Chalk Farm and adjacent Camden Town. The smoke reduced the desirability of the houses and many well-known residents (such as Mary Webb, Cecil Sharp and Stanley Spencer in Adelaide Road) found accommodation elsewhere in Hampstead. As the desirability of the area fell, houses were subdivided to provide lodging rooms.

The railways created numerous transient workers – drivers, firemen and train crews – that had to find overnight accommodation far from home, and many found temporary shelter in the area, close to the stations and goods yards where they worked. This transient population created its own needs. The presence of a male work force living in cheap lodging houses away from home resulted in the proliferation of drinking houses and brothels, the latter being documented even in streets now representing some of the most sought after in the area, such as Gloucester Avenue, St Marks Crescent and Park Village East.

10.10 Recollections of another world

Derek Sprange has recorded his impressions in *Primrose Hill Remembered (2001)*. This section draws selectively from his account but retains his voice.

His lifelong passion for steam trains was born in early childhood when he spent hours watching movements on the mainline to Euston from the window of his aunt's house at 51 Gloucester Road (now Gloucester Avenue) after having been tucked up early in bed. Ducking behind the curtain, he would observe the railway through the gap in the houses on the opposite side of the road, just south of the bridge over the Regent's Canal. His memories go back to 1918 and span the eighty years to the end of the century. He was intimately connected with the area for the rest of his life.

The houses in Gloucester Road backing onto the railway tracks were occupied by the full range of railway workers, the hundreds of men who worked on the railways: engine drivers, firemen, cleaners and other staff. A whole house was often occupied by several families, accommodation let by the room. Overcrowding, inadequate sanitation and primitive cooking facilities abounded.

Some houses had a landlady that let rooms for single male workers, providing her clients with meals. Prison welfare officers often got to know these landladies as they could make a room available for men coming out of jail. The hard and dirty unskilled work on the railways created its own labour demand, providing opportunities for ex-lags that wanted to go straight.

The houses were impossible to keep clean. One could not hang washing out to dry. Every few minutes flakes of soot, often an inch across, like black gossamer lace floated around in the air and settled on everything. But, as railway services improved with the introduction of dining and sleeping cars in the 1930s, laundries were established at the back of Gloucester Road houses, alongside the boundary wall, for washing all the railway linen and that from the Euston Hotel. All this laundry work was carried on indoors in substantial buildings and repacked in huge wicker hampers. This provided a lot of work for the wives and sweethearts of railwaymen.

The Lansdowne pub, located centrally on Dumpton Place, opened early for railway workers coming off shift. Pubs in Camden and Primrose Hill, many of which flourish to this day, served thirsty railway workers. Most had a private bar with a discrete side entrance. Once inside, frosted screens and shutters ensured that ladies could have a quiet tipple.

The major social change effected in Derek Sprange's lifetime was the transformation of an industrial area providing employment for a large working class, cohesive, sociable and self-supporting, to a much more disparate and less cohesive social mix, increasingly reflecting wealth and professional status.

11 Camden Depot from 1900 to end of steam

11.1 Railway Lands
11.2 New Warehouse
11.3 Electric Power Station
11.4 Oval Road entrance
11.5 1930s upgrade
11.6 Goods operations
11.7 Motive Power Depot
11.8 Camden Shed operations
11.9 Last days of the railway horse
11.10 Last days of steam

11.1 Railway Lands

The general layout of Camden Goods Depot in the mid 20th century is shown in §11.1. Most of the features identified have been described in earlier chapters.

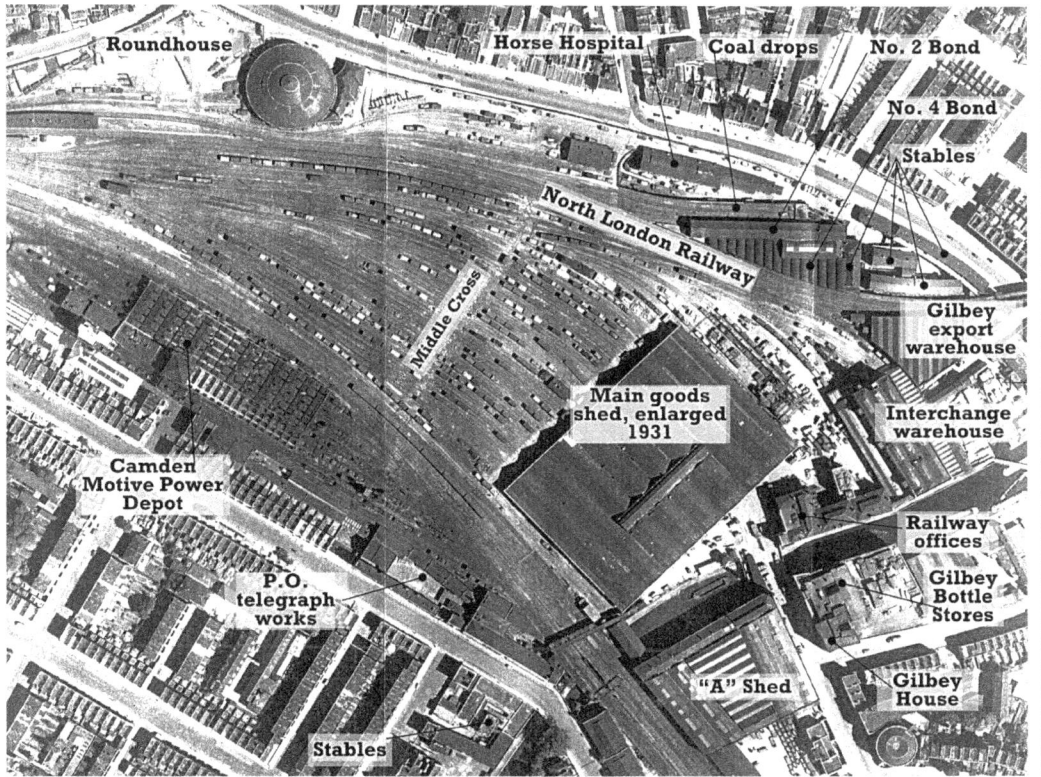

11.1 Camden Goods Depot from 1948 aerial photograph

Camden Goods Station was served by a fan of sidings intersected by Middle Cross (§11.1 and §11.2), a line of turntables, capstans and lamp standards that aided the assembly of goods trains. The building at the north end was the 'New Ale Stores' built by LNWR in 1892 for Benskins, the Watford brewers, whose name is prominently displayed on the façade facing Middle Cross.

The oblique aerial view from 1921 (§11.3) looks north along Oval Road, past the entrance to the Goods Station to the goods sidings in the distance. The high quality of the image allows detail to be picked out such as the three hoists on the western side of the Interchange building. Equally striking is the piano manufacturing complex of Collard and Collard in the foreground, extending on both sides of Oval Road and behind the fine villas of Gloucester Crescent.

The aerial photo shows how the offices provided by the LNWR for its main agents, Pickford and Chaplin & Horne, were built above the roof of the 1864 shed. They divide the shed into areas for local delivery/distribution on the near side and rail movements beyond.

11.2 Lined up for inspection on Middle Cross c1933

11.3 Camden Goods Station, 1921 oblique aerial photo

Part of the area between the North London Railway and Chalk Farm Road, running from the Roundhouse east to Benskins' Ale Stores, was the coal yard, as would be discerned, given sufficient magnification, from the sacks of coal stacked on the eastern side of the Roundhouse (just out of view) and the type of wagons and sidings in the area.

The Ale Stores was a traditional brick building with slate roof built by LNWR for the Watford brewers in 1892. This, and the stores with a corrugated roof immediately to the west, were taken over in the 1930s by Stanley Bros., manufacturers of glazed fireclay products and high-fired bricks and tiles, who used the yard as their London depot. Based at Nuneaton, a town on the East Warwickshire Coalfield with suitable supplies of clay and fuel, they were well placed to manufacture ceramic goods and took commercial advantage of the 1930s building boom in London and the southeast. It appears that their London depot did not survive a general retrenchment around 1940.

The name "Stanley Sidings" has since been used to refer to Stables Yard and was adopted as a company name by the developer of Stables Yard as a market. Both uses of the name appear inappropriate, serving only to confuse the history.

11.2 New Warehouse

The 'New Warehouse' of 1905 represents a singularly sophisticated example of storage and three-way transfer. Canal to rail transhipment had by then much declined and the new building was mainly devoted to transfers between railway and road vehicles and to storage in the warehouse on three floors above as seen in the schematic (§11.4).

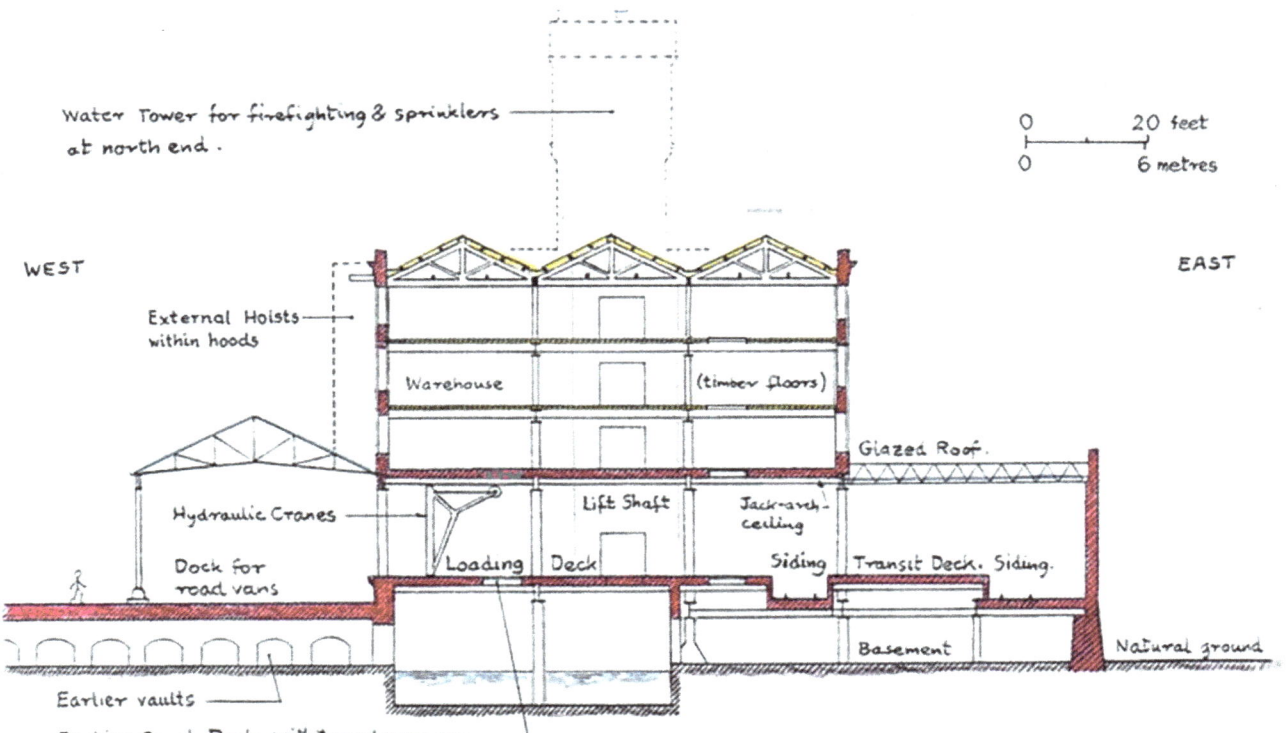

11.4 New Warehouse of 1905, schematic

The magnificent red brick building (§11.5) was designed to straddle the interchange dock. Bridged over with heavy girders supporting the tracks and platforms of a railway goods shed, the barges and narrowboats below were accessed through trapdoors in the platforms.

The towpath crosses the Interchange Basin, known popularly as 'Dead Dog Hole', by a bridge dating from 1846 (§11.6 and §13.13), built at the same time as the Roving Bridge when the LNWR started planning its first interchange facility (#5.13).

A line of massive octagonal riveted columns runs down the centre of the canal basin (§11.6 and §9.11) which the Interchange Warehouse straddles. The dock could accommodate six barges or twelve narrowboats. Internal cranes and hoists allowed goods transfer between storage levels.

11.5 Interchange Warehouse, 2013 (top left image)

11.6 Entrance to Interchange Basin from Regent's Canal with 1846 towpath bridge, 2008 (top right image)

11.7 Interchange forecourt on west side showing horse drawn vans being loaded c1910 (left image)

11.8 Loading platform or 'bank', here on east side. Note trapdoor above for transfer between storage and rail and large hatch for transfer by crane to/from basement warehouse, 1975 (right image)

11.9 Interchange Basement Warehouse, 2010

The ground floor of the Interchange opened on the west side to the Interchange forecourt where horse drawn vans. and later motor vans, were loaded under glazed canopies (§11.7).

Transhipment was mainly between rail and road via a raised loading platform running through the building west to east (§11.8). On the east side ran two rail sidings, the platform or 'bank' on the right of §11.8 being for inter-rail transfer. The trapdoor above was for transfer between storage and rail and the large hatch for transfer by crane to and from the basement warehouse.

The basement warehouse on the east side (§11.9) supported the rail side of the Interchange. It was used by Gilbey as a bottle store until the company's departure in 1964 (#9.11).

11.3 Electric Power Station

Camden goods station at night was so extensively lit by gas that it was described as an illuminated city. In 1906 the lighting was converted to electricity, served by an electric power station in Gloucester Road (§11.10), the power being provided by internal combustion engines running on gas. Called the 'Euston electric lighting plant', it must have served Euston as well as Camden.

The building was divided into a producer house in the northern part (on right in §11.10) and an engine room in the southern part (left). Gas was produced in furnaces called 'producers' by feeding a controlled supply of air through red-hot coke. Incomplete combustion of coke took place in an oxygen-limited atmosphere focused on maximising carbon monoxide and minimising carbon dioxide gases. Before being fed to the engines, the gas was purified by ascending through scrubbers, columns of coke continually sprayed by water to remove ammonia, tar and dust. Such producer gas could power gas engines more economically than gas from a conventional gas works.

11.10 Electric power station viewed from mainline railway side, 1906

The power produced and the voltage at which it was supplied are not known, nor if any purposes were served other than lighting.

The smells of by-products of gas production and the dangers of carbon monoxide dictated a need for adequate ventilation, evident from the lack of glazed windows in the producer house.

Stonebridge Park generating station, built in 1916 to power the LNWR suburban electrification may have rendered the power station at Gloucester Avenue obsolete, but the Goad insurance plan of 1921 confirms that the power station was still in operation at that time, the engine room with its DC generators being shown as a 'Dynamo House'.

11.4 Oval Road entrance

The road entrance to Camden Goods Station was alongside the goods offices at 30 Oval Road in which both LMS and agency staff worked (§11.11). The main goods shed, in its enlarged form, is seen in the background.

11.11 Horse drawn goods traffic emerging from goods station, 1934

The stairs serving the offices (§11.11) led through a gated LMS portal to the first and second floors where clerical and secretarial staff had their desks. A later extension of the offices in the 1960s, as part of a British Rail facelift, aligned part of the building façade with the LMS entrance portal (§11.12). The staircase then ran up the canal frontage to the first floor. Since the removal of the staircase the LMS portal has become an archaeological curiosity.

11.12 LMS portal, 2007 (left image)

11.13 Weighbridge office, Oval Road, c1933 (right image)

Goods vans entering or leaving the Goods Station through the Oval Road entrance were weighed at two weighbridges, one either side of the weighbridge offices, dating from 1931 (§11.13), the frames of which have survived.

In 1933 the railway commissioned Sir Giles Gilbert Scott to refurbish and extend the offices. He carefully enclosed the Horse Tunnel staircase, preserving its bollarded entrance and parapets below a stock brick piered structure, a design precursor of Battersea Power Station.

11.5 1930s upgrade

11.14 Additional warehouse accommodation, extension of goods shed, 1931

11.15 LMS goods shed, view of goods van delivery/distribution area on southeast side, c1933 (bottom right image)

The goods shed was enlarged in 1931 to the size seen in the sectional elevations of the north (actually the NW) side (§11.14). A photograph of the south (actually the SE) side is also shown (§11.15).

The disruption appears to have finally caused Allsopp to abandon the shed basement as a warehouse for beer, the enlarged basement now becoming a wool store, primarily for Merino wool imported from Australia. Those who worked there vividly recall the infestations in the wool.

At the same time, catering facilities for staff were much improved. A new mess room and stores with parking accommodation behind was built at 31 Oval Road, a building that is extant. This served staff working in the goods offices. Workers in the goods yard and goods shed were catered for by a second mess room that occupied a building on the Gloucester Avenue side of the mainline, in the complex that had previously included Allsopp's stables. A footbridge connected the goods yard with this second messroom.

One end of this footbridge is captured in §11.16, which also features the main goods shed as well as the Interchange Warehouse with its familiar water tower and the goods offices, where the external wooden staircase to the first floor rises from the LMS portal. The centre ground shows the original hydraulic accumulator tower, evidently well past its useful life.

11.16 Camden Goods Depot, from Fitzroy Bridge, 1975

11.6 Goods operations

Camden was the major goods yard in the London area. As well as its warehouse facilities, from which goods wagons were loaded, the yard received goods wagons from many London depots for despatch, together with its own wagons, by mainline trains to the Midlands and North. These London depots included Broad Street, Haydon Square, Poplar, Old Ford, Maiden Lane, Victoria Docks, Thames Wharf and St. Pancras Junction.

From about midnight to 12 noon the yard received incoming traffic, switching in the following 12 hours to the despatch of outgoing traffic (§11.17). Typically, 900-1000 wagons were handled between 6.00 pm and midnight, of which about 225 were loaded in the Camden warehouses. Broad Street despatched about 300 wagons with the rest emanating from stations east of Camden. All had to be rehandled on arrival.

11.17 Loading the Scotch Express (left image)

11.18 Assembling goods trains using capstans and turntables in front of the main goods shed (right image)

CAMDEN DEPOT FROM 1900 TO END OF STEAM

The timing of arrivals from the various depots, and their handling at Camden, was critical to the timely departure of trains given only a single departure line for mainline goods trains to the North – the crossover road, that led from the Depot to the down slow line. Shunting at this time was performed equally by locomotives and by hydraulic capstans and turntables (§11.18), with horses still used occasionally.

11.7 Motive Power Depot

Locomotives were stabled, cleaned, fuelled and given routine maintenance at motive power depots (MPDs). Camden MPD, known earlier as the Passenger Engine Shed and later colloquially as Camden Shed, had long been one of the most important. It was of a conventional straight shed design, but constrained on a narrow site between the villas of Gloucester Avenue and the mainline railway. The severe site restrictions prevented the shed from being enlarged and it was always over-crowded.

A view of the east end of Camden MPD in about 1900, before the 1930s upgrade, is shown in §11.19.

11.19 East end of Camden MPD c1900

The first mechanical ash lifting and coal plants were provided in about 1920. For a time there were two turntables, but the southern one eventually went out of use. The descriptions in this section generally relate to the upgrade and modernisation carried out in the early 1930s.

The upgrade saw some rearrangement of sidings, a coal plant with two 150-ton bunkers and wagon hoist, a 70-ft (21m) vacuum-operated turntable, an ash plant, and a number of water columns. The layout that resulted is shown in §11.20.

As part of the upgrade in the early 1930s the trussed roof of the original shed was replaced by a flat girder roof with a large area of glazing. The interior of Camden Shed is shown just before the roof was replaced (§11.21).

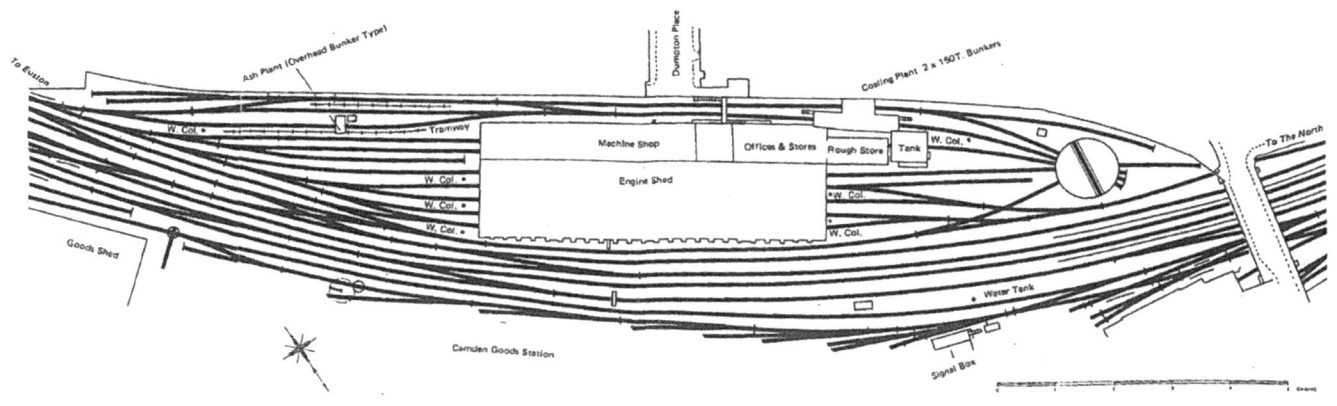

11.20 Track plan, 1950

The coaling plant was designed so that both bunkers fed a single coaling road, which required a large separation between bunkers to allow two locomotives onto the road at the same time.

The ash plant catered for two ashpits, sidings in which tubs received ashes from the engine ashpan via chutes. Ashes could also be thrown out from the footplate into ash trucks running alongside the pits as shown in §11.22. Bottom doors in these tubs and trucks allowed transfer of the ash into skips. Both ashpit tubs and ash trucks ran on narrow gauge tracks.

Two further views of the shed are shown in §11.23 and §11.24.

11.22 Disposal of ashes from smokebox and firebox into ash trucks

11.21 Shed interior before roof replacement in 1931

CAMDEN DEPOT FROM 1900 TO END OF STEAM

11.23 East side c1937, the two tracks of the 'back road' leading past the ash pits and ash handling plant under entrance footbridge to coaling plant and water tank (left image)

11.24 Unrebuilt Patriot 4-6-0 No 45546 Fleetwood is reversed in 1958 (right image)

Access to Camden Shed was via a narrow doorway in the brick wall at the end of Dumpton Place (§11.25), which opened to a footbridge that led to the main entrance passage, bridging two back road sidings. It passed the window of the Shed Master's office on the first floor, providing him with a view of any movements, which made access without a permit very difficult.

The narrow entrance feels at odds with the size and architectural treatment of the original Passenger Engine Shed. In the centre of the wall there is a set of granite steps, that now form an archaeological curiosity but may have provided access in the past to a wider entrance located centrally in the wall (§11.26). The 1894 OS map shows such an entrance with a footbridge, but earlier OS maps do not.

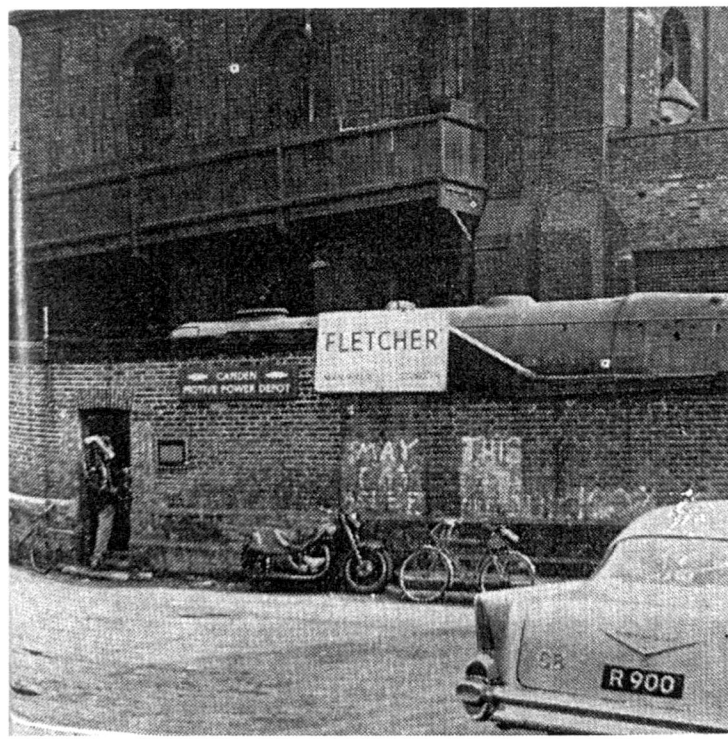

11.25 Dumpton Place entrance

After the opening in 1873 of a new shed at Willesden, housing freight locomotives and many locomotives in suburban service, the locomotive shed at Camden was used by large express passenger locomotives, together with a number of tanks for pilot work. Initially the Willesden shed was a sub-shed to Camden but later, under LMS, the roles were reversed, with Willesden becoming the 'concentration' depot at the head of the area. Camden had only to cope with some 50-60 engines.

The LMS introduced its twelve Princess Royal Class Pacific locomotives in 1933 and then enlarged the design with the streamlined Princess Coronation class of 1937, of which 37 locomotives were built by 1947. Coronation No. 6220, the first of the class, reached 114 mph (183 kph) on 29 June 1937 and briefly held the British speed record for steam traction until bettered by the LNER Mallard a year later. Some of these locomotives are captured in Peter Green's evocative oil painting depicting the west end of the shed in 1938 (§11.27).

CHALK FARM RAILWAY LANDS: A GUIDED TOUR 1830 TO 2030

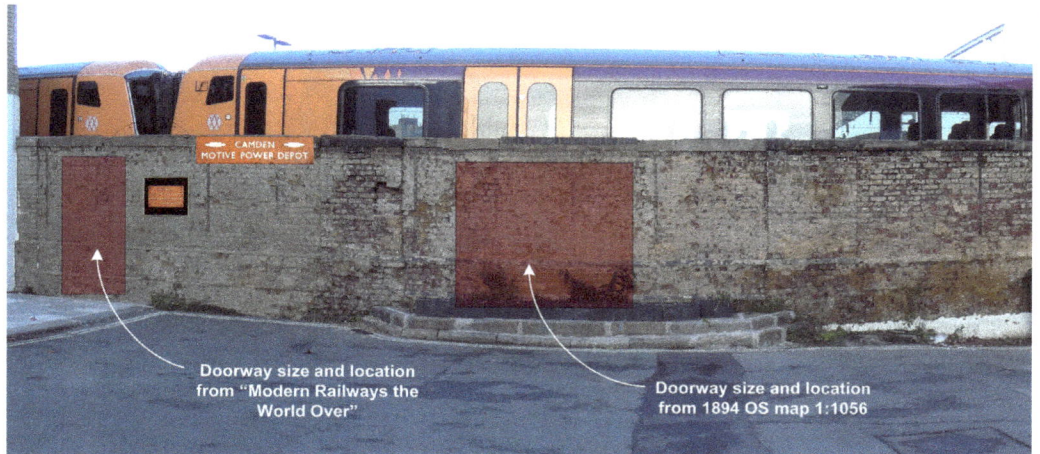

11.26 Dumpton Place end wall in 2023, showing former narrow entrance location and possible original entrance

11.27 West end of Camden Shed as imagined in 1938. Streamlined Pacific No. 6220 Coronation Scot, in original blue livery with silver stripes, passes Stanier 2-6-4 tank hauling up local train. Patriot class 4-6-0 No. 5512 *Bunsen* on turntable, *G Peter M Green*, 1958

Camden Shed's stabling of the larger passenger locomotives continued under the LMS and BR, tending to consist of Patriots, Jubilees, Royal Scots and Pacifics, with a pre-eminence in the 1950s of Coronation Pacifics. Locomotives of the Duchess, Princess, Royal Scot and Jubilee Class were all individually named, which added to the attraction of the Shed as a mecca for trainspotters in the 1950s until the end of steam.

Little remains of the heritage associated with Camden Shed. The major feature is the enginemen's hostel overlooking the line just west of Regent's Park Road Bridge (§11.28). Called Stephenson House when built in 1928, it served the aristocracy of the working class while off-duty – the long-distance drivers and firemen that were accommodated overnight awaiting their next assignments (§11.29). It has been renamed Iron Bridge House.

On the north side of the bridge lies the former Primrose Hill station building. In the mid 1950s part of the station building was provided with dance hall, bar and beer cellar as a social club for staff employed at Camden Shed.

CAMDEN DEPOT FROM 1900 TO END OF STEAM

11.28 Stephenson House, former hostel providing overnight accommodation for locomotive crews (left image)

11.29 Daily Assignments Board scheduling locomotive movements, 1936 (right image)

Locomotives discharged smoke and steam continuously as they shunted. Steam engines were fired and cleaned out at Camden MPD behind the wall close to Dumpton Place. In spite of the notices at the Shed warning engine crews to avoid the dreaded 'black smoke', at the risk of dark penalties, the smoke, dust and grit created an enormous and demoralising domestic cleaning effort, as well as a high incidence of respiratory diseases. Protests from among the well-to-do local residents were common and became an increasing issue from 1956 under the Clean Air Act.

11.8 Camden Shed operations

After an up train to Euston had been emptied of passengers, a pilot locomotive would take the empty carriages back to Willesden with the train locomotive typically providing assistance up Camden Bank. Arriving at Camden Shed, the passenger locomotive would fall back as the pilot and stock crossed from the down empty carriage line to the down fast and then down slow lines. Other moves also required banking assistance and would take a train locomotive onto the Shed from whichever direction was appropriate as it fell away from the rear of the stock. Some locomotives simply reversed onto shed along the down empty carriage line, which doubled as a down locomotive line.

In each case, locomotives were moving tender first along the north face of the Shed to the turntable, a 70 foot (21m) Cowans & Sheldon vacuum-operated turntable installed in the mid 1930s. The turntable was operated by the engine crew, the largest locomotives being turned through 180 degrees in 1½ minutes with no effort on the part of the engine crew.

The turntable was the scene of a remarkable accident when driver misjudgement allowed a locomotive to shoot over the rail stops to bury its tender in the cellar of the Pembroke Castle, much to the concern of the publican. In the chaos that ensued, it was decided to recover the locomotive to get the turntable back into service but leave the tender where it was until a recovery crew could be sent from Willesden.

After turning, locomotives continued to the coaling plant. Having coaled, they moved along the back road to the ash plant at the east end where their fire was cleaned and ash removed from the smokebox and ashpan. Following several hours working, the intense heat in the boiler of a locomotive caused the solids and ash content of coal to fuse and form thick solids called 'clinker' on the firebars, preventing oxygen from reaching the fire and thereby reducing steam pressure. Spent fuel in the form of ash settled in the smokebox under the chimney to quite a depth, which had to be emptied after every run – a very dirty job.

Before leaving the ashpit area, an engine's sandboxes were replenished with dry sand. The sand could be fed onto the rails at the push of a switch in the driver's cab to aid traction on steeper grades and slippery conditions. Locomotives that needed to be ready for their next workings immediately would then take up a position at the east end of the shed where they were prepared and watered in the open. Here locomotives would be given a general check by an examining fitter, usually equipped with a long wheel-tapping hammer. Locomotives were then ready for the engine crew to prepare them for their next workings by making up the fire, trimming the coal, oiling around the engine and watering. Some of this routine servicing was mechanised in the BR era with self-cleaning smokeboxes, rocking grates and self-emptying ashpans.

Locomotives now awaited reversing down the Bank to Euston to take a down train out of London. If a locomotive needed more work than simply servicing, it would move into the Shed itself, having had the fire completely dropped rather than just cleaning out the ash. The fire would be cleaned by withdrawal from the firebox with a long steel shovel and thrown onto the ground. Where possible, boiler washout and scheduled repairs took place inside the Shed, where locomotives could be kept apart from the servicing and preparation of active engines. Work in the Shed was characterised as a 'sooty claustrophobia'. After major servicing, it would take several hours to create sufficient steam pressure to move out of the Shed to take up a position outside at the west end of the Shed.

Part of this sequence of operations is illustrated in the following images (§11.30 to §11.32), and other parts have been shown in earlier images.

Maintenance of steam locomotives was highly labour-intensive, requiring an army of men (§11.31). Even aspiring locomotive drivers would start as cleaners, the lowest rung of a multitude of grades into which the Company separated their employees in military fashion.

11.30 *The Princess Royal* No. 46200 on the turntable at Camden Shed

11.31 Cleaners set to work on unrebuilt Scot on a hot afternoon in May 1935 (left image)

11.32 46200 on back road with ash plant behind, 3 June 1962 (right image)

The number of cleaners reflected the pride taken in the locomotives' appearance. Camden Shed had 32 at one time. As the labour market grew tighter in the 1950s, such dirty work created recruitment problems.

11.9 Last days of the railway horse

Many railway horses survived the cull after WWII. By the early 1950s what had become Camden Horse Department under British Rail stabled some 500 horses, covering Camden, Euston, St. Pancras and other smaller stable locations.

Horse numbers fell rapidly over the 1950s. the decline illustrated in §11.33. Most horses were sold, notably to charities that had been established to rescue horses after WWI. Two such charities accounted for 85% of charity purchases: Our Dumb Friends League (ODFL, now Blue Cross) and the International League for the Protection of Horses (ILPH, now World Horse Welfare).

§11.33 Main horse stables and numbers of horses (based on AN 35/19 at National Archives)

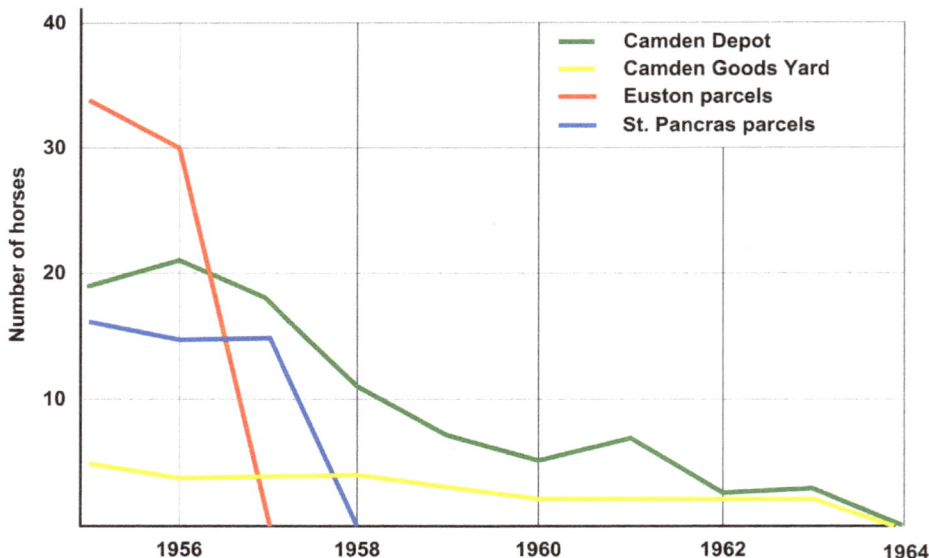

CHALK FARM RAILWAY LANDS: A GUIDED TOUR 1830 TO 2030

11.10 Last days of steam

The last four steam locomotives were banished to Willesden on 9 September 1962. One of the last, No. 46200 The Princess Royal, started its working life in Camden in 1933. Shown here on 3 June 1962, in its last year of operation, it stands on the back road next to the Shed having been coaled (§11.34).

11.34 No. 46200 The Princess Royal on the back road having been coaled, 1962 (left image)

After the banishment of steam, Camden enjoyed a brief twilight, housing diesels (§11.35). The lower servicing demands allowed the railway to operate with fewer traction units than with steam traction.

But after an undistinguished interlude, diesels were themselves evicted following electrification in 1966. Having already suffered the indignity of partial demolition, Camden Shed was closed completely on 3 January 1966. and pulled down the same year.

The view of the shed shortly before it was pulled down (§11.36) shows what remains of the original features on the right, and the partly stripped LMS 1930s roof on the left, as well as the footbridge from Dumpton Place. The area previously occupied by the Shed was converted to smokeless sidings and train washing facilities (§11.37).

11.35 The scene in front of the main goods shed c1965, with Classes 40, 08 and 86 diesel locomotives, has a rather tired atmosphere, anticipating its further decline (right image)

11.36 View south across the shed, 11 May 1964 (left image)

11.37 View from Pembroke Castle of carriage sidings, 2013 (right image)

CAMDEN DEPOT FROM 1900 TO END OF STEAM

12 Transformation in later 20th century

    12.1   Overview
    12.2   Gilbey departs
    12.3   Regent's Canal towpath opens
    12.4   Camden markets
    12.5   Gilbey House
    12.6   Camden Goods Station
    12.7   Roundhouse
    12.8   Pickford's Stables and Western Horse Tunnel
    12.9   Main line railway
    12.10 Primrose Hill Tunnel East Portals
    12.11 Electricity sub-station

12.1 Overview

Powerful forces were driving change in the decades after WWII. The Clean Air Act of 1956 and the electrification of the railways brought the middle classes back to the area, attracted by Victorian houses at reasonable prices that could be readily adapted for families.

By contrast, for the local authority the future was planned modernisation: bold, large-scale housing schemes containing up-to-date facilities and replacing Victorian terraced housing. The word 'Victorian' had become one of abuse in planning circles, connoting ugliness and impracticability. Wholesale replacement seemed the obvious way forward at a time when the recolonisation of inner London by the middle classes had only just begun.

The most dramatic manifestation of this trend was the rebuilding of Euston Station by British Rail and the demolition of its two finest features: the Euston Arch and the Great Hall. Euston Station is outside the scope of this account, but the strength of public opposition to the loss of such heritage was instrumental in fostering the conservation movement.

Camden Goods Station was also subject to adverse winds. Poor industrial relations in the 1950s contributed to a rapid decline in goods traffic, movement of goods becoming dominated by road traffic. The Beeching report of 1963 further speeded the demise of the sundries/small traffic associated with London depots such as Camden. The dominance of road was reflected in the GLC's grandiose scheme for the North Cross Route, a six-lane highway, part of the Motorway Box, which created planning uncertainty and blight before it was finally abandoned.

Nor was British Rail's main tenant at Camden, W & A Gilbey, in a healthier position. Predatory commercial wolves were circling an old-fashioned family firm. From its founding in 1856 up to the 1960s all board members had been from four families that were related by marriage. The directors faced difficult decisions simply to buy more time to assure the firm's survival.

The Regent's Canal also had an uncertain future as its trade collapsed with the disappearance of much of the industry along its banks.

12.2 Gilbey departs

Gilbey's lease with British Rail was due to expire in September 1953. The dilapidated state of much of the infrastructure did not leave any attractive options in the short term, most requiring planning permission and a subsequent period of construction. It was decided to renew the lease as a temporary measure. But a decade later another review became even more urgent if the company was to survive.

12.1 Gilbey's Gin distillery, Harlow New Town, built 1963, listed 1992, demolished 1993

The directors were courted by Harlow New Town where there was a central 19-acre (8ha) site available on condition that Gilbey created an iconic new head office building and gin distillery (§12.1). Gilbey moved its operations to Harlow in 1964 with 184 of its Camden staff. But the winds of change and company consolidation sweeping through the industry did not provide long-term respite.

Gilbey has been through several corporate amalgamations since its move to Harlow. It is now a minor brand in the Diageo portfolio, larger in the USA and Canada than in the UK. Yet it has perhaps the most interesting history, which this account has tried to elaborate in Ch. 9.

12.3 Regent's Canal towpath opens

The last horse-drawn traffic on the Regent's Canal was carried in 1956 and by the late 1960s commercial traffic had all but vanished.

The boat trip business had started on the Regent's Canal in 1951, as part of the Festival of Britain celebrations, growing from 1,500 to 100,000 passengers in ten years. The narrowboat 'Jason' was the first trip boat, seen here passing the stub of the Cumberland Market Branch and about to pass under Water Meeting Bridge (§12.2).

The Regent's Canal Group, formed in 1965 as a body embracing all the inner London canal-side amenity societies, campaigned effectively for opening the towpath to the public, championing a green and tranquil route for the public to enjoy. The regenerated towpath in Camden was opened on 20 May 1972.

The Pirate Club was founded by Viscount St Davids in 1966 to provide water-based activities for the young, initially from a Thames barge,

12.2 Jason at Water Meeting Point (left image)

12.3 Thames barge *Rosedale*, first base of the Pirate Club, 1975 (right image)

Rosedale (§12.3). It started a movement that spread widely across the country.

After a number of acts of vandalism, the Pirate Club needed more secure and permanent premises. The Pirate Castle, designed by Richard Seifert's practice, opened in 1977 and was enlarged in 2007-08 to provide better facilities and conference space.

The decaying remnants of the goods yard on each side of the canal include a length of hydraulic pipework that can be seen in §12.3 mounted on the retaining wall that ran between the two former accumulator towers (#8.5).

The regeneration of the towpath led to the restoration and upgrade of the Lock-keeper's Cottage at Hampstead Road Locks that dates from 1816 (§12.4). The crenellations are a 1970s addition.

12.4 Lock Keeper's Cottage, now a coffee bar and Regent's Canal Information Centre, 2013

TRANSFORMATION IN LATER 20TH CENTURY

12.4 Camden markets

The early transformation of the wharves and docks upstream of Hampstead Road Locks were used up to 1973 for various light industrial and storage uses including garaging. Market activities on the north side started later that summer in a rather *ad hoc* fashion, commencing with small stalls located externally to the stable buildings. This was followed by the opening of the crafts market at what was branded 'Camden Lock' (§12.5) in the former Dingwall's timber yards.

12.5 Camden Lock (left image)

12.6 West Yard in 1970s (right image)

The creative energy released was translated at weekends into an exciting retail market that grew and spread up the High Street into clothes, music, food and entertainment. Gradually shop units and canopies were added to the buildings (§12.6) and by the 1980s it was a fully-fledged market-place. A sample of the many wares on offer is shown in §12.7.

12.7 Baltic amber, trinkets, bags and other accessories in Camden Lock Market

CHALK FARM RAILWAY LANDS: A GUIDED TOUR 1830 TO 2030

12.8 The upper floor of the Horse Hospital in 1990s

The original market was joined by Stables Market (§12.8), Buck Street Market and Canal Street Market to form, together with Inverness Street Market, the largest and most popular street market complex in the UK.

Camden Market's success had much to do with the preservation of the historic setting. The panorama along the canal from the locks and the Roving Bridge is an exceptional vista of industrial buildings dominated by the Interchange Warehouse (§12.9).

12.9 View to west from Roving Bridge, 2019

12.5 Gilbey House

In 1996, 100 years after Hucks' Bottle Stores was built, the building was renamed Gilbey House and converted for residential use with a central light well and a seventh floor added (§12.10). The original Gilbey House, Gilbey's head office from 1937 to 1964, was renamed Academic House.

TRANSFORMATION IN LATER 20TH CENTURY

12.10 Gilbey House viewed from towpath bridge over Interchange Basin, 2013

Next to the building's Jamestown Road frontage, at Nos. 34-36, is a very large ice well built in 1839 at the head of William Leftwich's basin and deepened in c1846 to 100 feet (30m) to hold about 2400 tons of ice. The well is demarcated by a circle of bricks in the paving but is not accessible. There is an information panel at the site.

12.6 Camden Goods Station

The former Camden Goods Station closed c1980 and British Rail sold most of the site a few years later after demolishing the main goods shed. The former goods yard area can now be sub-divided as shown in §12.11.

12.11 Former Camden Goods Station area as subdivided in 1990s

The western triangle remains with Network Rail for maintenance of the main line and NLR. Juniper Crescent is a 1990s development for social housing, as is Gilbey's Yard in the southeast. The centre was acquired by Safeways (and later by Morrisons) which became Camden's first supermarket, with half of the site devoted to a car park.

Access to Safeway and Juniper Crescent was provided by construction of a new road from Chalk Farm Road, running under the NLR. To create this, much of the Great Wall had to be taken down and the land behind reduced from railway level to street level, where it provided for a petrol filling station. The retaining wall supporting the railway level was rebuilt as a concrete bored-pile structure on the northern side of the NLR. The access road passes under a bridge formed in this retaining wall.

One section of the original Great Wall remains to the west of the access road (§12.12). The thickness of the base reaches 6ft 9in (2.1 m), a vivid demonstration of its strength. Other sections remain east of the access road.

12.12 Remaining section of the Great Wall, 2013

12.7 Roundhouse

After Gilbey had vacated the site, the Roundhouse was purchased by Centre 42. Directed initially by Arnold Wesker, it was relaunched in 1966 with London's first all-night rave and soon became an iconic rock venue, hosting Jimi Hendrix, Led Zeppelin, Pink Floyd, Cream, the Rolling Stones, The Who, Elton John, David Bowie and many others (§12.13).

It also acquired a growing reputation for cutting-edge theatre and shows such as *Oh Calcutta* and *Hair*, which gradually displaced rock as noise and licensing restrictions took their toll. It closed in 1983 and had a chequered history for the next 20 years before the regeneration described in the next chapter.

12.13 The Roundhouse as music venue

12.8 Pickford's Stables and Western Horse Tunnel

Pickford's Stables, already much diminished after the WWII firebomb, were sold by British Rail in 1952 to Milliwatt, a manufacturer of electric blankets, which used the buildings for storage and light industrial purposes.

Given the nature of the surrounding streets, planning constraints effectively required that further development be residential. The complex was sold on for construction, over 1970-72, of 13 luxury family houses arranged around a paved courtyard and landscaped garden that became Waterside Place (§12.14).

Only parts of the eastern and western walls remain of the former stables. The most obvious is that along Gloucester Avenue, which forms an archaeological curiosity, part of which is seen in §12.15 adorned with opportunistic vegetation. A similar section of wall remains on the Primrose Hill School side.

12.14 Waterside Place, Google image, 2022

12.15 Remains of eastern wall of stables complex in Gloucester Avenue, 2023

An attempt has been made on the other side of the Gloucester Avenue wall, in the courtyard of Waterside Place, to create a fountain recalling the exit of the horse tunnel (§12.16). Simple comparison of the two sides of the wall suggests that this is not accurately located vertically in regard to the original tunnel exit.

The Western Horse Tunnel has now been sealed on either side of Gloucester Avenue but the public can enjoy a glimpse of the immediately adjoining section of tunnel from the sloping path that runs alongside 42 Gloucester Avenue and leads down to the Regent's Canal towpath. Those that would

12.16 Feature in courtyard of Waterside Place representing the exit of the horse tunnel, 2021 (left image)

12.17 West end of Western Horse Tunnel, 2023 (right image)

like a closer look can enter Michael Nadra's restaurant, which has incorporated the western end of the tunnel to form an integral part of the dining area (§12.17).

12.9 Main line railway

It was only when the full electrification programme had been completed in 1966 that the air became clean, the greatest change to the area since the original developments of the 19th century and a major stimulus to gentrification.

The next major upgrade was undertaken by Railtrack between Euston Station and the Primrose Hill Tunnels over 1998-2000, and included track renewal work, signalling and overhead electrification. Bridges and other structures were altered to clear the way for overhead electric wires. Individual small signal boxes were removed and replaced by large power-operated boxes sited at strategic points along the line to control the new colour-light signalling system.

12.10 Primrose Hill Tunnel East Portals

Around the time that steam traction ended, the leases of most of Eton College's Chalcots Estate fell in, some 650 houses, many above the Primrose Hill Tunnel. The future was planned modernisation, bold, large-scale housing schemes containing up to date facilities replacing Victorian terrace housing which had become something of an embarrassment. Camden Council took over part of the land being sold to erect four 23-storey tower blocks. This has dramatically affected the landscape and setting of the portals and the view from Primrose Hill.

British Rail followed the Eton Estate in selling land in the area on long leases to developers. A terrace of eight houses with shops on the ground floor (§12.18) was built over the south portal. It was not long before settlement over the fast tunnel was observed and the five most northerly of the eight units had

12.18 Flats with shops at street level as originally built (left image)

12.19 View of portals after part of terrace demolished, 2013 (right image)

to be demolished. The panorama of the two portals (§12.19) shows the terrace after being truncated.

Land on King Henry's Road next to the southern portal was sold to National Grid c1970 to erect a cooling station for the HV electricity cables between Tottenham and St. John's Wood transformer stations.

Close to the northern portal. on Adelaide Road, Camden erected a fifth tower block, Blashford Tower, that can be seen in §12.18. A surgery was built in a makeshift building next to this tower and, further along Adelaide Road, a repair garage. The embankment below these developments became Adelaide Nature Reserve.

The combined effect of these developments has left the portals very difficult to view and appreciate.

12.11 Electricity sub-station

Under British Rail, the larger part of the former electric power station, the engine room, appears to have been stripped of equipment and used as a diesel oil store.

12.20 Electricity sub station with residential development in former engine room, 2013

In the 1990a it was sold for residential development (§12.20), while the smaller northern part, formerly the producer house, was converted to a sub-station, providing DC to third running lines and 11 kV AC to overhead lines. The DC EHV cables were routed through the Western Horse Tunnel and into the Up Empty Carriage Tunnel.

13 Regeneration in the 21ˢᵗ century

    13.1   Overview
    13.2   Roundhouse
    13.3   Camden Lock
    13.4   Stables Yard
    13.5   Camden Catacombs
    13.6   Interchange Warehouse
    13.7   Camden Goods Yard
    13.8   The Henson
    13.9   Winding Engine Vaults
    13.10   Primrose Hill Tunnel East Portals
    13.11   Former Primrose Hill station

13.1 Overview

The Trust bears a responsibility to bring the unique nature of the Chalk Farm Railway Lands heritage to the attention of those primarily responsible for its protection. It tries to ensure that any development in the Railway Lands understands, respects, cherishes and celebrates the remarkable heritage that exists, creating long-term gain both for developers and the community. This account is one measure towards that end.

The threats to our heritage are well expressed by Sean Murphy, writing about the loss of heritage in Temple Bar, Dublin:

> Experience shows us that there is a deadly linkage between acts of planning vandalism and historical ignorance or apathy.

Ignorance about the heritage is prevalent, both among developers with their professional advisors and the statutory authorities to whom they make their applications. Given the resources that developers can muster, this ignorance can readily extend to misinformation, undermining proper understanding of the heritage and allowing the developers' professional advisors to mislead planning authorities. This account intends to provide a firm historical baseline against which all future developments will be assessed.

Overcoming the apathy to which Sean Murphy refers is more difficult in a climate where the planning authorities, starved of resources, fail to fulfil their democratic mandate by engaging with the community and lose expertise to developers as their staff pass through the revolving door.

This chapter is a review of regeneration in the Chalk Farm Railway Lands to date and a candid recognition of the successes and failures of the first quarter of the 21ˢᵗ century.

13.2 Roundhouse

The key milestone in the regeneration of the Roundhouse was its purchase by the Norman Trust in 1996. Established by Torquil Norman, owner of a successful toy business, this was to revitalise the Roundhouse as a centre for the performing arts and as a charity supporting the ambitions of young people to engage with a wide variety of the performing arts.

The major works undertaken over 2004-06 included creating an exo-skeleton (§13.1) that could support the structural needs of a modern venue in regard to lighting, sound and stage-sets while allowing the historical fabric (§13.2) to remain visually prominent. A new building was constructed alongside to provide a theatre, café and offices.

A charitable trust was established to provide a creative facility for young people at the ground floor (street) level, supported by commercial use of the Performance Space at railway level. The Performance Space is used for theatre and acrobatics, from dance to circus and for corporate events. Below the Performance Space, the vaults formerly supporting the locomotive shed have been adapted for studios and workshops.

The Roundhouse, through such major re-purposing, has regained its central role as a vibrant cultural landmark in North London, at the heart of Camden's music scene.

13.1 Exo-skeleton structure being clad, 2005 (left image)

13.2 The original cast iron columns give the Performance Space its character (right image)

13.3 Camden Lock

The elegant cast iron profile of the Roving Bridge (§13.3) makes it one of the best-known structures in Camden. Thanks to the popularity of Camden Lock Market, it has become an iconic symbol and an internationally familiar structure. From the bridge there are fine panoramas of the Regent's Canal and its industrial context, both upstream (to the west) and downstream (to the east).

An application by the Trust in 2019 to upgrade the Roving Bridge from II to II* was not successful but could be resubmitted if more information about the provenance of the bridge were obtained.

13.3 Panorama from south bank featuring, from right to left: Camden Lock Market, the Roving Bridge, Dingwall's Dock, the Interchange Warehouse and towpath bridge, and the former goods offices (now The Henson)

13.4 Stables Yard

The stables complex in Camden, as previously noted, is the most complete example of Victorian industrial stabling that has survived – in terms of scale, complexity and quality of structures. It includes associated features: horse tunnels, horse roads, ramps and galleries; the retaining wall that separated Stables Yard from Chalk Farm Road; the entrance to Stables Yard with its gatehouse; and the granite sett pavements. Stables Yard illustrates the evolution of stabling over the second half of the nineteenth century. All five stable ranges are now part of Stables Market, which includes retail outlets, workshops, bars and restaurants, and a variety of leisure activities.

The Horse Hospital is the outstanding architectural survivor in this rare complex of industrial stabling and was upgraded to II* as a result of the Trust's application in 2010. The image (§13.4) shows how well the building was adapted to the triangular site, stepping back three times from the original façade (refer #7.7 for more detail).

Stables Market was the subject of an almost continuous series of transformations in the early 2000s by the owner, Stanley Sidings Ltd. The spirit of place associated with the heritage of Stables Yard was assailed by inappropriate glass and steel buildings, prosaically called Buildings A, B and C, which were juxtaposed with Victorian stables, viaducts and vaults, a visible indictment of the planning process.

Construction of Buildings A and B in 2009 was combined with reconfiguration of the major element of the Catacombs, the 1847 vaults and arches under the NLR, as described in the next section.

The Gilgamesh complex (Building C) opened in 2005 providing market stalls at ground level where once had stood the Triangular Bottle Stores (#9.9).

13.4 Horse Hospital, view west to North Yard, Festival of Cheese, 2017

REGENERATION IN THE 21ST CENTURY

Horse Tunnel Market (Building D) was created in 2006 as an outlier of Stables Market. It incorporates one end of the Eastern Horse Tunnel, hence the name. Stalls of cast iron and timber create the illusion of historic materials being re-purposed.

Horse Tunnel Market is a sad pastiche of the former spectacular complex of 1839 goods sidings and vaults (§13.5), described in #3.6. Damaged by the construction of the car park for Safeway supermarket in the early 1990s, the vaults were then largely demolished on the basis of a planning application for Building D to create more retail outlets.

13.5 Original 1839 vaults, 1987 (left image)

13.6 Amy Winehouse statue in Stables Yard, 2021 (right image)

Given the research expertise of the two heritage consultants involved in the application, Heritage Architecture (*2004*) and AOC Archaeology (2007), both of whom failed to recognise the origins and significance of the structures that were to be demolished, one must ask what professionals can be trusted with the heritage. The same question is posed in the editorial and an article by Alec Forshaw in the *Journal of Islington Archaeology and History Society, 2016-17*.

A broad staircase descends from Stables Yard to a new basement level, provided in 2010 for yet more retail and other facilities. Seen in the snow behind the statue of Amy Winehouse (§13.6), it was intended to create the illusion of an original feature.

The new owners of Camden Markets, the Labs Group, have made some dramatic improvements, spurred by the stable ranges being placed on the 'at risk' register by Historic England. Surface mounted clutter, including pipes and electrical cables, has been removed leaving a much cleaner façade. Doors and windows have been upgraded and the bridge between Provender Stores and the Tack Room (§13.7) reinstated, all with a view to restoring their original appearance. The success of this may be judged by comparing photos §13.7 and §13.8 with earlier photos §7.5 and §7.6.

13.7 The bridge from Provender Stores (left) to the Tack Room (right) with container goods train passing on NLR, 2021 (left image)

13.8 Under the gallery of The Stables, with Provender Stores on left and east end of Long Stable, 2021 (right image)

13.5 Camden Catacombs

What was left of the key part of Camden Catacombs, vaults that originally supported the Construction Shop (#5.10) became part of Stables Market, accommodating a wide variety of retail outlets. Before the 2009 redevelopment, one could move relatively freely through both the major and minor vaults. The sense of anarchy that this created was very attractive to the predominantly young visitors. While it is almost impossible to re-capture this on camera, some images of the Catacombs from the early 2000s are shown in §13.9.

13.9 Area that became the Catacombs, early 2000s

One of the aims of the reconfiguration of Stables Yard in 2009 was to remove this anarchy by closing the arched openings of the smaller transverse vaults and converting this part of the Catacombs into a series of linear retail

REGENERATION IN THE 21ST CENTURY

13.10 View through minor vaults being refurbished, revealing inverted arches, 2009 (left image)

13.11 Saddle Row with main arches of former Catacombs on right and mock historic brickwork of the Atrium on left, 2013 (right image)

outlets based on the 25 major vaults. Both major and minor vaults were refurbished, in the process exposing the inverted arches of the minor vaults (§13.10) which had added strength to the original structure (§5.11).

The 25 main vaults were taken back to the NLR viaduct. Some were further shortened from the south, under what was then Morrisons' car park, where safety considerations placed a limit on their length. They opened onto a new passage, now called 'Saddle Row' (§13.11), opposite the mock Victorian façade of the Atrium, the name given to Buildings A and B in Stables Yard, also built in 2009 and seen on the left in the photograph.

13.6 Interchange Warehouse

The Interchange Warehouse (§13.12) was refurbished as offices in the late 1980s, retaining many of the original features and emphasizing the riveted steel columns. The glazed canopies on three sides were taken down. A new access route for pedestrians from Camden Lock Place was created with a staircase through the retaining wall.

In 2007 it was further restored by Associated Press, which for many years has leased the building, removing the more recent additions to expose the building's original features. Its current owner, the Labs Group, also owns Camden Markets.

13.12 Interchange Warehouse, 2007 (left image)

13.13 Refurbished and repainted 1846 towpath bridge over Interchange Basin, 2023 (right image)

CHALK FARM RAILWAY LANDS: A GUIDED TOUR 1830 TO 2030

The Interchange Basement Warehouse lies on the east side of the building, where rail sidings formerly ran. Adjoining it on the west, centrally under the main warehouse, is the Interchange Basin, known colloquially as 'Dead Dog Hole'. Waste from Camden Markets is currently removed by barge from the basin, using the basement warehouse for loading.

At the head of the basin, the Canal & River Trust has completed a major refurbishment of the 1846 bridge that carried the towpath over the basin. A forensic examination of paint layers revealed not only the original colour but also the succession of paints used over the last 175 years. The original paint is believed to be an L&BR wagon paint, which would have become surplus to requirements when the Company became part of LNWR. The bridge has consequently been repainted in a contemporary equivalent of the original colour – identified as 'Indian Red' (§13.13).

13.7 Camden Goods Yard

The plan of the Camden Goods Yard area is shown in §12.11, subdivided according to land ownership. The area formerly occupied by the Morrisons supermarket, including its car park and petrol filling station (PFS), is now subject to major redevelopment by St George, part of the Berkeley Group, as 'Camden Goods Yard', the name they have given the site.

The plan in §13.14 shows historical features in various shades of brown, later buildings in light grey and the new blocks under construction in dark grey.

The only road access to the new development is the existing connection with Chalk Farm Road, a narrow stretch of road that must serve all movements of pedestrians, cyclists, disabled users, buses and motor vehicles. No east-west connections across the site have been created, nor did Camden's Planning Framework envisage any at the start of these works. As a result, the Camden

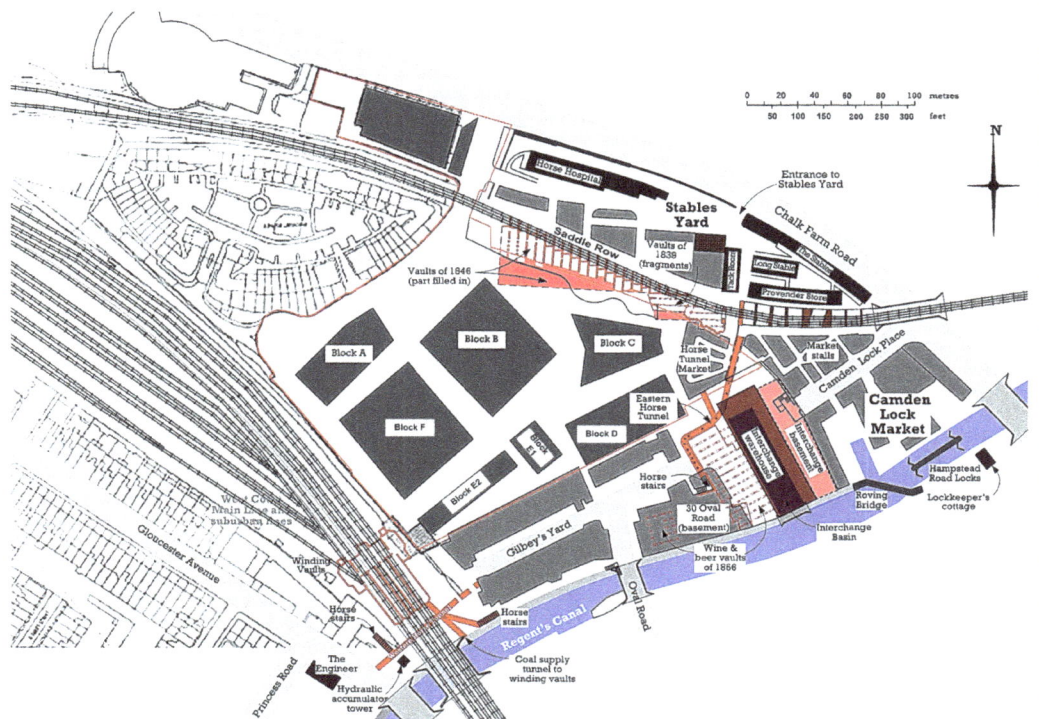

13.14 Camden Goods Yard site showing current redevelopment

REGENERATION IN THE 21ST CENTURY

Goods Yard site and its future residents and employees are effectively isolated from their surroundings, despite the usual estate agent hyperbole.

This isolation is compounded by the density of development with buildings 16 storeys (55 metres) high on land that is already up to five metres higher than the natural ground level in Chalk Farm Road.

Nor is there any celebration of the railway heritage on the site other than some street names that have no real connection with the past, notably the use of Stephenson's name for the access road from Chalk Farm Road. These are major opportunities lost by planners and developers. The next chapter describes how, by 2030, this situation had been, at least partially, remedied.

13.8 The Henson

The former goods offices at 30 Oval Road were redeveloped as 'The Henson' over 2007-2010, a new housing and office complex whose name celebrates the building that had housed Jim Henson's Creature Shop in the 1990s, creators of the Muppet Show.

Redevelopment involved sweeping away the goods offices and a large part of the basement Wine and Beer Vaults while retaining much of the older historic façade as shown in §13.15. The fragility of the supported brick façade became evident when parts collapsed or suffered structural damage. The southern façade along the canal, is shrouded in plastic sheeting in the image. The vaults can be seen under the temporary steel structure.

The walls in the foreground surround the exit of the Eastern Horse Tunnel, a listed structure. The north end of the tunnel is at Horse Tunnel Market. It winds around the Wine and Beer Vaults and emerges at 30 Oval Road via two flights of stairs. The planning application made no mention of the horse tunnel although the architect's plans showed demolition of the horse stairs and substantial alterations to the tunnel. Future access to the tunnel was to be blocked. These plans were initially approved.

13.15 Construction of The Henson, 30 Oval Road, viewed from The Interchange, June 2008

A three-month campaign by CRHT and others against these proposals resulted in new plans that preserved the horse tunnel but at the expense of very limited access via a gated entrance within the new housing development (§13.16). The tunnel should have had its own access from Oval Road, independent of the social housing entrance.

13.16 Entrance to Horse Tunnel via affordable housing with original granite bollards used to protect buildings from cart traffic, 2013

Historic features that have been retained in the redevelopment include the granite sett paving, LMS portal (§11.12), rail lines (§7.27), granite bollards used to protect buildings from cart traffic (§13.16), ventilation grilles to the horse tunnel (§7.27), turntable and the frames of two large weighbridges in Oval Road.

Speaker tubes in the building façade (§8.2) were demolished by the contractor but, after protest, new ones had to be recreated and installed.

13.9 Winding Engine Vaults

CRHT applied successfully in 2009 to raise the grade of the Stationary Winding Engine Vaults to II*. The determination by English Heritage declared the vaults to be of international importance:

> … for their historical and technological significance, as a remarkable survival of the London and Birmingham Railway, the first modern main line railway with a London terminus. The winding engine vaults represent a relatively brief transitional stage in the technological development of railway transportation, being one of the very last uses of rope haulage on a public railway. Their architectural interest lies in the grand scale and unique design of their underground brick construction.

13.17 Eastern Coal Vault, looking south, showing inverted arches of floor, 2016

Network Rail (NR), prompted by CRHT, subsequently commissioned consultants to carry out a Conservation Management Plan (*PPIY, 2020*). This started in 2014 but was held up pending works in 2016 to clear the vaults of accumulated debris and provide access, drainage and lighting.

Cleared of sediment, the inverted arches that form the invert and provide structural strength to the vaults can now be better appreciated (§13.17).

13.10 Primrose Hill Tunnel East Portals

The magnificent pair of portals gracing the entrance to Primrose Hill Tunnel are almost totally hidden from the public behind tawdry developments of the 1960s and '70s – a tower block, shops/flats, an electricity cooling station, car parks, garage and surgery (#12.10).

One of the Trust's first actions was to submit an application to English Heritage (now Historic England) for upgrade of the east portals to Grade II*. The decision to upgrade, received in June 2007, was unanimous declaring them to be of special interest:

> ...the first railway tunnel in London; the first nationally to negotiate the issue of competing claims for the use of land in an urban context; and the first tunnel to treat one of its portals architecturally. The portal is also of more than special architectural interest for its proud classical elevation which is indicative of the upmarket development Eton College hoped to undertake nearby. There are similarities in design with Brunel's portals to the Box Tunnel in the use of ashlar to imply strength, the classical features such as the treatment of the cornices and rusticated quoins, and the employment of quadrant arches to convey the sense of a grand entrance.

CRHT undertook an independent inspection, also in 2007, without breaching NR safety regulations. The Trust's report on the state of the structure, with architectural drawings by Anthony Richardson & Partners (ARP), was submitted to Network Rail later that year. This prompted a programme of maintenance works, budgeted for 2009, including removal of opportunistic vegetation, removal of graffiti, and rehabilitation of drainage works (§13.18).

As discussed in #12.10, the public is unable to view these magnificent structures, the finest in the area. This was briefly overcome in September 2007 when, with National Grid's cooperation, CRHT provided access for some 400 visitors to view the portals from the front of King Henry's Road electricity cooling station as part of London Open House.

13.18 Remedial works required to improve drainage and general appearance of the East Portals, 2007

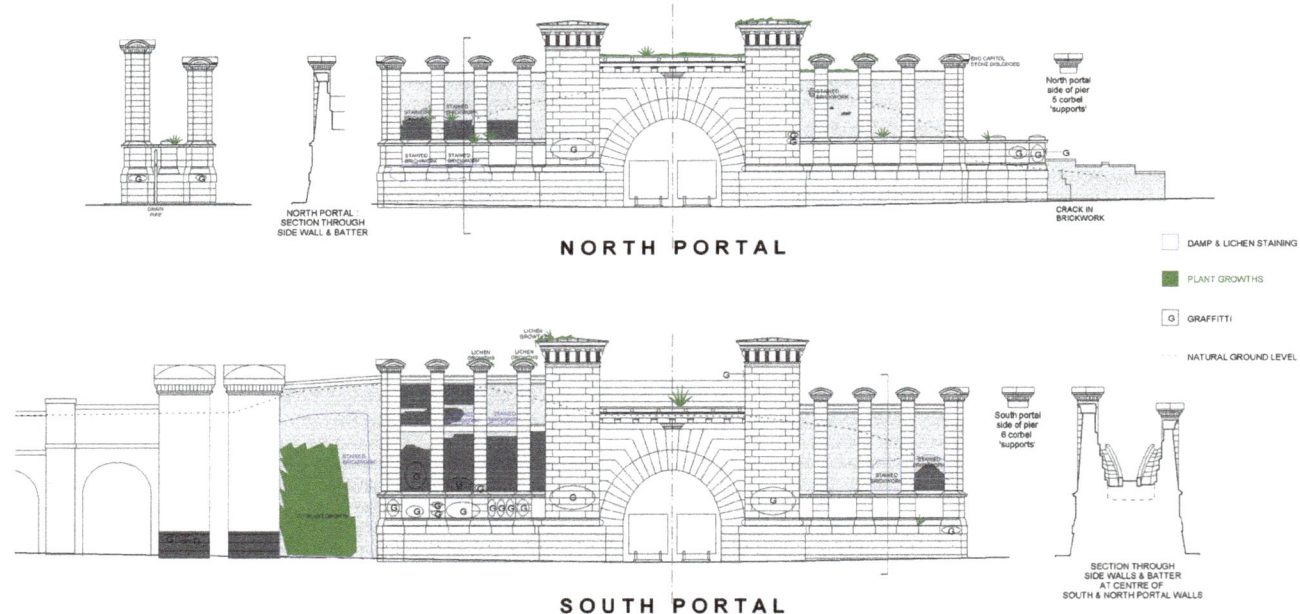

13.11 Former Primrose Hill station

In 1950 Chalk Farm station became Primrose Hill station and the street building was reconstructed. Primrose Hill station (§13.19) closed on 22 September 1992. The island platform with its 1871 buildings and fine ironwork remained (§13.20).

The razing on 6 December 2008 of the waiting room, wooden canopy and decorative cast iron columns and spandrels on the platform at Primrose Hill station destroyed a piece of almost unaltered classic mid-Victorian architecture.

Network Rail demolished the platform architecture on the grounds that the station was disused, unstaffed, not maintained, was a recognised hotspot for trespass and vandalism, raised problems of health and safety and would become an eyesore. There was no consultation or communication with the local community, which saw the demolition as a clandestine operation. Camden Council was advised shortly before the demolition and had no objection as the buildings were not in a conservation area.

Subsequent meetings with the Railway Heritage Trust and Network Rail revealed poor internal communications, lack of transparency and an undue haste to remove the architectural features, leading to quite unnecessary damage. CRHT was invited to inspect the salvaged but broken cast ironwork, which lay in the contractor's yard (§13.21), to assess the costs of restoration and to explore possible local reuse of the ironwork.

The views of the community were expressed at a full Council meeting on 2 March 2009, where CRHT led a deputation to highlight issues raised by demolition and raise the question of reopening the station. Broad agreement was expressed with these aims.

In the event, CRHT was, not surprisingly, unable to identify a suitable site for a rather unusual outdoor café and, alarmed at the costs of repairing the ironwork, had to abandon the attempt to restore it. Efforts to discover the destiny of the ironwork have not been successful. It would appear unlikely that any heritage railway could afford the cost of repairing the ironwork.

13.19 Primrose Hill station shortly before it closed, c1992 (left image)

13.20 Primrose Hill station platform architecture, c1992 (right image)

13.21 Murphy's Yard with broken platform architecture, March 2009

REGENERATION IN THE 21ST CENTURY

14 The Railway Lands: a guided tour in 2030

14.1 Camden Railway Heritage Trail
14.2 The Seven Wonders of Chalk Farm Railway Lands
14.3 Roundhouse to Hampstead Road Locks
14.4 Interchange and Dead Dog Basin
14.5 Wine and Beer Vaults
14.6 Stephenson Walk
14.7 Stationary Winding Engine Vaults
14.8 Pacific Village
14.9 Primrose Hill Tunnel East Portals
14.10 Improvements in access
14.11 Euston Square Gardens: an epilogue

This chapter imagines the Chalk Farm Railway Lands (CFRL) 200 years after the Stephensons took their Sunday stroll. Opening them to the public has been the motivation for researching the CFRL over the last two decades. I want to show you around what I hope we will be able to access in the year 2030. I use the personal pronoun and Camden Railway Heritage Trust (CRHT or the Trust) interchangeably, but we speak with the same voice. I make heroic assumptions regarding what heritage has been opened and re-purposed, based on proposals put forward by the Trust.

14.1 Heritage Trail guide

14.1 Camden Railway Heritage Trail

Visitors to the area today, in 2030, have very different motives from those of the Stephensons 200 years earlier. While many will be visiting the internationally renowned Camden Markets, an increasing number want to see the railway and canal heritage after learning from social media of the remarkable features now open to the public for the first time.

CRHT has long aimed to link key heritage sites to create a walk through the social and industrial past of one of London's most vibrant areas, the Camden Railway Heritage Trail. The Trust published a brochure for the Trail in 2008 (§14.1) that readily slips into a pocket or a handbag. It contains 24 pages of text and illustrations, a pull-out map of the Trail, a schematic plan of the former Goods Depot and information on the heritage and historical context.

It can also be downloaded from The Belsize Society website:

www.belsize.org.uk/events

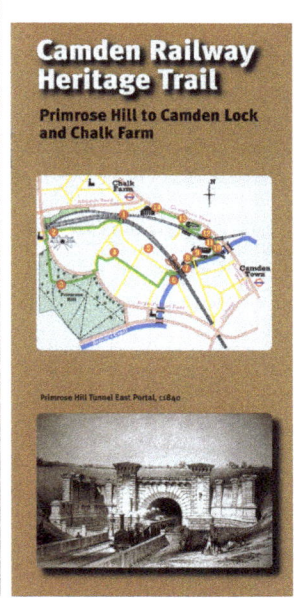

14.2 Railway Heritage Trail – Camden Goods Yard

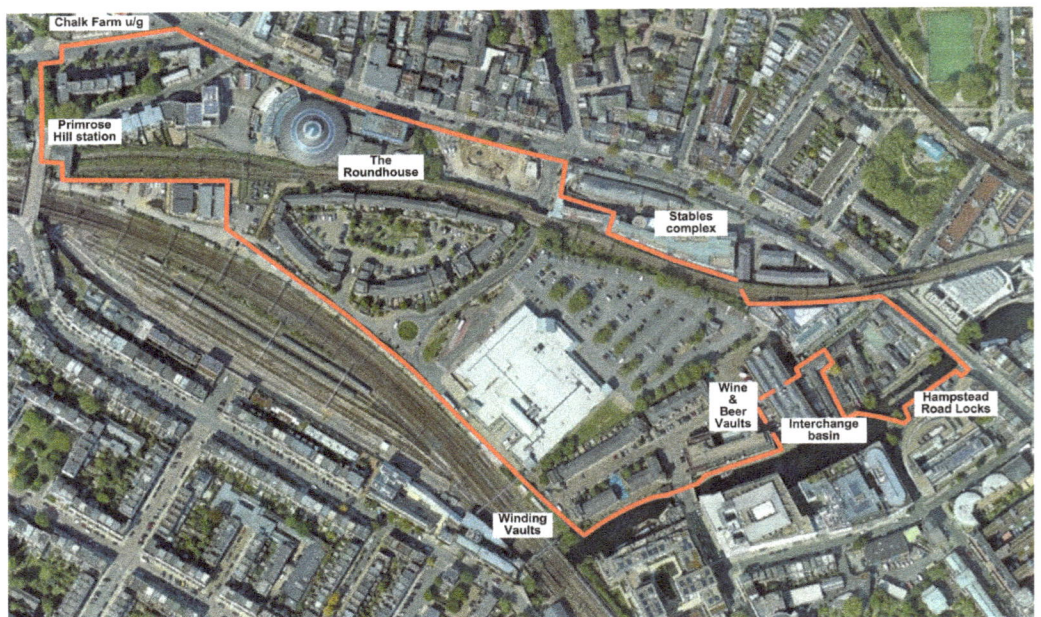

But what is accessible to the public now, in 2030, has moved on from 2008 and visitors need an updated guide to describe the Trail. In the absence of such a contemporary guide, which is on the Trust's action list, I shall describe here how the heritage of the area was revealed. I shall also consider what more could and should be done by the Trust and other stakeholders.

The 2030 Camden Railway Heritage Trail is divided into two parts: the circuit of Camden Goods Yard (§14.2) and a future extension to Primrose Hill Tunnel (§14.16). As well as the numerous stops to appreciate the heritage, there are watering holes and food halts *en route* as the Trail winds through Stables Market and Camden Lock.

But before embarking on the Trail, the most significant elements of the Chalk Farm Railway Lands are highlighted in the next section.

14.2 The Seven Wonders of Chalk Farm Railway Lands

No other area of London, and almost certainly the country, can celebrate such a rich 19th century railway and canal heritage as Chalk Farm Railway Lands. Within this limited area there are four Grade II* as well as a host of Grade II structures. I have picked out the most remarkable to define the Seven Wonders of Chalk Farm Railway Lands, described from our 2030 viewpoint.

1. **The Stationary Winding Engine Vaults:** a unique but hidden survivor of 1837 and the first mainline railway into London. Sited close to Camden Markets, the vaults have, since being opened to the public, created one of the most popular visitor attractions in London.
2. **Primrose Hill Tunnel East Portals:** also dating from 1837, they are an elegant reminder – now that they have been restored to view – of the first railway age and the use of such classical architecture to alleviate the public's concerns about rail tunnels.
3. **The Roundhouse:** a former goods locomotive shed of 1847 transformed into an iconic music and arts venue as well as a major media charity serving young people. The historic internal fabric of this structure is not generally accessible to the public other than through events.

4. **Stables complex:** the finest example of Victorian industrial stables in the country. Dating from the second half of the 19th century, the stables complex reminds us of the vital role horses formerly played in the movement of goods. It is largely accessible in its new role as Stables Market.
5. **Vaults, horse tunnels and catacombs:** dating variously from the first three phases of the goods yard, up to the mid 1850s, their elaborate Victorian brickwork, underground locations and air of mystery has become a magnet for visitors now that they are accessible, sensitively illuminated and re-purposed as part of the very popular Camden Markets.
6. **The Interchange Warehouse:** this magnificent building from 1905 recalls Camden's vital role as the first three-way interchange depot in London where goods were transferred between road, rail and canal, linking Camden to the Docks and to the world beyond. Opening the basement and canal basin has allowed the public to comprehend its former role as well as creating exhibition space and providing new access routes through the vaults and horse tunnel.
7. **Hampstead Road Locks:** canal and railway heritage is concentrated here, at Hampstead Road, with the iconic Roving Bridge of 1846 providing historic industrial views in both directions and the Lock-keeper's Cottage of 1816 serving as a Regent's Canal Information Centre.

14.3 Roundhouse to Hampstead Road Locks

The first part of the Trail is treated succinctly as this will not have changed very significantly from its description in the 2008 Trail Guide.

From the Roundhouse, readily accessed from Chalk Farm underground station, the 2030 Trail continues along Chalk Farm Road past the surviving vestige of the Great Wall to enter the North Yard of Stables Market. The Horse Hospital (Grade II*) can be explored here, commercial interests permitting access, before diverting to Saddle Row (§13.11) along the former North London Railway. This passage, along some of the original but much altered Catacombs, leads out of Stables Market to Paddock Lane, following the line of the NLR. Note the skewed arch under the NLR viaduct and relate this to the first LNWR interchange warehouse (§5.18). We exit to Camden Lock Place.

Where Camden Lock Place joins Chalk Farm Road, turn right at the iconic 'Camden Lock' NLR railway bridge and proceed south, passing over the Regent's Canal at Hampstead Road Bridge (Grade II), and turning right to enter the precinct of the Lock-keeper's Cottage (Grade II), nestling alongside Hampstead Road Locks (Grade II). The Trust has helped create the Regent's Canal Information Centre in what has been re-purposed as a coffee bar.

From here the Trail leads across the Roving Bridge, a Grade II feature that the Trust believes should be re-designated II*. From the bridge there are views both upstream (west) and downstream (east) that make this whole site one of the Seven Wonders.

The Trail continues into the West Yard of Camden Lock Market, which is awaiting further restoration following the planning decision earlier in the year to remove the controversial ferris wheel, which has been in operation for the last five years. We continue over West Yard, emerging back into Camden Lock Place and turning left to find the entrance to the Basement Warehouse.

From here the recent changes made to public access are described in the following sections.

14.4 Interchange Basement Warehouse and Dead Dog Basin

The redevelopment and re-purposing of the Interchange Basement Warehouse is shown in an artist's impression (§14.3). The Basement Warehouse has become an art gallery and exhibition space. It has fire door openings at the canal end to enable passengers to board the waterbuses that operate between here and Paddington Basin. Outside waterbus operating hours the canal basin allows the mooring of barges for removal of the waste generated by all Camden Markets.

The Trail now passes through another opening in the west wall of the Basement Warehouse that leads onto a broad pontoon bridge with security railings. This takes us across the Interchange Basin to the Wine and Beer Vaults (§14.4). The brick infill has been removed from two vaults, restoring these to their original open character.

14.3 Cross-section east-west with Wine and Beer Vaults (left), mooring for waterbus and barge (centre) and exhibition space (right), 2023

14.4 Wine and Beer Vaults, brick filled east face, view across Interchange Basin, 2010

At the head of the Interchange Basin, a side branch from the pontoon bridge leads to Dead Dog Café, a café/restaurant that has adopted the colloquial name of the basin and become a popular meeting place and watering hole.

We cross the pontoon bridge and enter the Wine and Beer Vaults.

14.5 Wine and Beer Vaults and Eastern Horse Tunnel

One arm of the L-shaped Wine and Beer Vaults, about 50% of the original area, was incorporated into the basement of The Henson in 2008 (#13.8) and is not only inaccessible to the public but was largely demolished.

The remaining half has been redeveloped as part of a linked series of historic underground spaces, that includes the Eastern Horse Tunnel, the Interchange Basin and the Interchange Basement Warehouse. Despite the loss of such a large part of the original vaults, the remaining area is an impressive size as can be appreciated by Trail followers (§14.5).

14.5 Wine and Beer Vaults, view through side vaults, 2010

14.6 Eastern Horse Tunnel with side entrance to Wine and Beer Vaults, *Geoffrey Fletcher,* c1960

Two new means of access to the Wine and Beer Vaults have been created. We have just gained access from the Interchange Basement Warehouse via the pontoon bridge. Access is also provided from the Regent's Canal towpath via an opening close to the western foot of the 1846 towpath bridge over the Interchange Basin.

A third entry point already exists as an opening in the Eastern Horse Tunnel, close to the foot of the horse stairs, on the west side of the vaults, as seen in plan in §9.10. This opening is best illustrated in one of Geoffrey Fletcher's sketches from *The London Nobody Knows,* a sketch described in his book as "The Catacombs of Camden Town" (§14.6). Before the development of Horse Tunnel Market (#13.4) the tunnel used to connect with not only the 1856 Wine and Beer Vaults but also with the original 1839 vaults and through these with the 1846 vaults, as shown in §9.10.

However, access to this opening from the horse tunnel has proved challenging, as four separate freeholders and leaseholders are involved in ownership of the Eastern Horse Tunnel. Opening the entire horse tunnel to the public is an important next step that I hope will be realised before long.

The Wine and Beer Vaults have had to be adapted for public access. The main vaults are about 2.92 metres high. The side vaults are only about 1.80 metres high at the crown of the low-rise arches (§14.7). The stepped brick foundations are 600mm deep to a concrete base.

THE RAILWAY LANDS: A GUIDED TOUR IN 2030

Re-purposing has required that the floor be lowered to gain head room. After lowering the floor to the base of the brickwork, the brick foundations were exposed, reducing the effective width of the side vaults from 3.5 metres to 3.0 metres but raising their height to 2.4 metres. The stepped brickwork around the base has proved useful both as informal seating and for display of artifacts for sale.

The accessibility of the whole area would be greatly enhanced if a solution could be found to creating a separate and independent entrance to the horse tunnel next to the gated entrance to the affordable housing at 30 Oval Road (#13.8). This would provide the Trail with another exit from the vaults. As matters stand, Trail followers must exit from the vaults onto the Regent's Canal towpath.

From here the Trail continues west along the towpath, passing the recently completed stairs at Southampton Bridge that lead up to Oval Road via the historic LMS portal (§14.8) that once provided access to a staircase to the railway offices above.

We continue along the towpath from here to the railway bridge and to the gated opening in the retaining wall. This opens onto the concourse that forms the south-eastern access to Stephenson Walk.

14.7 The author in the Wine and Beer Vaults, showing height of side arches, during campaign to save the horse tunnel, January 2007 (top image)

14.8 The LMS portal marks the stairs from the towpath to Oval Road (bottom image)

14.6 Stephenson Walk

Stephenson Walk is a 500 metre pedestrian and cycle path alongside the West Coast Main Line railway in Camden linking the Regent's Canal towpath with Regent's Park Road Bridge. Conceived by CRHT in 2019, the Trust was commissioned by the local authority to carry out a feasibility study (*Adams & Sutherland, 2023*). Further stages of design development were followed by implementation and Stephenson Walk was opened in 2028.

The Walk has provided new connections to the otherwise very isolated site of the former Camden Goods Yard, now a dense residential area. The Regent's Canal towpath entrance leads to the Walk through the concourse. Access from the other end, from Regent's Park Road Bridge, is via an entrance into the former Primrose Hill station building (§14.9) with a new exit onto the Walk.

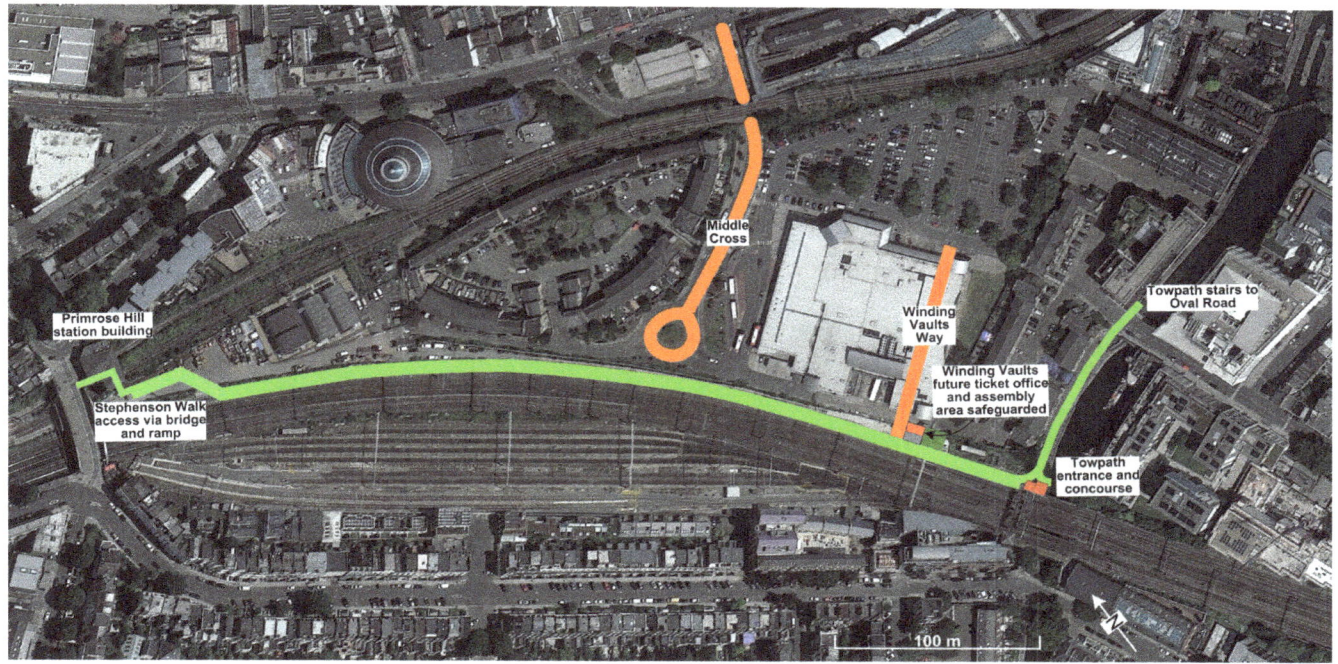

14.9 Stephenson Walk, showing key links

Stephenson Walk celebrates one of our greatest engineers, who was intimately involved with this length of mainline railway and goods depot for a decade and took personal responsibility for its engineering and construction. A major purpose of the Walk has been to highlight and safeguard access to Robert Stephenson's Grade II* listed early Victorian Stationary Winding Engine Vaults, sited under the mainline railway (#14.7).

Creating the Walk faced restricted space and the challenges of working alongside an operational mainline railway and other infrastructure. In particular, the six-metre level change between Camden Goods Yard and Regent's Park Road Bridge had to be accommodated. Oversite development of the railway maintenance yard west of Juniper Crescent allowed a ramp to be created in the centre of the triangular site (§14.10).

At the canal towpath, alterations made to the 1930's diversion of the horse tunnel have facilitated public use of the historic horse stairs. Both these alterations and the new ramp leading from the concourse have improved access to the Winding Vaults.

Stephenson Walk is characterised by robust ground surface treatments and regularly placed structures to support lighting and assist wayfinding. These have celebrated the railway fabric of timber sleeper, rusty steel, and overhead gantry as well as the naturally opportunistic vegetation.

The success of Stephenson Walk has led to plans for its extension along the Primrose Hill Tunnel approach cutting as far as the tunnel portals (§14.16) where another major element of Robert Stephenson heritage remains (#14.9).

Having led from the towpath through the concourse up to Stephenson Walk, the Trail has now reached the Winding Vaults Reception Centre at the junction of Stephenson Walk and Winding Vaults Way. The Reception Centre is a site of 20m x 10m that was safeguarded by the local authority well before

THE RAILWAY LANDS: A GUIDED TOUR IN 2030

14.10 Stephenson Walk approaching raised ramp, artist's impression looking west, *Adams & Sutherland*, 2023

14.11 Robert Stephenson's bronze statue by Baron Carlo Marochetti at Euston station

the Camden Goods Yard redevelopment got underway. It now features the ticket office, a refreshment kiosk, an outdoor seating and assembly area, as well as a base for the statue of Robert Stephenson.

The wealth of heritage in Chalk Farm Railway Lands dating back to the advent of the L&BR can be compared with the poverty of heritage at Euston, where nothing that Robert Stephenson built survives. For this reason, his Grade II listed statue, seen here on the Euston forecourt (§14.11) and currently in storage, will be moved to the Reception Centre, close to his winding vaults, where he will overlook the railway he built and the rope haulage system he devised.

After a stop for tickets and refreshment, Trail followers are ready to descend into the Winding Vaults.

14.7 Stationary Winding Engine Vaults

The Grade II* listed Stationary Winding Engine Vaults were a notable feature of the London and Birmingham Railway (L&BR), the first modern main line railway with a London terminus, that opened in 1837. They have survived the almost two centuries since they ceased operation remarkably well (§14.12).

Restoration has included treating the structure to prevent damp penetration and providing adequate ventilation to accommodate a large number of visitors. The Winding Vaults were only opened at the end of last year.

Re-purposing has allowed the public to appreciate their form, fabric and history for the first time. A building with 1125 square metres net area at basement level and an additional 20% available at higher level could have had many uses. It has been re-purposed as a mixed-use development (§14.13), including a heritage centre, exhibition centre and café for daytime

14.12 Eastern rope tensioning vault with well at end, showing distinctive water level mark, 2013

visitors combined with evening/night-time use as restaurant, bar and performance space.

Modifications and additions that were made to the structure are shown in red. Commercial use has helped support a Stephenson Museum and heritage gallery, a major, and very popular, feature of which is a working model of rope haulage between Camden and Euston at a 1:20 scale.

The Winding Vaults Visitor Centre has been erected over the eastern boiler room and is accessed from Stephenson Walk. This is where we now enter the Winding Vaults. After passing a security check we enter a concourse with cloakroom, stairs and a lift to carry visitors to the mezzanine and basement floors. The lift is formed within the remaining structure of the eastern chimney. A glazed canopy covers the eastern boiler room and rises above the lift to an architectural feature that recalls the tall chimney that once stood there. The mezzanine floor features a bookshop/souvenir shop and offices. The basement has a foyer/reception area.

From the basement, visitors have access to almost all parts of the vaults and can follow numbered routes with wayfinding signs and divisions of the space by ropes that mimic the rope once used for train haulage.

Emergency escape exits have been provided at all four corners of the vaults as shown in §14.13. The exit from the western boiler room is combined with the supply of services to the vaults from the Primrose Hill side, separating these services from the access for visitors on the Camden side.

The Winding Vaults remain the property of Network Rail and their re-purposing has been implemented under a long lease. Under Network Rail's supervision they will continue to perform a vital structural role in supporting West Coast Mainline and other trains that operate on Camden Incline.

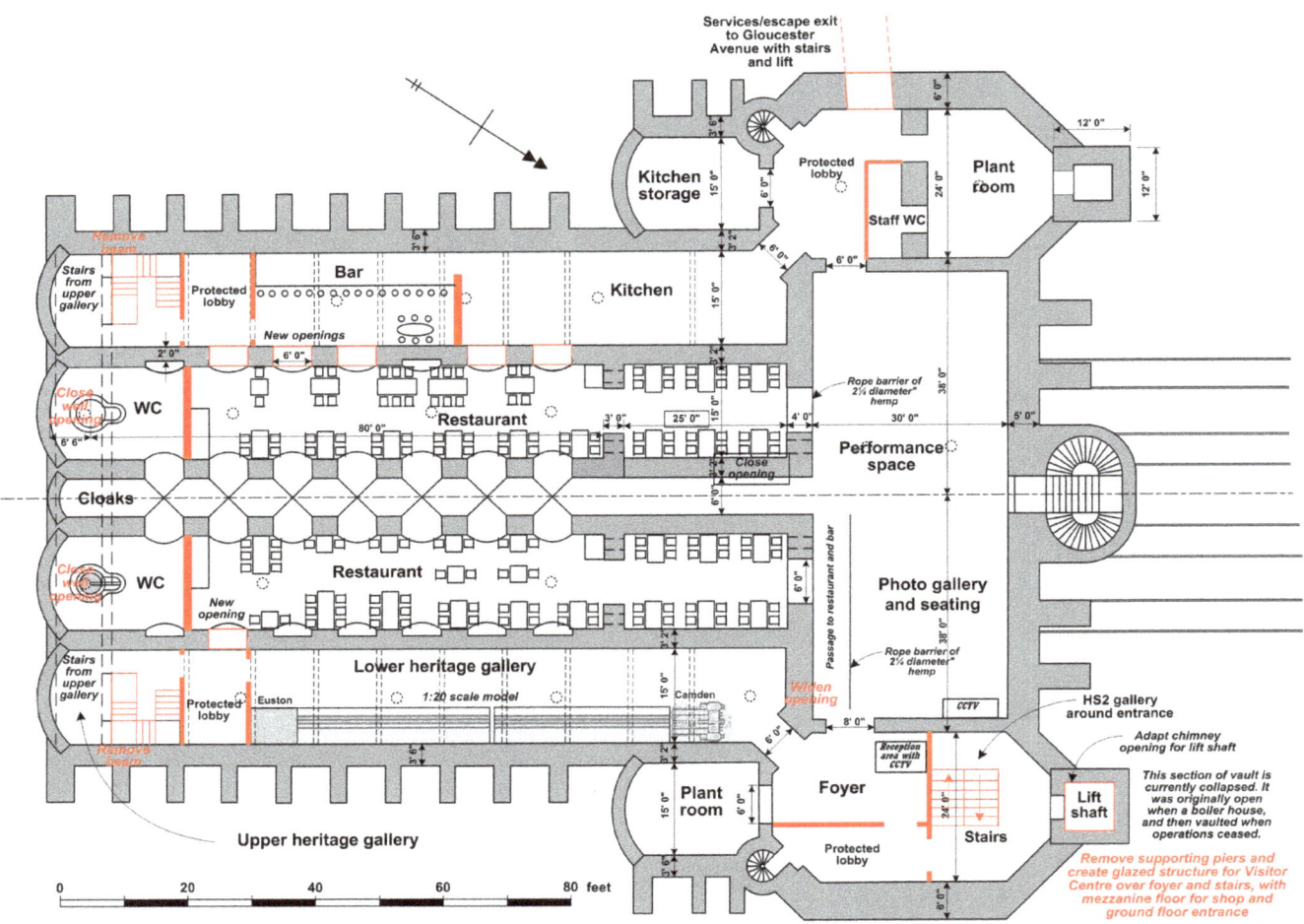

14.13 General plan of Stationary Winding Vaults showing preliminary structural works required before re-purposing for commercial use and as heritage centre

14.8 Pacific Village

After exploring the Winding Vaults, the Trail now continues along Stephenson Walk. Trail followers will observe the building works underway on the opposite side of the mainline railway. These can be seen more clearly as Stephenson Walk gently rises up the ramp at Juniper Crescent. From the start of construction in 2027, this neighbouring building site, covering much of what were formerly train sidings, has become the largest residential development in Primrose Hill since the last quarter of the 19th century. Work started with the provision of access from 42 Gloucester Avenue for servicing the Winding Vaults and is expected to be completed in 2033.

The train sidings that ran between the main line railway and Gloucester Avenue (§11.37) stretched from the Engineer to the Pembroke Castle public houses. They represented an exceptional opportunity for residential and mixed development in an area where the value of land encouraged a search for an alternative site for sidings. Much of the land was subsequently sold or leased by Network Rail for redevelopment, with some retained for its own purposes.

The area has been called 'Pacific Village' to celebrate the fact that Camden Shed, which occupied the site up to 1966, housed more Pacific express locomotives than any other locomotive shed. Princess Royal Pacific No. 6201 *Princess Elizabeth*, the second of its class and one of the most famous, is shown in §14.14 on the turntable at Camden Shed with the terraced Gloucester Avenue houses behind. Named after the seven-year-old princess, the class was soon known as 'Lizzies'. *Princess Elizabeth* sounded her whistle on 3 June 2012 on Battersea Railway Bridge to signal the start of the Thames Diamond Jubilee pageant, the Queen waving to the crew. It is now based at Crewe Heritage Centre.

A schematic layout of Pacific Village is shown in §14.15. Uncertainty over how much of the land occupied by sidings could be redeveloped was resolved in 2025 when a new site for sidings was found. The 1.5 hectare site measures about 350 metres long by 50 metres wide at its Dumpton Place entrance. It features a tree-lined spine service road that runs centrally between two roundabouts, intended to mimic former turntables. The development is car-free.

Pacific Village, in planning terms, divides into zones divided by the spine road. On the south side the development is in sympathy with the Primrose Hill Conservation Area and the Victorian stucco terraces of Gloucester Avenue while on the north side taller buildings can be accommodated. reflecting those in the Camden Goods Yard redevelopment area, while substantially lower in height. The site will eventually accommodate some 200 residential units. A security fence separates Pacific Village from the main line railway.

As well as the main access from Dumpton Place, Pacific Village will be accessed by pedestrians and cyclists at either end via the two green spaces. At the west end

14.14 Princess Royal Class No. 6201 *Princess Elizabeth*, built in 1933, on vacuum turntable at Camden Shed. *G Peter M Green*, 1975

14.15 Railway sidings adapted to serve Chalk Farm Railway Lands and Pacific Village

THE RAILWAY LANDS: A GUIDED TOUR IN 2030

an approach ramp will be created from Regent's Park Road Bridge, as once led to an LNWR platform (#10.6). The garden of the Pembroke Castle will form part of this ramp, its loss compensated by a new garden for the pub created at track level. At the east end of Pacific Village, a Network Rail gated opening at 42 Gloucester Avenue formerly provided access to the train sidings. This now provides access to the east end of Pacific Village. It is also used to supply the Winding Vaults from the Primrose Hill side via a service building with a lift to the vaults two floors below, a supply route that becomes an escape tunnel in emergency.

Public spaces will be provided at either end for recreation. Camden Shed could be recalled with a scale model of the *Princess Elizabeth* as part of a children's playground near the western roundabout.

The Trail continues along Stephenson Walk, rising gently as it approaches the Triangle, the area used for maintenance by Network Rail west of Juniper Crescent. Traversing the Triangle at a level that allows for railway maintenance activities below, it passes through an opening in the side of the former station building and exits onto Regent's Park Road. This ends the Camden Goods Yard part of the Trail.

14.9 Primrose Hill Tunnel East Portals

In a future stage the Trail will be extended to Primrose Hill Tunnel East Portals as shown in §14.16. The route has yet to be developed and faces several constraints, including defining a passage past the HS2 Adelaide Road vent shaft.

Primrose Hill Tunnel East Portals (Grade II*) are an elegant reminder of a former railway age. They convey the sense of a grand entrance. Hidden from the public until recently, and so largely unappreciated, the Trust's intention,

14.16 Railway Heritage Trail – Primrose Hill Tunnel extension

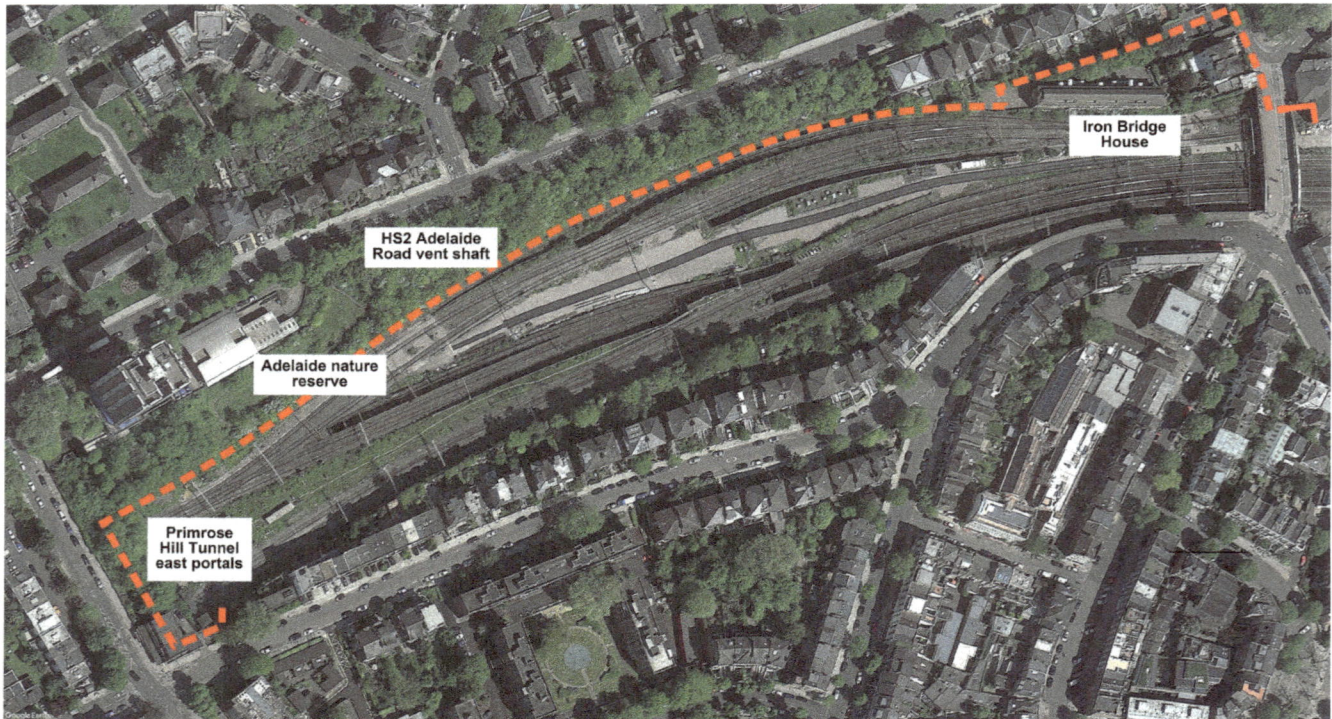

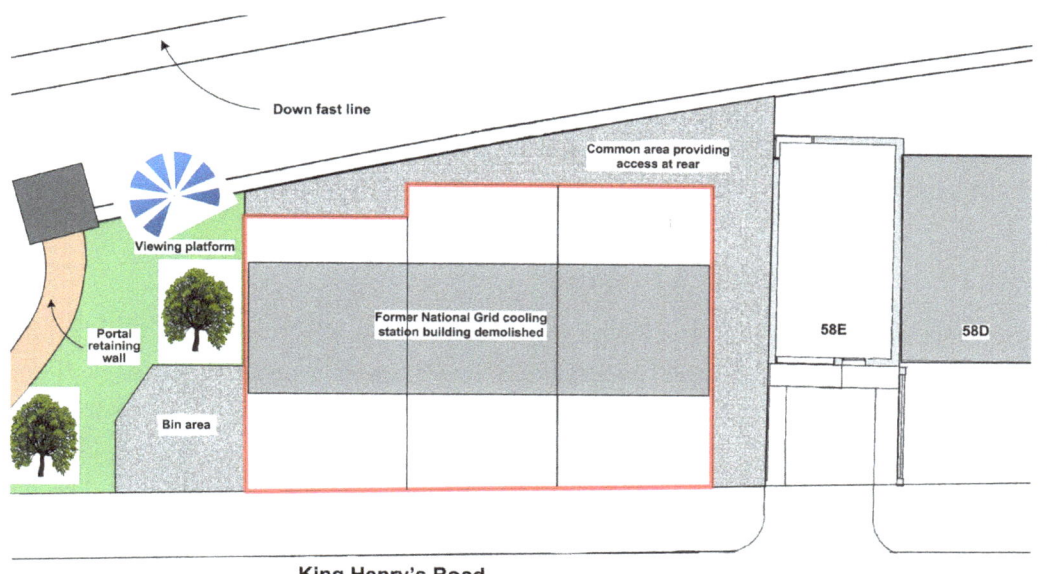

14.17 Schematic plan showing proposed site of viewing platform in King Henry's Road

since being established in 2007, has been to provide public access and suitable viewing platforms on either one or both sides of the tracks.

National Grid decommissioned and sold the site in King Henry's Road, close to the junction with Primrose Hill Road, together with the building that had been a cooling station for HV electricity cables. The Trust has promoted the concept of a viewing platform close to the portals as part of redevelopment of the site (§14.17). The release of the land shown in green for this community asset was agreed with the new owner in 2026 as part of a pre-application process and now, following planning approval, awaits completion of the terrace of three houses, which is expected within the next 12 months. Network Rail has been an interested party in these negotiations and remains responsible for the structural stability and maintenance of the portals and retaining wall.

Primrose Hill Tunnel East Portals include both the original (northern) portal completed in 1838, seen in the two photos (§14.18 and §14.19), and the later (southern) portal dating from 1879.

A heavy modillion cornice, with six carved lion masks, links to massive stone piers on vermiculated stone pedestals with hipped capitals (§14.19).

14.18 Original east portal of Primrose Hill Tunnel, October 2006 (left image)

14.19 Close-up of classical features of original portal, 2013 (right image)

THE RAILWAY LANDS: A GUIDED TOUR IN 2030

The later portal, nearer to King Henry's Road, faithfully replicates the classical elevation of the original portal down to decorative detail but is taller in order to retain land rising up to Primrose Hill. It represents the railway's rapid expansion in the second half of the 19th century. It is now the entrance to the 'fast' tunnel used by West Coast Main Line trains (§10.1).

14.10 Improvements to access

Given that the area is already a magnet for visitors, anything done to enhance access to these exceptional heritage assets will encourage further footfall and inevitably raise concerns about transport links and movements around and within CFRL.

This is not the forum to discuss wider access improvements and their timing, but recent improved transport links, and those in the pipeline, include the following:

- The upgrade of Camden Road station as part of the first phase of the Camden Highline.
- The planned construction of a satellite Camden underground station in Buck Street.

Improvements in movement through the Railway Lands, shown on §14.20, have included the following, some of which have been described in earlier sections:

14.20 Improving access and movement through Chalk Farm Railway Lands

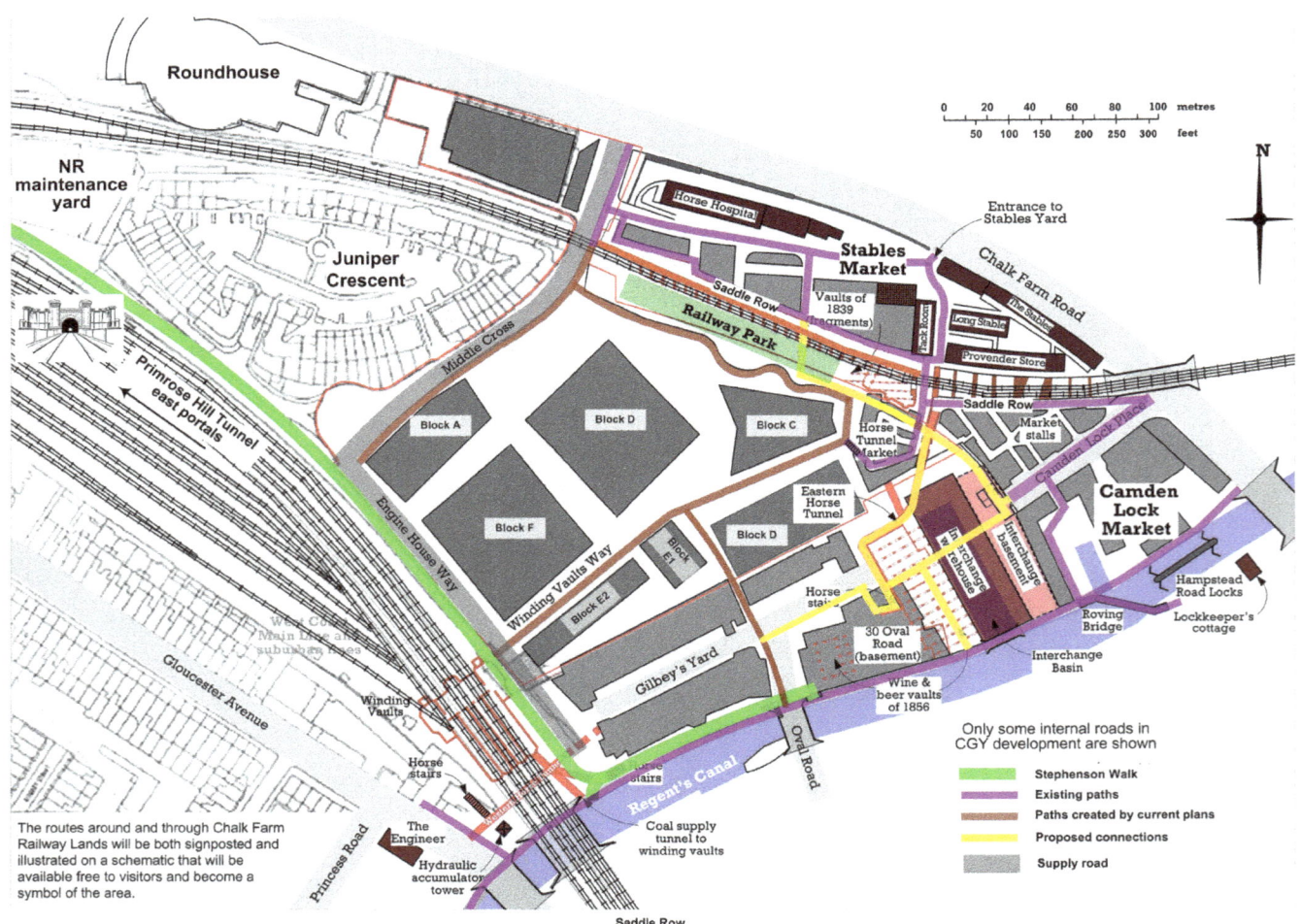

The routes around and through Chalk Farm Railway Lands will be both signposted and illustrated on a schematic that will be available free to visitors and become a symbol of the area.

202 CHALK FARM RAILWAY LANDS: A GUIDED TOUR 1830 TO 2030

- Construction of Stephenson Walk linking the Regent's Canal towpath to Regent's Park Road Bridge.
- Reinstatement of the stairs leading from Camden Lock Place to the Interchange east forecourt.
- Creation of a passage through the Interchange Basement Warehouse and across the Interchange Basin to the Wine and Beer Vaults, with exits from there both to the Regent's Canal towpath and to the Eastern Horse Tunnel (#14.4 and #14.5).

Additional permeability would be created if the following access routes could be agreed:

- adapting the entrance to 30 Oval Road to provide separate and secure entry both to the affordable housing entrance to the building and to the Eastern Horse Tunnel (#14.5);
- opening a passage from Saddle Row through the former Catacombs into the Camden Goods Yard redevelopment, revealing some of the vaults in their original form (see below).

The second of these could, in principle, be created from Stables Market to the Camden Goods Yard side by extending one of the major vaults (§14.21) under the North London Line to rise via stairs into Railway Park (§14.20), a public open space in the new development. The difference in level is about five metres. This would help ameliorate the lack of permeability caused by the barrier that is the North London Line.

14.21 Passage through 'The Atrium' could be extended through former Catacombs

At the same time, each of the adjacent major vaults could be opened up, revealing the minor vaults, so that the public gets a glimpse of the character of the former Catacombs.

14.11 Euston Square Gardens: an epilogue

The destruction of the Euston Arch in 1962 was a seminal moment for the conservation of our railway heritage and ultimately for the survival of King's Cross and St. Pancras stations.

The future of Euston station remains shrouded in uncertainty and is outside the scope of this account. However, the Trust over the last decade has consistently promoted the reinstatement of Euston Square Gardens where, as a consequence of HS2 and its failures to involve the community, mature plane trees have been wantonly felled and the public deprived of an important open space.

Reinstatement of Euston Square Gardens should not only be an obligation on the owner, Network Rail, but should be enhanced by including stones from the Euston Arch in any new landscaping. Fragments of the stone facing of the Arch have been recovered from the River Lee and the larger of these could be strategically placed both to create an aesthetically pleasing landscape and as an essential reminder of the Arch's destruction. We do not wish to see a reconstruction of the historic arch, which would now be demeaned by the scale of the surrounding developments. On the other hand, a modern representation of the Arch would serve as a further reminder of its past role.

The grit stone from the Bramley Fall quarry in Yorkshire that was used as facing material for the Arch is nearly as hard as granite. The stones could therefore provide seating or play areas as well as structural icons in the landscape, all as part of the vital restoration of public amenity.

The loss of the heritage at Euston would achieve some closure with the creation of a memorial garden in Euston Square. But the focus of this account has been not on Euston but on the Chalk Farm Railway Lands and on understanding the infrastructure created to support the first mainline railway into London. Re-purposing and opening to the public of these remarkable structures, the finest closely associated with Robert Stephenson, would be a celebration of our railway heritage and a final act of atonement.

Bibliography, References and Sources

Bibliography

Allen, Geoffrey Freeman, *Modern Railways the World Over,* Ian Allen, 1962

Bourne, John C., *A series of lithographical drawings of the London and Birmingham Railway,* Ackermann, 1839

Bailey, Michael R., *Robert Stephenson – The Eminent Engineer,* Routledge, 2003

Bonavia, Michael, *The Four Great Railways,* David & Charles, 1980

Bradley, Simon, *The Railways: Nation, Network & People,* Profile Books, 2016

Brees, Stanley Charles, *Railway Practice. A Collection of Working Plans and Practical details of Construction*, London, 1838

Britton, John, *Introduction to Drawings of the London & Birmingham Railway,* Ackermann, 1839

Camden History Society, *Streets of Camden Town,* 2003 (updated 2023)

Camden Railway Heritage Trust, *Camden Railway Heritage Trail, Primrose Hill to Camden Lock and Chalk Farm,* 2009

Catford, Nick, *Secret Underground London,* Folly Books, 2013

Conder, Francis Roubiliac, *Personal Recollections of English Engineers,* 1868

Cossons, Neil, *The BP Book of Industrial Archaeology*, David & Charles, Newton Abbott, 1993

Darley, Peter, *Camden Goods Station through time*, Amberley Publishing, 2013

Darley, Peter, *The King's Cross Story: 200 years of history in the Railway Lands,* The History Press, 2018

Davies, Caitlin, *Camden Lock and the Market,* Frances Lincoln, 2013

Dempsey, George Drysdale, *The Practical Railway Engineer,* John Weale, London, 1855

Denney, Martyn, *London's Waterways,* Harper Collins, 1977

Elmes, James, *Metropolitan Improvements; or London in the Nineteenth Century,* Jones & Co., London, 1827

Faulkner, Alan, *The Regent's Canal, London's Hidden Waterway,* Waterways World Ltd, 2005

Fletcher, Geoffrey, *The London Nobody Knows,* The History Press, 1962

Godwin, Fay, *Bison at Chalk Farm,* Routledge & Kegan Paul, 1982

Gold, Alec, *Four-in-Hand: a History of W. and A. Gilbey Ltd, 1857-1957,* 1857

Gordon, William John, *The Horse World of London,* 1893

Hughes, S. H., *Panoramic View around the Regent's Park from Drawings Taken on the Spot,* Richard Morris, R. Ackermann, London, 1831

Jack, Harry, *Locomotives of the LNWR Southern Division,* The Railway Correspondence and Travel Society, Amadeus Press, 2001

Jackson, Peter, *George Scharfe's London sketches and watercolours of a changing city, 1820-1850,* John Murray, 1987

Jeaffreson, J. C., *The Life of Robert Stephenson, F.R.S.,* 1864

Kidd, Jane, *Gilbeys: Wine and Horses,* Lutterworth Press, 1997

Knight, Charles & Co., *The Pictorial Gallery of Arts, Vol. 1 Useful Arts,* London, c1847

Lecount, Peter, Lt., R.N., *The History of the Railway Connecting London and Birmingham,* 1839

McKenna, Frank, *The Railway Workers, 1840-1970,* Faber, 1980

Mountford, Colin, *Rope and Chain Haulage,* Industrial Railway Society, 2013

Osborne, Edward Cornelius and William, *Osborne's London & Birmingham Railway Guide,* London, 1839

Reed, M. C., *The LNWR – a History,* Atlantic Transport Publishers, 1996

Roscoe, Thomas and Peter Lecount, *The London and Birmingham Railway,* Charles Tilt, 1839

Russell, Janet, *Great Western Horse Power,* Oxford Publishing, 1995

Simmons, Jack, *The Railway in Town and Country 1830-1914,* David & Charles, 1886

Simms, Frederick W. (Ed.), *Public Works of Great Britain,* John Weale, 1838

Smithson, Alison and Peter, *The Euston Arch and the Growth of the London, Midland and Scottish Railway,* Thames and Hudson, 1958

Scott, George Gilbert, *Remarks on Secular & Domestic Architecture, Present and Future,* John Murray, London, 1857

Spencer, Herbert, *An Autobiography,* Volume 1, D. Appleton, 1904

Steele, Rod, *LMS Steam at Euston & Camden,* Amberley Publishing, 2013

The Friends of Chalk Farm Library, *Primrose Hill Remembered,* 2001

Thompson, Prof. Francis M. L., *Hampstead: Building a Borough, 1650-1964,* Routledge & Kegan Paul, 1974

Thomson, David, *In Camden Town,* Penguin, 1963

Thornbury, Walter and Edward Walford, *Old and New London: Illustrated,* Vol. 5, Cassell, London, 1887

Turner, Leopold (Ed.), *50 Years on the London and North Western Railway and Other Memoranda in the Life of David Stevenson,* McCorquodale, London, 1891

Turton, Keith, *The Early Years of London's Coal Trade,* Railway Archive, Nº. 13

Wade, George A., *The Horse Department of a Railway,* Railway Magazine, Volume 8, 1900

Walford, Edward, *Old and New London: a Narrative of its History, its People, and its Places – The Western and Northern Suburbs,* Volume 5, Cassell Petter & Galpin, London, 1878

Waugh, Alec, *Merchants of Wine,* Cassell & Co., London, 1957

Wishaw, Francis, *The Railways of Great Britain and Ireland*, Simkin Marshall, 2nd edition, 1842, reprinted by David & Charles, 1969

Whitehead, Jack, *The Growth of Camden Town: AD 1800-2000*, privately published, 2nd Edition, 2000

References

The major sources are the Board and Committee Minutes, letters, newspaper and other reports relating to the L&BR, LNWR, LMS, GWR and RCC, obtained over many visits to the National Archives and other sources, translated into a document of 280 typewritten pages. These entries have not been specifically referenced for reasons of space and continuity. Those who actively seek further substantiation are invited to comment, contribute, challenge and correct by contacting the author through the Camden Railway Heritage Trust.

Adams and Sutherland, *Stephenson Walk: Feasibility Study*, Final Report, May 2023

AOC Archaeology, *Buildings A, B and D, Stables Market, London Borough of Camden: Results of an Archaeological Watching Brief and Historic Building Record,* October 2007

Armstrong, William G., *On the Application of Water Pressure, as a Motive Power, for Working Cranes and other Descriptions of Machinery,* Proceedings ICE, Volume 9, 1850

Darley, Peter, *Stables Complex and Underground Features in Former Camden Goods Depot: Historic Area Assessment,* for English Heritage, August 2016 (unpublished)

Dockray, Robert Benson, *Description of the Camden Station of the London and North Western Railway*, Proceedings of the Institution of Civil Engineers, 13 March 1849, pp 164-187

Feinstein, C H, *National Income, Expenditure and Output of the United Kingdom 1855 to 1965,* 1972

Firth, J. F. B., *The Coal and Wine Dues: the History of the London Coal Tax and the Arguments for and against its Renewal,* Municipal Reform Pamphlet No. 20, reprinted from The Times of December 7 1886, The Anti-Coal Tax Committee, 1887.

Forshaw, Alec, *Paying the Piper,* Journal of the Islington Archaeology and History Society, Vol 6 No 4, Winter 2016-17

Heritage Architecture, *Stables Market, Stanley Sidings, Building "D": the Horse Tunnel, PPG 15 Statement,* prepared for Stanley Sidings Ltd by Stephen Levrant, 2004.

Household Words, *Navvies as they used to be,* H. J. Brown, Vol XIII, pp 543-550, June 21 1856

Humber, William, *On the Design and Arrangement of Railway Stations, Repairing Shops, Engine Sheds, &c.,* Proceedings of the ICE, No. 1,137, February 13 1866

Layton, W and G Crowther, *An Introduction to the Study of Prices,* 1935

Office for National Statistics, *All items RPI, 1947-2023*

Perryman, J A, *Handling of Traffic by Rail Transport, Camden Yard,* LMS Magazine, Nov. 1928

Petticrew, Ian, *The Train Now Departing,* Tring Local History, Notes and Extracts on the history of the London and Birmingham Railway, 2014

Phelps-Brown, E. H. and S. Hopkins, *Seven Centuries of the Prices of Consumables compared with Builders' Wage-rates,* Economica, Nov. 1956

PPIY Ltd, for Network Rail, *Camden Winding Vaults: Conservation Management Plan, Final,* September 2020

Railnatter, Episode 71, 21 July 2021

Roenisch, Pauline, Transcript of interview of Walter Looney, former stable hand at Camden Stables Yard from c1913, at his home on 20 December 1976

Roenisch, Pauline, Transcript of interview of Walter Gilbey at his home in Henley-on-Thames on 7 February 1977

Scudamore, Mr, *Reorganisation of the Telegraph System of the United Kingdom,* report presented to the House of Commons. London, 1871

Sprange, Derek, *How the Railway Influenced the Development of Primrose Hill,* undated manuscript

The Builder, 19 December 1846, pp 602-603

The Pictorial Times, 4 January 1845

The Post Office, *The Post Office and the Electric Telegraph,* 1867

Thorne, Robert, *The Railway Vaults, Gloucester Avenue, NW1,* English Heritage London Division, September 7 1989

van Laun, John, *John Cooke Bourne (1814-1896) lithographer: Drawings of the London & Birmingham Railway (1836-1838),* Journal of the Railway & Canal Historical Society, Nos. 219 to 225.

van Laun, John, *British Railway Topography and Politics in John Cooke Bourne's (1839) 'Drawings of the London and Birmingham Railway',* thesis submitted for M.Phil., UCL Department of Science and Technology, two volumes, 2021.

Sources

ASLEF Journal

British History Online (Euston and Works LXXIV)

British Library

Camden History Society, Newsletter and Journal

Camden Local Studies and Archives Centre

Canal & River Trust

Diageo Archive

Eton Archives

Gilbey Archive

Greater London Industrial Archaeology Society Journal

Historic England, London and Swindon
Institution of Civil Engineers
Ironbridge Gorge Museum
London Metropolitan Archives
London Railway Record
Museum of London
National Archives
National Railway Museum
Network Rail Archive
Parliamentary Archives
Railway and Canal Historical Society
RMWeb
Wellcome Library

Image credits

Every effort has been made to contact all copyright holders. The publishers will be happy to make good in future editions any errors or omissions brought to their attention.

All the images unattributed here are the copyright of the author.

Copyright holder	Images credited
Adams and Sutherland	14.9
Alison Kemp	Front cover, 7.38, 7.39, 7.40
Alan Faulkner Collection	1.1, 1.9
Anthony Richardson & Partners	13.18
Brian Morrison	10.15, 11.24, 11.30
Camden Local Studies & Archives	1.12, 2.2, 2.5, 3.3, 3.4, 3.10, 3.14, 3.15, 3.16, 3.19, 3.20, 3.21, 4.8,
Camden Market Ltd	12.7, 12.8, 13.4, 13.6, 13.7, 13.8, 13.9 (3 images)
Canal & River Trust	12.2, 13.13
Celia Kelly	13.1
CRHT Collection	1.14, 2.1, 2.3, 2.4, 3.7, 4.2, 4.4, 4.5, 4.6, 4.7, 4.13, 5.1, 5.10, 5.15, 5.16, 5.17, 5.24, 5.25, 5.26, 6.4, 6.8, 7.2B, 7.3, 7.28, 7.35, 8.15, 9.6, 9.8, 9.20, 10.7, 11.1, 11.2, 11.7, 11.11, 11.13, 11.15, 11.17, 11.18. 11.20, 11.21, 11.22, 11.23, 11.25, 11.35, 12.18,
Cumbria Image Bank	1.13
David Thomas	7.29, 9.15, 11.8, 11.16, 12.3,
Diageo Archive	9.3, 9.4, 9.5, 9.10, 9.12, 9.16, 9.17, 9.18, 9.19, 9.21, 9.24, 9.25, 9.26, 9.27, 9.28, 9.29, 9.30, 9.32, 9.33, 9.34, 9.35, 9.37, 9.39, 9.41, 9.42, 9.43, 9.44, 9.45, 12.1
Elliot Sinclair	10.9, 10.10
Eric Braun	7.9, 13.9 (1 image), 13.15
Fay Godwin	6.12
Geoffrey Fletcher Estate	14.6
G Peter M Green Estate	10.16, 11.27, 14.14
Graham Larkby	13.19, 13.20
Harry Jack Collection	5.8
Harvard Map Collection	1.2, 1.10
H C Casserley Collection	11.29
Historic England	7.37, 9.38, 11.3
Imperial War Museum	1
Institution of Civil Engineers	2.8
J E Connor Collection	10.11

London Canal Museum	8.3
London Metropolitan Archive	5.27
Malcolm Tucker	5.19, 7.6, 7.19, 7.34, 9.14, 9.36, 9.40, 11.4, 11.9, 12.13, 14.4, 14.5, Rear Cover
Mark Alper	13.17, Rear Cover
Michael Nadra	12.17
National Archives	5.18, 6.1, 7.12, 7.15, 7.20
National Railway Museum	3.18, 5.3, 5.14, 7.2A, 10.14
Network Rail Archives	2, 2.7, 2.10, 2.11, 3.8, 3.13, 4.3, 4.9, 4.10, 4.11, 4.12, 5.2, 5.4, 5.9, 5.11, 5.12, 6.6, 6.7, 7.5, 7.25, 8.4, 8.5, 8.6, 8.7, 8.11, 8.13, 9.13, 9.31, 11.10, 11.14
Nick Catford	5,13, 8.9, 8.10, 8.14, 9.9, 9.11, 13.5, 14.12
Nik Newman	7.26
Northside Archives	5.22, 12.5, 12.6
Piercy & Company	14.3
Private Collection	2.6, 11.19
Proud Camden	7.23
Railway Gazette	10.3, 10.4, 10.5, 10.12
R C Riley	11.32, 11.33
Science Museum	3.2, 5.5
Stuart Leach	13.2
The Guardian	1.3
The Roundhouse	5.7
Trustees of the British Museum	3.1, 3.6, 3.12
Westminster City Archive	2.9
Yale Centre for British Art	1.4, 1.5, 1.6, 1.7, 1.8, 1.11, 3.5, 3.9, 3.22, 3.23, 3.24, 3.25
53A Models of Hull Collection	11.34

www.ingramcontent.com/pod-product-compliance
Lightning Source LLC
Chambersburg PA
CBHW041242240426
43668CB00025B/2464